Open the Door to Understanding

Humanity has always been in awe of the heavens. There is something wondrous and inspirational about the world above on a clear night. We sense the mystery. What is it that is out there? What do planets and stars out there have to do with life here on Earth? How are we part of this miraculous system? Questions like these have piqued the mind of humankind for millennia.

As the heavens were studied and observed, awe-inspiring correlations *were* found between the motions of the planets and events on Earth. These observations led to an understanding of our connection with the heavens; that connection and our study of it is what we call astrology.

Astrology rests on the major, spiritual premise that the soul picks its time and place to be born in order to refine and fulfill itself best. We have this guiding imprint caught (encapsulated) within the birth moment, within time, and at a particular place on Earth; this is when these planets become individualistically ours. That is what the horoscope is—a planetary drawing of the "hour," of the moment of becoming; a map of our individual microcosm within the macrocosm of Natural Order.

The most celebrated astrologer of our time, American Noel Tyl, in his more than two dozen textbooks, has brought the presentation of astrology into the dawn of the twenty-first century with the development of a course of study. In this book, Basil Fearrington presents the Noel Tyl Method, as it has been taught and tested at the Noel Tyl Study Center for Astrology and New Age Exploration in South Africa. Now this holistic, humanistic study can become part of *your* life, opening you to knowledge and understanding of your own special place in the scheme of things, on Earth and in the Heavens.

Once you begin reading this fascinating orientation to astrology, you will immediately see life around you differently, insightfully—and you won't be able to stop learning! You will be giving yourself a gift indeed!

About the Author

Basil Fearrington was introduced to astrology at the age of thirteen when he began studying the discipline. He began practicing astrology professionally in 1980, for three years co-hosted a Philadelphia area radio show, and his articles on astrology have appeared in *The Mountain Astrologer, American Astrology Magazine, Dell Horoscope Magazine*, the NCGR magazine, and many more. He was a contributing writer to *Astrology Looks at History*, compiled and edited by Noel Tyl (Llewellyn Publications, 1995). He was invited to speak on the faculty of the prestigious United Astrology Conference in 1998, and at Astro2000 in 1999. He taught the extraordinary Noel Tyl course at MilleyDome/Johannesburg, in South Africa.

In addition to his work in astrology, Basil has also been a full-time musician, touring, recording, or playing with performers such as Roberta Flack, George Benson, Stevie Wonder, and many others. In 1980 he was a member of a production team that won a Grammy Award for the best R&B Song of the Year.

To Write to the Author

If you wish to contact the author or would like more information about this book, please write to the author in care of Llewellyn Worldwide, and we will forward your request. Both the author and publisher appreciate hearing from you and learning of your enjoyment of this book and how it has helped you. Llewellyn Worldwide cannot guarantee that every letter written to the author can be answered, but all will be forwarded. Please write to:

Basil Fearrington
℅ Llewellyn Worldwide Ltd.
P.O. Box 64383, Dept. K739–0
St. Paul, MN 55164-0383, U.S.A.

Please enclose a self-addressed, stamped envelope for reply or $1.00 to cover costs.
If outside the U.S.A., enclose international postal reply coupon.

For Llewellyn's free full-color catalog, write to New Worlds at the above address, or call 1–800–THE MOON. Also visit our web site at www.llewellyn.com.

the New Way

TO LEARN ASTROLOGY

Basil Fearrington

Presenting the Noel Tyl Method

1999
Llewellyn Publications
St. Paul, Minnesota, U.S.A., 55164–0383

FIRST EDITION
First Printing, 1999

Cover design by Lisa Novak
Interior design and editing by Connie Hill

Library of Congress Cataloging-in-Publication Data
Fearrington, Basil, 1954–
      The new way to learn astrology / Basil Fearrington. — 1st ed.
         p.   cm.
      Includes bibliographical references and index.
      ISBN 1–56718–739–0
      1. Astrology—Study and teaching.   2. Tyl, Noel, 1936–   .
   I. Title.
   BF1708.1.F43   1999
   133.5—dc21   99–33969
                                                              CIP

Llewellyn Publications
A Division of Llewellyn Worldwide, Ltd.
P.O. Box 64383, Dept. K739–0
St. Paul, Minnesota, 55164-0383, U.S.A.
www.llewellyn.com

 Printed in the United States of America on recycled paper

To the Lights of my life:
my sons,
Ameer and Kijano

Contents

Chapter 14 ... Integrated Transits ... 201

Introduction

THIS BOOK REPRESENTS A CULMINATION, AND, at the same time, an open door to a lifetime of learning, understanding, and knowing. It is the fruit of seeds planted within me during the mid-seventies: I was studying astrology, searching for answers about so many things. Much of what I read and the way it was presented were nebulous and not very useful. Something was missing.

Enter Noel Tyl and his best-selling, twelve-volume series, *The Principles & Practice of Astrology*. Here was a presentation of astrology that brought it into the so-called "Psychological Century." This was a view of astrology that made sense. Quite simply: it worked, and it worked better than anything I (and most others) had seen up to that time.

The approach, the understanding, was/is holistic, a utilization of astrology that demands recognition of the human being first, above all measurements, fitting the horoscope to the reality of the person. Every single horoscope is given distinct individuation.

This holistic approach to astrology has been extraordinarily successful: Noel Tyl is perhaps the most celebrated astrologer of our time, with his over two-dozen textbooks indispensable to any professional's practice. The approach has taken astrologers away from doing "readings" and brought them to holding consultations; a very important distinction, the former describing a static, fatalistic astrology all too popular for all too long in our history, and the latter clearly describing an enriching discussion about life using astrological symbolism as a guide.

I recently relocated from Philadelphia, Pennsylvania to Johannesburg, South Africa for the express purpose of teaching this approach to astrology with Noel Tyl. This astrology has worked now for a quarter century and it continues to work every day, class after class. Our beginning students learned, in just twenty weeks (eighty hours of study), the basics of sophisticated analytical techniques in astrology. They learned how to take the many crayons of technique and draw a coherent, artfully-colored portrait of identity.

I am honored and happy to share this wonderful course with you, exactly as I presented it in its highly concerted format at MilleyDome/Johannesburg!

You will be amazed at how quickly and fulfillingly this holistic, humanistic study will become part of your life; and how, for the rest of your life, you will understand and you will know; and best of all, you will help so many others appreciate their life more than they ever did before.

Basil Fearrington
Philadelphia, Pennsylvania
Johannesburg, South Africa
December, 1998

Chapter 1

• • •

The Planets

IN MODERN TIMES ASTROLOGY HAS STILL SUF-
fered criticism and doubt, not because of its store of
knowledge and breadth of application, but because it is
presented improperly by many of its practitioners. In
times past, generally from 1500 to 1750, astrologers were
indeed privileged members of society and were held in
very high regard. This esteem has dissipated throughout
the years, in large part because the application of astrology turned pointedly fatalistic, favoring the idea that
planets somehow dictate life, controlling people and
assigning them to an unalterable fate. This is certainly not
productively consonant with sophistications in the
present "psychological century." In its embrace of time
and eventuation, astrology can not leave the human
being's needs, dreams, and will behind.

Astrology in Perspective

It is quite easy to think and expect that studying astrology provides a sense of control over others and thus a control over life. The reality and magic of astrology are quite different: astrology teaches us about the controls of the life process, that which helps us to make life happen. In modern times, it is extremely important for a new astrologer to know and understand that astrology, a horoscope, does not describe a static fate of any kind, but a dynamically integrated holistic system. Indeed, planets do nothing; it is people who dictate the direction and quality of life. We people are motivated by psychological and biological needs that are reflected in the wonder of the heavens—our Solar System—through the personalized drama of our planetary symbology. The planets symbolize our needs, and it is needs that make things happen.

There are several holistic principles we must understand when we begin the study of astrology:

1. There is no good or bad in astrology. There is no such thing as a bad Sign or bad planet. There are only potentials of energy. People are free to use these potentials as they desire, for growth or for waste.

2. A horoscope is a symbolic representation of a person as he or she can be, not necessarily the person as he or she is. The horoscope is a holographic guide of potentials. We could suggest that it is a map of the absolute best an individual can be. Or further: fulfillment and happiness are certainly emphasized in life when one follows the guidelines of the horoscope, learns lessons in life, and follows a strategy of will.

3. Environmental influences play a most important role in how a person reflects the horoscope. For example, we are all born into a certain family environment that is influenced by our parental history, by our neighborhood, educational system, city, state, and religion. These considerations play vital roles in shaping the development of the individual, and the horoscope must be analyzed in these terms. In the process of circumspect analysis, we adjust the horoscope to the reality being lived by the individual. Otherwise, since the environment plays such a pivotal role in the

development of the individual, judgments made before assessing that environmental profile are confining for the individual.

4. Astrology can not be proved or disproved. When a person's development deviates from the ideal suggested in the horoscope, we must recognize that it is not the astrology that is wrong! The manifestation reflects individuation and personal choice or something within personal development that has stifled potential. And there very well can be an instructive purpose within that process and state of affairs.

5. Astrology is not fortunetelling. For example, we can certainly tell when a personal relationship is likely to be challenged, but we can rarely determine specifically why; there can be any number of factors at work that will cause the tension, such as unemployment, infidelity, financial problems, etc. Although many times it *is* possible, it is not the astrologer's chief function to categorize the specifics of energy (behavioral) manifestation.

   Another example: astrology can not tell an individual that he or she will be walking down Main Street next September 3 and, while doing so, find a pink suitcase with $102,000 in it! Instead, today's astrologer can see that a period of great potential is ahead, one in which very strong financial developments are likely to manifest if the effort is made to succeed. This can mean selling a home, getting a raise, receiving an inheritance, etc.

   For these concerns, since astrology is not fortunetelling, any reference to horoscope delineation should be referred to as analyzing the horoscope, not reading it. When a person comes to an astrologer, they are coming for a consultation, not for an abject reading of fate. The consultation is a discussion about life experience and plan, using astrological symbols; it is not a discussion about astrology.

6. Astrology in no way contradicts or interferes with any religious belief. It is simply something to know about in order to aid and guide fulfillment in life. Its beauty in its nearness to the mystery of life suggests the premise of religion: that an all-pervasive creative spirit prevails in life, within time.

Orientation to the Heavens

Mankind has always been in awe of the heavens. There is something wondrous and inspirational about staring at the heavens on a clear night. We sense the mystery. What is it that is out there? What would it be like to be on a star? Questions like these have piqued the mind of humankind for millennia.

Centuries ago, humans were first awed by the Sun as it rose from darkness in the east and set to darkness in the west. This passage created a fearful drama: the light of life disappears; will it return? What will bring it back? The miracle of resurrection, the base of world religions in one way or another, is linked to this natural drama. As darkness set in, man observed millions of tiny, fixed, flickering lights that, like the Sun, were also given to a schedule of rising and setting. Amid all this, humans noticed that some of these flickering white dots were not so fixed in space and that five of them seemed to wander in and out among more stable stars. These "moving" stars were the planets, the "wanderers": Mercury, Venus, Mars, Jupiter, and Saturn.

As man studied and observed the heavens more and more, he found awe-inspiring correlations between the motions of the planets and events on Earth: floods, good and bad harvests, wars, and more. Wars seemed to occur most frequently when Mars and Jupiter were linked in certain ways, for example, in certain sectors of the heavens. Correspondences like these were recorded and preserved on tablets in Egypt. This was the beginning of our astrology. Students of life and nature from the land of Sumer (Mesopotamia) and, much later, Greece, all studied for decades with the wise priests, the scholar/magicians of ancient Egypt.

Hermes Trismegistus (Thrice Master) is the Roman name for the Egyptian God, Thoth. Hermes is famous for the dictum, "As Above so Below." What this means is that what is below on Earth is reflected above and what is above is reflected below. This is the core of the so-called Hermetic doctrine. In the late fifteenth century, the Swiss seer Paracelsus (doctor, astrologer, and alchemist) personalized the doctrine even further: he said, so simply, so illuminatingly, "The Planets are Within." This was an eloquent statement of the relation between the microcosm here below and the macrocosm of all around us, the integration of the all-pervasive creative principle.

How is this all brought together in the horoscope? Astrology rests on the major, spiritual premise that the soul picks its time and place to be born in order to refine and fulfill itself best. We will see that the planets upon which astrology is based become archetypes of needs in human behavior. They are the symbols of behavioral faculties that guide the astrologer to anticipate, appreciate, guide, and counsel behavior in many, many significant ways. We have this guiding imprint caught (encapsulated) within in the birth moment, within time and at a particular place on Earth; this is when these planets become individualistically ours. That is what the horoscope is—a planetary drawing of the "hour," of the moment of becoming; it is a map of our individual microcosm within the macrocosm of Natural Order.

Planets as Gods

In the beginning, planets were looked upon as gods because we observed that certain things seemed to occur when a certain heavenly body was at a certain position in the heavens. An awareness of causal relationship was established. And since humans could not control these heavenly bodies and because they seemed to have this enormous power from their positions in the heavens, the planets were given names that associated them with gods. Indeed, the names of the days of the week were based on the gods drawn from Egyptian, Teutonic, and Nordic lore: Sunday is the Sun's day; Monday is the Moon's day; Tuesday is named after Tiw, the German God of war (corresponds to Mars); Wednesday is named for Odin, the Norse counterpart to Mercury; Thursday, or Thor's Day, is related to the Roman Jupiter; Friday, or Freyja's Day, (the god of beauty) is the day of Venus; Saturday is Saturn's day, the end of the week, named so because the ancients saw Saturn as the end of the line, the last visible planet. Saturday therefore became Saturn's day. The day of great light, the Sun's Day, began the next week—the new cycle, the new life.

We begin our study of the planets with the heart of the matter, the Sun, and present the planets as they are ranked in distances away from the Sun.

The Sun's symbol is a circle enclosing a dot in its center. The circle represents eternity and the dot represents mankind's place within the All, at the center of the solar system, benefiting from the solar influence. It is the position of the Sun in the sky that determines each person's so-called "birth sign." On or around the twenty-first of each month, the Sun moves into certain areas of the heavens called constellations. These constellations are defined by our zodiacal Signs—Aries, Taurus, Gemini, Cancer, Leo, Virgo, Libra, Scorpio, Sagittarius, Capricorn, Aquarius, and Pisces. When you were born, the Sun was in one of these Signs; for the period between July 23 and August 23, for example, the Sun was in the Sign of Leo; Leo is your Sun Sign. Popular astrology, seen in newspapers and magazines is "Sun Sign Astrology," presenting a singularly simplistic and incomplete view of commonly shared life energies delineated through the Sun's position alone; the Moon, all the other planets, and all their interrelationships are largely ignored.

The Sun, of course, is what defines day from night. In a horoscope, the Sun symbolizes a particular kind of life energy that fuels the individual, that is essential to individual vitality. **The Sun in a natal horoscope represents the quality and form of the life energy. It is the gravitational center of your identity. It is ego.** It is the kind of fuel that your systemic engine depends on. And just as the Sun in the heavens shines its light upon all the planets in its Solar System, its energy in the horoscope shines upon all of the other planets in a horoscope, illuminating them accordingly. The Sun is so important and so central that it rules the most vital parts of the body, the heart and the eyes—and also because it is so central, it is associated with the father, kings, people in authority, royalty, etc. It is thoroughly masculine.

☽ The Moon's symbol is quite easy to remember: it is the Crescent Moon. The most important thing to realize about the Moon, from an astronomical point of view, is that it has no light of its own; its light is a reflection of the Sun. And because it is a reflector taking in the masculine energies of the Sun, it is feminine, the symbol of the maternal and nurturing. The Sun and Moon are yin and yang, day and night, masculine and feminine.

In a horoscope, **the Moon takes the Sun's energy, the Sun's fuel, and expresses it in a personality form that is dependent upon the Moon's position in the overall planetary scheme. The Moon represents everything that the personality needs in order to be fulfilled.** By Sign, it is a most incisive, decisive force in the horoscope. This is why, so often, you know people who do not obviously act like the Sun Sign under which they were born; what you actually experience in such a person is his or her Moon Sign. The Moon takes 27.32 days to orbit around the Earth and the Sun. It moves very swiftly and is the symbol of the mother in a horoscope, often indicating how one views one's mother subjectively. The Moon is thoroughly feminine. It rules the stomach and breasts.

☿ In mythology, Mercury was known as the messenger of the gods. As the closest god to the Sun, never more than 28 degrees away, Mercury took in the Sun's message and traveled swiftly to communicate this message to everyone else. It is because of this that Mercury is associated with everything having to do with thinking, communicating, and travel; the mind.

The symbol that we use in our astrology for Mercury can be seen (in order to facilitate learning it) in two ways. First of all, the symbol is formed by a half Moon on its back that sits upon a circle atop a cross. If you recall pictures of Mercury, the ancient messenger of the gods, you can recall the half-moon part of the symbol as the "wings on the messenger's helmet." Your second option to facilitate memorization of the symbol is to see the glyph as a hand-held microphone. This makes it easy to associate the symbol with communication and speaking.

In a natal horoscope, **Mercury represents the way you need to think and communicate in order to fulfill needs.** It takes 88 days to circle the Sun. It is its quick orbit of the Sun that links Mercury with qualities having to do with eagerness, quickness, moving around, and diversity. Primarily, Mercury rules the lungs, arms, shoulders, hands, and fingers.

♀ The symbol for Venus is drawn as a circle atop a cross. In ancient times, Venus was the goddess of love. We see Venus as the planet representing romantic, social, relational, and aesthetic concerns. In order to facilitate memorization of the symbol, imagine it as a hand-held mirror for personal reflection. This gives you the sense of wanting to look good, to be pleasing, qualities that are important in the Venus archetype.

Venus is farther from the Sun and nearer to the Earth and is therefore closer to man's horizon. Its orbit around the Sun takes 224.5 days and it is nearly the same size as Earth. Where the Sun is the King and the Moon is the Queen, Venus is the Court Charmer whose job it is to sweep everyone up and away with scintillating mannerisms. **Venus represents how you need to relate to others in order to fulfill needs.** Venus rules love attractions, marriage, beauty, aesthetics, finery, attractiveness, art, music, sweets, anything that is pleasing to the senses. Specifically in a natal horoscope, it has dominion over the social, romantic, aesthetic needs. It also rules money and has rulership over the throat, lower back, kidneys, bladder, and hair.

♂ The symbol for Mars is very well known in our culture. It is a circle with an arrow drawn from the upper right side of the circle, 45 degrees or so from the top position. This arrow should be seen as being a "Pow!" point: emphatic, definite! It is an athlete in the heat of competition; a red sports car driving fast; it is thrust, inflammation, assertion, impulse, temperament, and courage. Indeed, it is warrior-like, always stirring up whatever it touches in the horoscope—POW!

Mars is just outside Earth's orbit and, both astronomically and astrologically, is the bridge to the larger planets. It follows the life-energy of the Sun, the mind of Mercury, and sense of relating we see in Venus. **Mars represents the kind of applied energy we use to fulfill needs.** Mars is the utilization of what we are.

Mars takes 22 months to orbit the Sun.

④ The symbol for Jupiter is most easily memorized as a sleek combination of the number "24." The most immediate awareness about Jupiter is its size: it is, by far, the largest planet in the Solar System, larger than all the other planets and Moon together. Whenever you think of Jupiter, your mind should automatically associate its size with the concepts of **expansion, enthusiasm, and excess,** and, because it expands what it touches, it brings in the concepts of **luck, reward, and benefit, the sense of "much."**

In ancient lore, Jupiter was the Greek Zeus, the god who bestowed immortality upon those whom he deemed worthy. Zeus had the power and authority, as sovereign ruler, to reward or condemn based upon his judgment of what a person had done. It is through this lore that we see Jupiter's association with the spirit of the law and people who are important through law (lawyers, judges, etc.). Jupiter also has to do with the higher mind, academia, religion, faith, and internationalism. **In a natal horoscope, Jupiter represents one's hope for reward, whatever it takes for one to feel a sense of having been rewarded.**

In health, Jupiter rules the liver, upper leg, sciatic nerve, and more.

Jupiter takes 12 years to orbit the Sun (2 orbits in 24 years; "24" the mnemonic for the planet's symbol).

♄ The first thing to notice about Saturn's symbol is that, in its basic form, it is Jupiter turned upside down! This suggests a profile that is diametrically opposed to Jupiter's symbolism. Where Jupiter is happy-go-lucky, excessive, and enthusiastic, Saturn is unfortunate, conservative, often melancholy; thrifty, cold, cynical, hierarchical, ruling, regulating, and doubting; often lacking emotion, being materialistic and self-sufficient, alone, ministerial, very organized with a strong control factor. The ancient Greeks knew Saturn as Chronus, their word for "time." Time is the natural control of life and development.

We have a drive to be efficient in life that is wholly dependent upon operating through and within certain rules, regulations, and controls. Without these controls, people would run amuck, rivers would overflow their banks, cars would have no organized traffic pattern for safe operation. These are all necessary controls for essential efficiency. **Saturn is the symbol of necessary controls and of ambition.** It is the lessons of time.

Prior to the discovery of Uranus, Neptune, and Pluto, Saturn was regarded as "the end of the line" as far as planets were concerned. Everything seen as a negative influence in human life was related to Saturn because it was seen as the planet farthest away from the Sun, thus being the coldest (and its 29.5-year orbit around the Sun paralleled the general human lifespan in times long ago). It is restriction, disappointment, frustration, and delays—in order to learn the important lessons of life—that bring maturity and wisdom; it is things that are old. Saturn also represents the kind of reward that is gained from the longtime pursuit of a goal. It is form, structure, a CEO. **Saturn is about learning life lessons through the management of obstacles.**

Saturn rules all the parts of the body that hurt badly when they cause problems—bones, knees, teeth—in general, the skeleton and the skin that keep the body in form.

♅ BZZZZZZZZZ! BZZZZZZZZZ! BZZZZZZZZZZ! Feel that jolt, that electrical intensity! That is Uranus: it adds its great intensity to whatever it touches in the horoscope. Uranus was discovered March 13, 1781 by a German-born English teacher, William Herschel (the symbol for Uranus is based on the monogrammatic "H", and can be seen as a pair of rods that are constantly buzzing a current from one to the other) at a time of revolution (American and French Revolutions in 1776–1781), of invention and scientific discovery throughout the world (electricity). It is from all this that we take Uranus to symbolize independence, revolution, and invention. The Uranian influence is one that wants to go against the grain, to be different, innovative, and ahead of one's time. Uranus rulership is linked to astrology, air travel, computers, wireless communications, space travel, and modernity. **In a personal horoscope, Uranus intensifies, individuates, and/or makes eccentric.** Uranus questions authority, transcends social and cultural boundaries, is stubborn, inflexible, quirkish, and always wants to fight against oppressed states of being. Uranus loves to break rules.

In the body, Uranus rules the nervous system and all nervous conditions, or illness that comes on suddenly, such as epileptic seizures. It also rules the ankles.

Uranus orbits the Sun every 84 years. The European symbol for the planet Uranus is ♅.

♆ Neptune is the Roman name of the Greek god Poseidon, god of the sea; in ancient mythology, when Ulysses was returning home from his travels, he was tormented and confused by Poseidon. Neptune corresponds to the confusion of mankind, the chaos of impressionability and human emotions, the elements of self-deception and camouflage.

When one stares at the sea or sails upon it far from land, a different consciousness and a dreaminess are inspired, fantasy and imagery are stimulated. These are important concepts for Neptune. When a person steps into a role as an actor, for example, he or she is utilizing Neptune's energy. Neptune is foggy. It represents intangibles, the unseen, that which is spiritual. It is deception, illusion, and the idea that **things are other than what they seem: idealism and camouflage.** Neptune is confusion, uncertainty, the suppression of Self, interest in psychic phenomena, parapsychology, daydreaming, the esoteric, New Age-ness, lack of direction, laziness, problems associated with drugs and intoxication, delusions of grandeur, mirages, actors, musicians, spiritual leaders.

Neptune was discovered by Johann Galle on September 24, 1846 in Berlin, Germany. Neptune moves very, very slowly, taking 165 years to orbit the Sun. Its symbol is obvious: the trident of Neptune.

Neptune rules the blood and refers to the feet.

Pluto was discovered by Percival Lowell on February 18, 1930 in Flagstaff, Arizona. The symbol that we use for Pluto, ♇, is the monogram of his name. (An optional symbol is used for Pluto in astrology: ♀). Its discovery coincided with a rise in world turmoil, the first use of the atom bomb, and the strong rise of crime and underworld activity. Pluto's symbolism plays an **adverbial function in the horoscope:** it is "how much," "how many," "how large," "how long." Pluto strongly adds perspective to what it touches. **Pluto is empowerment.** It is an all-or-nothing influence.

Pluto generally takes 230 years to rotate the Sun in its irregular, erratic orbit. It rules the sexual organs and everything around them, including the colon, and suggests situational concerns associated with end-of-life matters.

Interpreting Speeds and Distances

Although you have just started your journey with the planets, it is not too soon to introduce some examples of the art of interpretation in astrology! To do this, we need to cover a few technical details of the relative speeds of the planets.

The farther a planet is from the Sun, the slower its movement is. In terms of speed, from fastest to slowest, the order of speed among the planets (how the planets were presented on the previous pages) out from the Sun is as follows: Sun, Moon, Mercury, Venus, Mars, Jupiter, Saturn, Uranus, Neptune, Pluto. *Know this well.* As you practice writing the symbols for the planets, write them in this order, over and over and over again. In just a few days, the symbols and their order will be second nature for you. It must be that internalized, as soon as you can manage it.

Planets gain further descriptive significance through their distances from the Sun. Since the Sun represents the core form of one's life energy, the planets closest to it—Moon, Mercury, Venus, and Mars—are the planets that symbolize the most personalized processes of development. We classify these planets through Mars, as the *inner* **planets.** These planets symbolize the core being: the life energy (☉); the reigning need of the personality (☽); the need to think and communicate in a certain manner (☿); our romantic/relational needs (♀); and the kind of energy and effort we use to get things done (♂).

The slow-moving planets: Uranus, Neptune, and Pluto, are classified as the outer planets. They represent archetypes that condition development more emphatically, more slowly **and with longer ranging impact**. The planets Jupiter and Saturn represent archetypes bridging the gap from the inner to outer planets.

Planetary Orientation

⊙

☽

☿

♀

These are the inner planets, the core Self, the archetypes of behavior that represent the processes of development

♂

♃

♄

} **Action**

Reward

Efficiency

♅

♆

♇

These are the outer planets; they condition development more emphatically, more slowly, and with more impact

Now: Some Interpretation!

How do we combine the planetary archetypes to make a determination about identity that is enlightening, useful, and helpful? **Remember this primary rule: the archetype of the slower moving planet always, always conditions the archetype of the faster moving planet to which it may relate.** For example, you have learned that Mars represents the principle of applied energy. You know that it stirs up whatever it relates to in the horoscope. If Mars and Venus are relating, what is going to be stirred up?

Answer: that which is romantic, social, etc.

So quickly, easily, and with confidence, you can appreciate that Mars relating to Venus is indicative of passion. Actor Clark Gable, basketball star Earvin "Magic" Johnson, and singer/entertainer Tom Jones, all have conspicuous relationships between ♀ and ♂ in their horoscope. Gable was the matinee idol of his time, known for his attractiveness and sex appeal. Johnson, megawealthy extremely popular athlete, contracted the AIDS virus, presumably as a result of having unprotected sex with many, many women. Tom Jones, like Gable, is an extreme attraction for the opposite sex. His appearances on stage quite frequently find women so attracted to him that they litter the stage around him with personal clothing items. These are real-life, strong manifestations of Mars relating to Venus.

Now suppose Saturn is in relationship to Venus! Can you appreciate that there would be a **control** factor placed on the Venus need to express itself in a certain manner? Of course! Actor Robert DeNiro, Jackie Kennedy-Onassis, and Nicole Brown-Simpson, the murdered ex-wife of O. J. Simpson, all have conspicuous relationships between ♄ and ♀ in their horoscope. DeNiro, a talented but elusive actor, has obvious difficulties in self-expression that easily spill over into relationship challenges. Jackie Onassis had a very definite control factor (her coolness and aloofness) placed upon her ability to relate; there were deep self-worth concerns linked to the relationship with her father. Nicole Brown-Simpson left this world remembered for being controlled and victimized in her marriage to O. J. Simpson. These are real-life, strong manifestations of Saturn's relationship to Venus.

If **Uranus** is in relationship to Venus, then romance and relating can become highly intense, possibly unusual or erratic. Bzzzzzzzz! Singers

Michael Jackson, Julio Iglesias, and Elvis Presley are all examples of this Uranus (♅) and Venus (♀) relationship. All three entertainers are extraordinarily magnetic and unique in their individual expressions of sensuality, sexuality.

If **Neptune** is in relationship to Venus, the sense of confusion or deception or aesthetics or art is introduced to the need to relate in a certain manner. Might this possibly make one susceptible to pain in relationships, as a result of seeing a relationship differently than it really is? Three strong examples of this relationship between Neptune (♆) and Venus (♀) include singers Tina Turner and Whitney Houston, and Ethel Kennedy, wife of Robert Kennedy, younger brother of President John F. Kennedy. For years, Tina Turner was in an abusive relationship that she would not leave because of idealistic inclinations. Whitney Houston is married to a singer named Bobby Brown, well known for his various arrests and his "bad-boy" image. Most people wonder what Houston sees in Brown. Ethel Kennedy's marriage to Robert was enshrouded in massive doses of confusion and uncertainty due to her husband's womanizing. The aesthetic dimensions of the Neptune-Venus relationship are seen in the great Russian ballet dancer, Vaslav Nijinsky, French composer Maurice Ravel, artist extraordinaire, Rembrandt, and many other celebrated performers and artists.

And if **Pluto** is in relationship to Venus, a tremendous, empowering perspective is given to the relational/romantic needs, which may be extreme. Conspicuous examples of the ♀–♇ relationship include actors Elizabeth Taylor and Richard Pryor, who, between them, were married thirteen times! In addition, famous actor Rock Hudson, who succumbed to the AIDS virus, also had a conspicuous relationship between ♀–♇.

If, say, Saturn is in relationship to Mercury, the concern is with the control factors that are placed upon the mind in development, somehow necessarily (as are the cases in the life of actors Steven Seagal and Robert Redford, and former U.S. First Lady, Betty Ford). These control factors may aid the mind or depress it. If Saturn is in relationship to the Sun, the core life-energy fuel will be colored by strong control factors, usually in relation to the father in early development (U.S. General Norman Schwarzkopf). If Venus is in relationship to the Moon, can you see the potential of a personality that needs to express itself in a cordial, charming fashion (actress Brooke Shields)? Think about these vignettes; feel them in relation to the contact between the two specifically exampled planets.

These examples demonstrate how easy—how natural—it is to learn interpretation in astrology. By combining the basic planetary archetypes of two symbols, knowing that the intrinsically slower moving archetype conditions the development of the intrinsically faster moving planet, you can quickly begin to make valid judgments of interpretation in a horoscope. You are off to a good start!

Planetary Behavioral Archetypes

Planet		Behavioral Function
Sun	☉	The Energy of Life
Moon	☽	The Reigning Need of the Personality; how the Sun's Energy is expressed in Personality Form
Mercury	☿	Mind; Nervous System, Movement, Communication
Venus	♀	Social, Romantic, Relational, Aesthetic Concerns
Mars	♂	Applied Energy, Assertion, Aggression
Jupiter	♃	Expansion, Optimism, Enthusiasm
Saturn	♄	Ambition, Necessary Controls
Uranus	♅	Intensification, Eccentricism, Individualism
Neptune	♆	Creative Visualization; Camouflage
Pluto	♇	Perspective; Empowerment

Now, it is important, at this point, before you read the next chapter, **To memorize backwards and forward what the symbols and basic meanings of all the planets are.** You must learn to draw their glyphs clearly with precision and associate the essential meaning of the planet with its glyph every time you write it! Spend some doodling time when you have "downtime" during the day; draw each glyph "into your consciousness" some forty or fifty times a day, in all orders. Really get the feel of it all—it will pay off, and soon it will be instinctive. It is essential (and it's fun!).

Summary

1. It is important to understand the perspective in which one views astrology. Astrology is not fortunetelling! The horoscope is a map of a person as he or she can be, not necessarily the person as he or she is. Environmental (including family) influences play a most important role in how a person reflects the horoscope.

2. Astrology presumes that the soul picks its time and place of birth in order to refine and fulfill itself in a grand scheme of things.

3. Planets represent important behavioral faculties: Sun—the life energy; Moon—the reigning need of the personality; Mercury—the need to think and communicate; Venus—the need to relate socially and romantically; Mars—applied energy; Jupiter—reward needs; Saturn—necessary controls; Uranus—individuation, intensification, and eccentricism; Neptune—creative visualization; Pluto—perspective and empowerment.

4. The inner planets are those closest to the Sun: Moon, Mercury, Venus, and Mars. These planets represent core needs.

5. The larger planets—Jupiter and Saturn, and especially Uranus, Neptune, and Pluto, represent qualities that condition behavior slowly and with decided impact.

6. The faculty of an outer planet almost always conditions the behavioral faculty of a planet intrinsically faster-moving (closer to the Sun) when they are in contact within the horoscope. This is the key to interpretation of planets in contact with each other in the natal horoscope.

Test Yourself

Answer the following questions without referring back to the book text, on a separate piece of paper if you prefer. [The answers to this test and all those that follow appear in the appendix (beginning on p. 229), as answered by Noel Tyl, who took the tests himself (!), at my request. —B.F.]

1. Write the symbols for the outer planets in backward order into the Sun.

2. Write the symbols for the all planets in order of their relative speeds to one another.

3. Label each planet with its basic, most essential behavioral faculty, its key words.

4. Mercury and Uranus are making contact in a horoscope. How would you interpret it?

5. The Moon and Venus are making contact in a horoscope. How would you interpret it?

6. Venus is making contact with Mars **and** Pluto, how would you interpret it?

7. What do planets represent in human beings?

8. Which planet is closest to the Sun?

9. Which planet here is misplaced? ♄ ☉ ☽ ☿ ♀

10. Draw the symbol for the planet that represents excess.

11. What does the dot in the symbol for the Sun represent?

12. What are the advantageous and difficult possibilities of a Mercury-Saturn contact in a horoscope?

13. Which planet might have more of an impact, Jupiter or Neptune?

14. When a person needs to think in large, expansive ways, what planetary contact does that bring to mind? Why?

15. The life energy and the reigning need of the personality are given great perspective—name the planets that would symbolize this statement within the horoscope.

16. You see in a horoscope that Mercury is in contact with Mars and Saturn. How might a person represent this contact? What would you expect? Why?

17. Quickly, without looking at anything but this question, write the symbol for the planet that looks like Jupiter turned upside down.

18. Which planet best represents a host or hostess? Why?

19. When Mars is together with Uranus, is there a planned, deliberate application of energy? Clarify your answer. Be careful!

20. The number "24" makes you think of which planet? Why?

Chapter 2

•••

The Signs of the Zodiac

WE KNOW THAT ASTROLOGY EVOLVED AS A result of centuries of observation of heavenly bodies; these bodies seemed to be positioned strategically above in the heavens *in relation to events that occurred on Earth.* Through these observances, it was also noted that certain planets seemed to act with special significance when they were in certain sectors of the sky. For example, Mars in a certain sector, as it were, coincided remarkably often with the birth and tracked the activities of warlords on Earth, people whose character traits closely manifested the energetic, competitive, warrior-like qualities associated with Mars. And when this observance disclosed that Mars operated with such strength in the area of the sky mapped out as Aries, for example, the assumption was formulated that Mars somehow "ruled" Aries. Mars was "comfortable and expressive" there. This process of observation is what has given us our astrological Signs. **The Signs of the zodiac developed their characteristic qualities from the planets "ruling" each of them.**

The Sun, for example, is the light of our lives. It is the absolute center-piece of the heavens (our Solar System), that which *everything* depends on for illumination and for life. Its importance can not be questioned. The ancients observed that the Sun's strength was at its most dramatic level in Leo. Therefore, the qualities, as you will see, that are associated with the Leo archetype have to do with recognition, being the center of attention, being influential. These qualities and more will need to be present in the behavioral manifestation of anyone with a pronounced Leo emphasis in the horoscope. Doesn't it make sense, then, that Leo is the Sign of the entertainer, of theatricality, of drama, royalty, presidents, chieftains? Sure it does!

Symbology in Astrology

There are many ways to describe a person, place, or thing. Language evolved to serve our complex demands for description; a common medium of expression is essential for people to recognize and understand each other.

As many parts of speech as we have in language, they sometimes do not do justice to what is being described. For example, to describe something that is lethal upon ingestion, we may use the word "poison." While that *word* says a great deal, when you see a *symbol* of a huge skull with crossbones, the thrust of that *symbol* is much more dramatic; its meaning is more dramatic! *That's* descriptive! The word "water," tells us one thing, but that doesn't quite measure up to the symbol H_2O, which tells us that two atoms of hydrogen and one atom of oxygen have combined miraculously.

And so it is in astrology. The word Mars "says" something that cannot compete with the aggressive, direct nature of its symbol, ♂. So, as we proceed with our study of the astrological Signs, to facilitate memorization of each Sign, and to appreciate its archetype, *we must appreciate what the symbol describes.*

Aries ♈

The symbol for Aries, "The Ram," suggests an upright, bold scepter of authority with the horns of a ram flaring from its top end. You can feel the ram's attack! Aries is the first Sign of the zodiac. What's suggested here is the combination of authority with the Arian tendency to forge ahead individualistically, courageously, with aggression, a thrust of spirit, usually without caution. Aries is ruled by Mars and, just that quickly, you are able to tie together in your mind why Aries characteristics are as they are.

Thomas Jefferson, Otto von Bismarck, Marlon Brando, Steven Seagal, and Diana Ross have the ☉ in ♈.

Aries represents **ego importance, assertion, the exertion of force, and the self-positioning as number one** (in the sense of not being subordinate and not being in the background). The Sun is in Aries from approximately March 21 to April 21.

Taurus ♉

The symbol for Taurus, "The Bull," when compared to the Aries symbol, immediately shows heaviness, organization; it is stolid, stubborn. And if you observe a cow or bull in life, it does the same thing, the same way, every day. It grazes in the meadow, chews grass, and is really quiet, calm, and collected within its daily structured routine. It is when you try to take the bull out of its pattern that it becomes agitated and shows its temperament. This description of the bull's nature coupled with its stolid symbol gives us a clear explanation of the Taurean archetype.

Taurus represents **keeping things as they are or making them as they should be, to maintain structure, organization, and security.** This is the kind of influence that will tolerate an unfulfilling (but predictable) situation rather than make risky, insecurity-causing changes for the new. The Sun is in Taurus from approximately May 21 to June 21, and is ruled by artistic Venus.

Niccolo Machiavelli, Liberace, Cher, and Barbara Streisand have the ☉ in ♉.

Gemini ♊

The symbol for Gemini, "The Twins," immediately projects the idea of duality, of more than one thing at a time. It shows two staves or scepters or two arms or both lungs. One feels parallel polarity issues. Ruled by *Mercury,* Gemini symbolizes a quick, cerebral, intellectual, conversational influence with an active nervous system and an extremely active, facile mind. The Gemini experience is antithetical to boredom. There is constant activity and stimulation and, because of this, energies will tend to go from one thing to another to maintain the sense of new excitement.

Gemini represents **diversity, communication, cleverness, inquisitiveness, wit, and the idea of being scintillating.** The cerebral element is dominant in this influence. The Sun is in Gemini from approximately May 21 to June 21.

Bob Hope, John F. Kennedy, Marilyn Monroe, Paul McCartney, and Donald Trump have the ☉ in ♊.

Cancer ♋

Cancer's symbol depicts the breasts. This is a very easy symbol to remember both in its drawing and in its life manifestation. Simply think of a child suckling at the breasts of its mother, the sense of comfort, security, and satisfaction. Everything is safe and secure at that moment. There is no threat. All is at peace. In addition, the association of Cancer with the crab constellation reveals an archetype with a very protective outer nature that serves to hide a very soft, sensitive core. **Cancer represents emotional and home security.**

Cancer's ruler is the Moon. The Sun is in Cancer from approximately June 21–July 21. Nelson Mandela, Bill Cosby, Sylvester Stallone, and Harrison Ford have the Sun in ☉ in ♋.

Leo ♌

The symbol for Leo, "The Lion," has two different meanings traditionally. We can see it as the tail of an aroused lion or as the symbol of the heart and its two valves.

Leo is ruled by the most radiant body in our Solar System, the Sun. Just as the Sun is the central dynamo of the zodiac, Leo energy commands the center stage position in life. It is a strong, domineering, prideful, vain, creative influence with a central **requirement for recognition, respect, love, and honor. There is a command for ego triumph found in Leo.** It is the archetype of the king. The Sun is in Leo from approximately July 21 to August 23.

Mae West, Bill Clinton, Mick Jagger, Madonna, Arnold Schwarzenegger, and Basil Fearrington have the ☉ in ♌.

Virgo ♍

Virgo is misleadingly given the name "Virgin." This naturally leads the mind into thoughts connected with sexual inexperience. The virginity associated with Virgo actually relates to discernment, to the idealism of choice. Think of a woman cutting down virgin wheat stalks with a scythe. This harvesting must be done at the right time in the right way! This idea of waiting for just the right time and being exacting in technique tells the story about the Virgo archetype. There is the sense of worried patience within Virgo.

In addition, the symbol for Virgo may be seen to depict the intestines, the long tubing inside our abdomen where food is managed.

The Virgo archetype reflects **refinement, fastidiousness, discrimination, being exact, the cerebral nature, the practical and correct.** Virgo's ruler is Mercury. (Yes, Mercury rules two Signs: Gemini and Virgo).

The Sun is in Virgo from approximately August 23 to September 21. Mother Teresa, Yassar Arafat, David Copperfield, and Michael Jackson have the ☉ in ♍.

Libra ♎

The symbol for Libra shows two halves of one unit, signifying Libra's zodiacal reign over partnership and marriage. In addition, the symbol shows a setting Sun balanced between day and night, the operative word being "balanced." Ruled by Venus (which also rules Taurus), Libra is the sign of balance, fairness, justice, and popularity. Where Aries seeks ego recognition on its own, Libra seeks to gain ego recognition through the societal reflection by others. Picture the attractive host or hostess who greets and seats you at a restaurant—she gains satisfaction by pleasing you and hearing your appreciation.

The Libra archetype is **to please and gain appreciation socially, to be popular, fair, and attractive.**

The Sun is in Libra from September 23–October 22. Mahatma Gandhi, Charleton Heston, Julie Andrews, and Michael Douglas, have the ☉ in ♎.

Scorpio ♏

The symbol for Scorpio is easily confused with the symbol for Virgo. The important distinction between the two is that the Scorpio symbol has a pointed tail on it to show the Scorpion's sting. This is a deeply complex, emotional archetype that runs the gamut from being extremely emotional and passionate to soaring the high realms of mystery, to being inspired by spirituality and religion. Symbolically, Scorpio can soar as high and free as an eagle or dove, or crawl as low and threateningly as a scorpion.

Like its opposite Sign, Taurus, Scorpio is very fixed and structured. Its strong link with passion has given Scorpio the zodiacal archetype that is most connected with sexuality. It is a very passionate, unyielding, strong area of the zodiac that is quite capable of harboring grudges, being revengeful, spiteful, and sarcastic.

The Scorpio archetype represents **control by knowing about things; getting to the bottom of things, plumbing the depths in order to reach the heights; to be regarded as deep and significant, self-sufficient and right.**

Scorpio is ruled by Pluto (with Mars as its co-ruler) The Sun is in Scorpio generally from October 21 to November 21. Picasso, Billy Graham, Richard Burton, Larry King, and Charles Manson have the ☉ in ♏.

Sagittarius ♐

The traditional symbol for the Sagittarius constellation depicts an arrow being shot from its bow by a centaur. You will gain a great feeling for the Sagittarian archetype by focusing on the arrow as it thrusts through the air. What would its thoughts be as it looked through the sky and at the ground below it? Wouldn't there be questions about the universe, about life itself? Wouldn't there be the most ultimate feeling of freedom? Definitely!

Sagittarius is connected with a **strong thrust of thought**—often idealistic—an outpouring of ideas in an enthusiastic, to-the-point manner that is often seen by others as impulsive, even brusque. It is an outdoors archetype (remember the joy of that arrow is it soars through the air unimpeded). It is the Sign of physical exercise. There is a strong concern for justice in Sagittarius, the need to assert oneself in matters of justice in order to make things right. This is a bold, fiery, enthusiastic, optimistic, and idealistic archetype.

Ruled by Jupiter, the Sagittarius archetype shows **arch opinionation, self-assertion, knowing what is right; affecting thought.**

The Sun is in Sagittarius from approximately November 21 to December 21. Charles de Gaulle, Alexander Solzhenitzen, Tina Turner, Kirk Douglas, and Frank Sinatra have the ☉ in ♐.

Capricorn ♑

The Capricorn symbol is the most difficult to learn to draw. It takes practice. Formulate in your mind the sense of a knee: the organization of the lines will begin to make sense. Why the knees? What is the association? The Capricorn archetype is essentially connected with affecting progress and making things happen. When one's knees are bad, mobility and advancement are impeded. Additionally, the knees can be strategic weapons.

Ruled by Saturn, Capricorn is a Sign of leadership, ambition, practicality, and patience. In personality, there is frequently a strong projection of austerity that is almost ministerial in manifestation. Practicality, punctuality, and efficiency are prized attributes and concerns connected with Capricorn. It is the Sign of the do-or-die leader or hard-working business person.

The Capricorn archetype is connected with **making things happen; organization, strategy, and deployment of resources; ambition, responsibility, and finality.**

The Sun is in Capricorn from approximately December 21 to January 20. Konrad Adenauer, Mao Tse-tung, Anwar Sadat, Richard Nixon, Anthony Hopkins, and Noel Tyl have the ⊙ in ♑.

Aquarius ♒

Aquarius is called "The Water Bearer." This is the name given to this Sign from the constellation in which it was formerly found. It is unfortunately misleading, since Aquarius has nothing at all to do with the water element in astrology. The "water bearer" is simply pouring new ideas, innovation, inspiration, and concepts into a stream of influence upon the world, in the name of social progress and humanitarianism.

Ruled by Uranus (co-ruled by Saturn), Aquarius, like Sagittarius, is very freedom-oriented. It symbolizes a highly social, humanitarian influence that is quite detached in its nature, can be given to strong doses of eccentricism, and is better focused with groups of people in an impersonal manner than in one-on-one situations. It is a very group-oriented Sign, very comfortable with friends, especially like-minded friends in groups or clubs. Aquarius is very interested in reaching out to help others. The Aquarian archetype is connected with **innovation, uniqueness, the social view, and humanitarian thrust.**

The Sun is in Aquarius from approximately January 21 to February 19. Abraham Lincoln, Ronald Reagan, Boris Yeltsin, and Oprah Winfrey have the ☉ in ♒.

Pisces ♓

The symbol for Pisces shows two fish (also looking like two lunar crescents), back to back, swimming in opposite directions, both joined by a horizon line of earthly experience. That there are *two* fish suggests the inherent duality of the Sign. Swimming in opposite directions *in water* suggests **emotional confusion**, the importance of finding one's way in the higher realms. If you view the symbol as two crescent moons, joined by a horizon line of earthly experience, there is the idea of Pisces bringing deep, subconscious sensitivity down to earth, joining consciousness with the subconscious.

Ruled by Neptune (co-ruled by Jupiter), Pisces is a deeply empathic, compassionate, emotional, idealistic, and sensitive archetype. It feels things strongly, easily taking on a martyr complex when feelings have been badly hurt or as an emotional strategy. Pisces also includes strong dimensions of spirituality and artistic creativity within its archetype.

Pisces represents *feelings, understanding, compassion and empathy with the ideal; working with the intangible.*

The Sun is in Pisces from approximately February 19 to March 20. Mozart, Michelangelo, Edgar Cayce, Mikhail Gorbachev, and Elizabeth Taylor have the ☉ in ♓.

It is very important that you memorize the symbols for the Signs and it is crucial that you learn them in zodiacal order, BACKWARD AND FORWARD so that you can repeat them with ease. Although there are twelve Signs, they are actually six sets of two each. It is extremely helpful and of essential necessity that you learn them as pairs of opposites as well (see below).

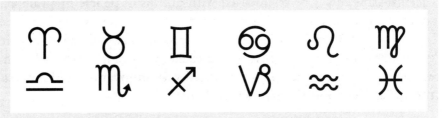

The Question of Dual Rulerships

Mercury and Venus rule two Signs each: Mercury rules Gemini and Virgo; Venus rules Taurus and Libra.

How can this be? How do we work with this? With Mercury and Venus so close to the Sun, it is reasonable that their influence permeates the emanation of selfhood, out from the center, touching more than one sphere of activity, symbolizing more than one very important developmental dimension. In Gemini, Mercury focuses intelligence in terms of *intellectual curiosity*, whereas in Virgo, the intelligence is directed toward cerebral *discrimination and idealism*. The emphasis in both Signs is intellectual.

Venus has a duality about it too: one side, the Libra-rulership, symbolizes the *charming, aesthetic, popularity-seeking* dimension; the other side is the security-seeking Taurean dimension, which *refers to money*!

More Interpretation

In Chapter 1, we learned that **each planet represents various human behavioral faculties.** In this chapter, we have seen how **each Sign of the zodiac reflects certain personality dynamics.** We know that Aries is assertive, Taurus is structured, Virgo is detailed, etc. Now, the first part of extending our interpretation process involves **combining the behavioral faculty of a planet with its PLACEMENT IN A SIGN, with its personality dynamic.**

For example, the behavioral faculty associated with Mercury has to do with thought and communication. We can ask, "How does this particular person's Mercury need to think and communicate in order to be efficient and fulfilled?" The answer to that question is found, in large part, **in its Sign placement in the person's horoscope.**

Let us assume that a person is born when Mercury is in Aries. What does this suggest? How do you interpret it? You would say that *there is a need to think and communicate in terms of ego importance, assertiveness, fire and drive,* etc. In other words, while Mercury represents thinking and communicating, its placement in Aries suggests that the person *needs* to think in a manner that is *like the archetype of Aries,* in order to feel personally fulfilled!

Another example: Mars represents the principle of applied energy. If Mars is in Gemini, the application of energy becomes nervous, cerebral:

perhaps there is a need *to apply energy in more than one direction at a time.* If Mars is in Taurus, the need to apply energy becomes distinctly different than when Mars is in Gemini. Taurus is more structured, organized, and fixed so the energy application would be best fulfilled for this person by being in a position to apply energy *in a structured, organized fashion.*

How important would information like this be to an employer or the coach of a professional sports team? The knowledge of how a person needs to apply energy allows a more efficient deployment of that person's energy; and taking action on that knowledge would greatly benefit, in this case, both employer or coach and employee or athlete.

The Moon, next to the Sun the most important planetary considera-tion, represents the **reigning need of the personality,** the personality's drive for fulfillment. What is that need? If the Moon is in, say, Sagittarius, the reigning need of that personality is to have its opinions respected. If it is in Cancer, the reigning need of the personality is for emotional secur-ity. In Leo, you are expecting the kind of behavior that needs to attract recognition in order to assure ego triumph. **ABOVE ALL ELSE, THE REIGNING NEED OF THE PERSONALITY IS EMPHAT-ICALLY THE DRIVER OF LIFE BEHAVIOR AND LIFE DEVELOPMENT.**

The behavioral faculty of a planet is expressed through the Sign of its placement at birth. Together, planet and Sign synthesize; they show how the various needs (of life energy ($\odot$), of the general per-sonality ($\mathangle$), mind ($\mercury$), relationships ($\venus$), energy application ($\mars$), reward needs ($\jupiter$), ambition ($\saturn$), individuality ($\uranus$), creative visualiza-tion ($\neptune$), and personal perspective ($\pluto$)) in an individual all come together to depict the process of life development.

It is important, at this juncture, to remind you that the horoscope is a guide that is used to anticipate, appreciate, and direct behavior. A planet placed in a particular Sign is telling you, the astrologer, what the *opti-mum* way of expression is for that particular behavioral faculty. It is what the person needs *naturally!* It is **not always** going to be expressed that way or be successful, because there are **influences from the environ-ment**—family, other people with *their* needs, and society as a whole— that may alter individual expression, as the individual works in life to develop in the best way possible.

The Ephemeris

There are two ways to determine in what Sign a planet is at any given time. One way is obviously through astrological data displayed by the computer, from astrological software. The other is through a detailed set of tables called an Ephemeris. An Ephemeris contains a daily listing of the planetary positions in the heavens. Ephemerides (the plural; eh-phe-meh-reeds) are sold in book form (an entire century is available in one book!) and are available in software form with almost every professional astrology program.

Reading an Ephemeris is simple. Our example Ephemeris (p. 30) shows the planetary positions recorded for the period from September 1, 1998 through September 29, 1998. If you wanted to know the positions of the planets on September 1, you would first find that date in the far-left corner of the Ephemeris page. Then you would read across the columns from left to right. The first column is headed by the Moon. It shows a position of 28°♐44'. This means that the Moon is located at 28 degrees and 44 minutes of Sagittarius.

The next column is headed by the Sun. It shows a position of 08°♍22'. This tells you that the Sun is located at 8 degrees and 22 minutes of Virgo.

The next column is headed by Mercury. It shows a position of 20♌12. This is telling you that Mercury is located at 20 degrees and 12 minutes of Leo on this date. It is just that simple! (Indeed, there are more intricate measurements presented on an Ephemeris page, not illustrated here. For example, there is an important conversion factor, called *Sidereal Time*, that we must understand [explained later in this book], and there are other time and motion factors as well).

We will return to the Ephemeris and its data soon. Hold on!

Ephemeris

GMT + 0:00 Tropical Geo Long	The Moon ☽	The Sun ☉	Mercury ☿	Venus ♀	Mars ♂	Jupiter ♃	Saturn ♄	Uranus ♅	Neptune ♆	Pluto ♇
Sep 1 1998	28°♐44'	08°♍22'	20°♌12'	22°♌49'	07°♌10'	25°♓00'℞	03°♉23'℞	09°♒41'℞	29°♑48'℞	05°♐21'
Sep 2 1998	11°♑33'	09°♍20'	21°♌18'	24°♌03'	07°♌48'	24°♓53'	03°♉22'	09°♒39'	29°♑47'	05°♐22'
Sep 3 1998	24°♑45'	10°♍18'	22°♌30'	25°♌17'	08°♌27'	24°♓45'	03°♉20'	09°♒37'	29°♑46'	05°♐22'
Sep 4 1998	08°♒21'	11°♍16'	23°♌48'	26°♌31'	09°♌05'	24°♓38'	03°♉18'	09°♒35'	29°♑45'	05°♐23'
Sep 5 1998	22°♒22'	12°♍14'	25°♌12'	27°♌45'	09°♌43'	24°♓30'	03°♉16'	09°♒33'	29°♑44'	05°♐24'
Sep 6 1998	06°♓45'	13°♍12'	26°♌41'	29°♌00'	10°♌21'	24°♓23'	03°♉14'	09°♒31'	29°♑42'	05°♐24'
Sep 7 1998	21°♓25'	14°♍10'	28°♌14'	00°♍14'	10°♌59'	24°♓15'	03°♉12'	09°♒29'	29°♑41'	05°♐25'
Sep 8 1998	06°♈16'	15°♍09'	29°♌51'	01°♍28'	11°♌37'	24°♓07'	03°♉09'	09°♒27'	29°♑40'	05°♐26'
Sep 9 1998	21°♈10'	16°♍07'	01°♍32'	02°♍42'	12°♌15'	23°♓59'	03°♉07'	09°♒25'	29°♑39'	05°♐27'
Sep 10 1998	05°♉59'	17°♍05'	03°♍16'	03°♍56'	12°♌53'	23°♓52'	03°♉04'	09°♒24'	29°♑38'	05°♐27'
Sep 11 1998	20°♉36'	18°♍03'	05°♍03'	05°♍11'	13°♌30'	23°♓44'	03°♉02'	09°♒22'	29°♑37'	05°♐28'
Sep 12 1998	04°♊56'	19°♍02'	06°♍51'	06°♍25'	14°♌08'	23°♓36'	03°♉00'	09°♒20'	29°♑37'	05°♐29'
Sep 13 1998	18°♊57'	20°♍00'	08°♍41'	07°♍39'	14°♌46'	23°♓28'	02°♉56'	09°♒19'	29°♑36'	05°♐30'
Sep 14 1998	02°♋38'	20°♍58'	10°♍32'	08°♍54'	15°♌24'	23°♓20'	02°♉54'	09°♒17'	29°♑35'	05°♐31'
Sep 15 1998	15°♋59'	21°♍57'	12°♍25'	10°♍08'	16°♌02'	23°♓12'	02°♉51'	09°♒16'	29°♑34'	05°♐32'
Sep 16 1998	29°♋02'	22°♍55'	14°♍17'	11°♍22'	16°♌39'	23°♓04'	02°♉48'	09°♒14'	29°♑33'	05°♐33'
Sep 17 1998	11°♌49'	23°♍54'	16°♍10'	12°♍37'	17°♌17'	22°♓56'	02°♉45'	09°♒13'	29°♑32'	05°♐34'
Sep 18 1998	24°♌22'	24°♍52'	18°♍03'	13°♍51'	17°♌54'	22°♓48'	02°♉41'	09°♒11'	29°♑32'	05°♐35'
Sep 19 1998	06°♍45'	25°♍51'	19°♍56'	15°♍06'	18°♌32'	22°♓40'	02°♉38'	09°♒10'	29°♑31'	05°♐36'
Sep 20 1998	18°♍57'	26°♍50'	21°♍49'	16°♍20'	19°♌09'	22°♓32'	02°♉35'	09°♒08'	29°♑30'	05°♐37'
Sep 21 1998	01°♎01'	27°♍48'	23°♍41'	17°♍35'	19°♌47'	22°♓24'	02°♉31'	09°♒07'	29°♑29'	05°♐38'
Sep 22 1998	12°♎59'	28°♍47'	26°♍32'	18°♍50'	20°♌24'	22°♓16'	02°♉28'	09°♒06'	29°♑29'	05°♐39'
Sep 23 1998	24°♎53'	29°♍46'	27°♍23'	20°♍04'	21°♌02'	22°♓08'	02°♉24'	09°♒04'	29°♑28'	05°♐41'
Sep 24 1998	06°♏43'	00°♎44'	29°♍13'	21°♍19'	21°♌39'	22°♓00'	02°♉21'	09°♒03'	29°♑28'	05°♐42'
Sep 25 1998	18°♏34'	01°♎43'	01°♎02'	22°♍33'	22°♌16'	21°♓53'	02°♉17'	09°♒02'	29°♑27'	05°♐43'
Sep 26 1998	00°♐27'	02°♎42'	02°♎51'	23°♍48'	22°♌54'	21°♓45'	02°♉13'	09°♒01'	29°♑27'	05°♐44'
Sep 27 1998	12°♐27'	03°♎41'	04°♎38'	25°♍03'	23°♌31'	21°♓37'	02°♉09'	09°♒00'	29°♑26'	05°♐46'
Sep 28 1998	24°♐36'	04°♎41'	06°♎25'	26°♍18'	24°♌08'	21°♓30'	02°♉05'	08°♒59'	29°♑26'	05°♐47'
Sep 29 1998	07°♑00'	05°♎39'	08°♎11'	27°♍32'	24°♌45'	21°♓22'	02°♉01'	08°♒58'	29°♑25'	05°♐49'

30

Elements and Modes

Chapter 5 of this manual introduces an extremely important and creative discussion of aspects, a subject we will study in great detail. **Aspects are celestial longitudinal distances between planets, measured in degrees.** They are geometrical angles formed between planets or between planets and other points in the horoscope. To facilitate our ability to measure aspects (as well as allowing us to assess Signs in terms of temperament), we must learn to see the zodiac in terms of **special divisions that we call ELEMENTS and MODES.**

The Four Elements (Qualities of Experience)

The four elements in astrology are **Fire, Earth, Air, and Water.** They represent qualities of experience within us; our diversity of temperament. As an element, for example, fire has a direct relationship to the vernal equinox in the Northern hemisphere. It is the beginning of Spring, the time of year when life seems to "come alive" and when plants thrust through the cold ground to reach for the Sun. Fire represents action, energy, thrust, heat, and impulse. **The fire Signs are Aries, Leo, and Sagittarius.**

In the traditional order of the elements, Earth always follows Fire, just as Taurus always follows Aries. The Earth element is associated with the winter solstice in the Northern hemisphere, that time of year when darkness is at its acme, a time that begins a season of grim determination to make it through to spring and warmer weather. The Earth element refers to practicality, strategy, and building. **The Earth Signs are Capricorn, Taurus, and Virgo.**

The Air element is associated with the autumnal equinox, the beginning of the fall season in the Northern hemisphere. It is the time of year when the senses begin to anticipate winter and that anticipation seems to heighten awareness. The Air element refers to dimensions of communicating, thinking, social poise, intellect, and unification. **The Air Signs are Libra, Aquarius, and Gemini.**

Our final element in the traditional order is Water. The Water element is associated with the summer solstice, a time when the light of the Sun reaches its maximum power in the Northern hemisphere. Plants grow quickly and easily. All of life seems to flourish, it appears protected and nurtured by the heat of the Sun. The Water element refers to emotion, feeling, sensitivity, compassion, nurturing, instincts, and sympathies. **The Water Signs are Cancer, Scorpio, and Pisces.**

Metaphor of the Seasons

With the introduction of the elements, we are using a metaphor that relates the archetypal derivation of the signs to the seasons of the year: Aries, the first sign of the zodiac is related to Spring, and that is related to March 21. It is initially bewildering to note that all of this celebration of newness of life beginning to bloom in March, springtime, and of its culmination around July 21 at the height of Summer is dependent upon references within the *Northern hemisphere*. Below the equator in the *Southern hemisphere*, the seasons are reversed, of course: March and July, to begin with, are times of fall and winter!

Yet, the archetypal profiles of the Signs DO prevail in the Southern hemisphere as in the North.

The explanation is that the poetical metaphor of the seasons, used by the observers who formulated astrology so beautifully over so many centuries, is essentially valid in general terms of personality development but unfortunately narrow in terms of seasonal reference. The observers sought to understand all this in terms of their life experience only in the Northern hemisphere. Lands and life elsewhere were not known.

What is being described here, apart from the concepts of the four seasons, is really the concept of *life rhythm*, which "in terms of plant life and other occurrences of Nature" are highest (the Sun highest in the sky) in the North between March and July and highest in the South between September and December (the seasons created by the Earth's tilt on its axis). *In other terms*, in a *different* metaphor, one based upon social relations, for example (keying on *Libra, opposite Aries*) and societal accomplishment (Capricorn, opposite Cancer), the September and December periods for the South would reflect the highest development periods (the Sun highest in the sky there). In the North, at that time between September and December, in this other metaphor, people begin to withdraw from barren fields and the ensuing cold.

It seems that the beauty of the seasonal metaphor was a fortunate vehicle for appreciation and teaching of archetypal development of the Signs *in the North*; that the system has been accepted with grace by the South. We continue this in our learning now. But, metaphor aside, something primal, relevant, and enduring was/is being depicted through these signs and THAT is what we must capture in our learning of astrology and in our application of it to understand life North *and* South.

—Noel Tyl

The Three Modes (Ways of Expression)

There are three archetypal phases of human life. There is the beginning of a cycle, which we call birth. There is existence itself, which we refer to as life. Finally, we know that all things born must die. These three life archetypes—a beginning, an organization of that beginning, and an end to the beginning—form the basis of the archetypes of modes in astrology, the ways of expression given to us in Nature.

The first mode is *Cardinal*. Cardinality refers to action, activity, initiating, leading, birth, and leadership. **The Cardinal Signs are: Aries, Cancer, Libra, and Capricorn.** These Signs represent the times of the year when the seasons begin.

Following cardinality is the *Fixed* mode. This mode has the connotation of organization, stolidity, rootedness, fixity, stability, and solidarity. **The Fixed Signs are: Taurus, Leo, Scorpio, and Aquarius.** These Signs represent the times of the year when our seasons are stable, when a new season has clearly established itself.

We are born into life; as we live it, it is organized in myriad ways many times over. Within the patterns of development we gradually grow old, and there is a gradual breakdown in health and efficiency. Life is falling away from birth and reaching to a point of death, which, in turn, *allows new birth*. This process of change from a fixed state through metamorphosis in a new birth is reflected in the mode of *mutability*, changeability. The mutable mode in astrology refers to change, adaptability, responsiveness, blending, compromise, compliance, and reacting. **The Mutable Signs are: Gemini, Virgo, Sagittarius, and Pisces.** They represent the times of the year when the seasons are in a state of change from what was to what will be.

In your growing study of astrology, you will find that **planets in any Signs emphasize an Element and a Mode**; you will find horoscopes that, through the planets, have an element or mode highly emphasized or conspicuously absent! An emphasis of a given element highlights the qualities of that element. An absence or low number of planets in the *Fire* element, for example, suggests a difficulty with that element, *with entering into activity or experience with enthusiasm, inspiration, or spontaneity;* sometimes a lack of motivation. (Richard Nixon, J. Edgar Hoover). An absence or low number of planets in the *Air* element suggests a difficulty dealing with what is expected, socially or intellectually.

It can also refer to an inability to see oneself the way others do (Napoleon, Lyndon Johnson).

An absence or low number of planets in the *Earth* element suggests *a lack of practicality or a feeling of inner instability that causes one to over-analyze and criticize everyone else*, a displacement of personal insecurity, of feeling ungrounded (Judy Garland, Marilyn Monroe).

An absence or low number of planets in the *Water* element suggests the absence of an inner frame of reference for close emotional orientation in life. Such a person finds the need to become associated with something far outside the Self to which to direct emotional allegiance. Quite frequently we see a person becoming involved in religion, spirituality, or a complex philosophy as a substitute for interpersonal intimacy (Hitler, Charles de Gaulle, Muhammad Ali).

An absence of articulation of a certain mode is rarely seen in a horoscope. However, when that absence or a low count is present, say, in the cardinal element, you can expect a de-emphasis of the behavioral manifestation of that mode in the person's behavior, i.e., a lack of forcefulness, enterprise, leadership. An absence or low count in the Fixed mode suggests a difficulty holding fast, a feeling of not being rooted. An absence of the Mutable element suggests fundamental problems with change, cooperation, and compromise.

Before proceeding to the next chapter, **please let's be sure that you have memorized the Sign archetypes, and the elements and modes of the Signs, as presented in the charts that follow here and in the Summary of the chapter.** The scheme of elements and modes is of paramount importance for you to continue and progress in astrology. The following is the key to all of this discussion—the key to reading aspects. It is a chart we will refer to many, many times. Please, make copies of this chart; put them everywhere in your house (on your TV set, refrigerator, bedroom ceiling!), in your car, at work on your desk—so that, in a few days, it will be emblazoned on your retina! You will know it so well, and together we will be able to use the magic contained in it.

Sign Archetypes

Aries	♈	Ego importance, assertiveness, exerting force, being number one
Taurus	♉	Keeping things as they are, or making them as they should be, to maintain structure, organization, and security
Gemini	♊	Diversity, communication, cleverness, inquisitiveness, wit, and the idea of being scintillating, clever
Cancer	♋	Emotional and domestic security
Leo	♌	Recognition, respect, love and honor; ego triumph
Virgo	♍	Refinement, discrimination, being exact, cerebral, practical, correct, accuracy
Libra	♎	To please and gain appreciation socially; being popular, fair, attractive
Scorpio	♏	Control by knowing; get to the bottom of things; research; being significant, self-sufficient, right
Sagittarius	♐	Opinionation; self-assertion to know what is proper; affecting thought
Capricorn	♑	Making things happen; organizing; strategizing and deploying resources; ambition
Aquarius	♒	Innovation, social outreach, humanitarianism
Pisces	♓	Feeling, understanding, having compassion and identifying the ideal; working with the intangible

Master Chart: Elements and Modes

	C	F	M
F	♈	♌	♐
A	♎	♒	♊
W	♋	♏	♓
E	♑	♉	♍

Summary

1. The Signs of the zodiac get their characteristic qualities from the planets ruling them.

2. To help with remembering each Sign, understand what the symbol is describing.

3. The behavioral faculty of a planet is expressed through the Sign it is in. *Planet and Sign synthesize* to show how the various planetary behavioral archetypes in an individual come together to portray the important psychological needs of the individual, to depict the process of life development.

4. An Ephemeris contains a daily listing of the planetary positions in the heavens.

5. Although there are twelve Signs, they are actually six sets of two each. It is essential that you learn them as pairs of opposites.

6. The Four Elements are the qualities of experience, the different states of consciousness that allow us to gauge temperament. They include Fire (Aries, Leo, Sagittarius), which represents energy, action, thrust, and impulse; Air (Libra, Aquarius, Gemini), which represents dimensions of communicating, thinking, and social poise; Earth (Capricorn, Taurus, Virgo), which represents practicality, strategy, and building; Water (Cancer, Scorpio, Pisces), which refers to sensitivity, sympathies, emotion, feeling, compassion, nurturing, and instincts.

7. The three Modes are ways of expression: Cardinal (Aries, Cancer, Libra, Capricorn) leadership, initiation, making things happen; Fixed (Taurus, Leo, Scorpio, Aquarius) organizing, dramatizing, controlling; and Mutable (Gemini, Virgo, Sagittarius, and Pisces) diversifying, cooperating, reacting.

8. A heavy articulation or absence of an element or mode in a horoscope is an important analytical tool. Know these manifestations well.

Test Yourself

Here's test number two. Answer the following questions, at best *without referring back to the book text*. You're learning so much so well. Really nail it down with these tests. Take real time with them. The answers are in the Appendix (p. 231), as answered by Noel Tyl, who took the tests along with you, at my request! He does add some things you'll enjoy!

1. Draw the Sign symbols in forward and then backward order. How quickly can you do it?

2. Draw the Sign symbols again, this time with the symbol for the planet that rules each Sign. How fast can you do THAT?

3. Where did the characteristic meanings for the Signs come from?

4. Circle the Sign that does *not* belong in the following groups:
   ♋︎≈♏︎♓︎, ♌︎♏︎♐︎≈, ♎︎♈︎♉︎♋︎, ♑︎♓︎♊︎♐︎.
   [You must learn the chart on page 37. You can not imagine how important this chart is to freeing up your analytical ability once the memorization process is over.]

5. Which Sign is associated with opinionation?

6. List the four Signs of the Cardinal Mode: List them in proper zodiacal order.

7. Emotional/home security is the dominant characteristic associated with which Sign?

8. The Earth Signs are:

9. "I *need* to be 'numero uno'! My Moon's Sign is _____."

10. The Mutable mode includes which four Signs? List them in proper zodiacal order.

11. What does Mercury in Cancer suggest in synthesis?

12. The three Signs of the Water element are:

13. What does the Moon in Taurus suggest?

14. List the four Signs of the Fixed mode: List them in proper zodiacal order.

15. Venus in Virgo suggests:

16. What difference is suggested between Mars in Aries and Mars in Capricorn?

17. List the three Signs of the Air element:

18. "The reigning need of my personality is to be diversified. I am pretty heady and quite clever." What planet-in-Sign does this describe?

19. What is suggested when a horoscope lacks the Water element?

20. What is suggested when a horoscope has a dominant emphasis in the Fire element?

Chapter 3

• • •

The Houses

ASTROLOGY CONCERNS ITSELF WITH OUR place in the "scheme of things." We want to know where we stand in relationship to experience and to others: in relationship to ourselves, to purpose, to God, etc. Astrology provides an inspired perspective of the human condition. Astrology is the most fundamental and vital tool that we have available in the humanistic sciences to answer our questions about life. We get these answers by bringing the symbolisms of the heavens down to Earth for individual reference, **down to Earth** and **into Houses**. The astrological Houses are arbitrary divisions of space and time in the horoscope, above and below our horizon. (In metaphor, they are mail addresses for delivery of the planets!)

The circle that describes the ring of any horoscope is called the **ecliptic**. It represents the apparent path of the Sun around the Earth and is the projected path along which planetary movement occurs.

Within the vault of the heavens, which is symbolized by the horoscope itself, the horizon—the ground that you are standing on right now—is projected into space to the East and West; it cuts into and across the vault to establish personal perspective. The horizon is represented by the horizontal line that separates the wheel into upper and lower divisions. This axis is called the **horizon line**.

The Sun in its daily journey appears to travel around the wheel in a clockwise direction. When it is sunrise outside, the Sun is located exactly on the **left side** of this horizon line. It is **east**[1] and that is the point where the Sun and all planets rise above the horizon for visibility in the open sky. Because this is the point in the horoscope where things are ascending, we give it the name: **Ascendant**. The Sign that is rising at the time and place of birth is also named the Ascendant or **Rising Sign** because it is the Sign rising above the horizon at the moment of birth, as seen from the birth location. This is the single most important, individualistic point in the horoscope. We will see later that the Ascendant is, as well, the health center of the horoscope. **The Ascendant is SELF, the identity.**

The opposite end of the horizon line represents the point where the Sun sets below the horizon to allow darkness. Because it represents the point where the Sun (and planets) descends from view below the horizon, it is given the name **Descendant**. The horoscope's horizon axis represents the place of experiential awareness in the horoscope in the same way that Earth's horizon allows humans to have an awareness of day and night. **The Descendant complements the Ascendant. The Descendant is OTHERS.**

Going back to our circle of the vault of the heavens, when the Sun reaches the uppermost point on the wheel (the 12:00 position), it is directly overhead in the sky in the middle of the heavens. We therefore name this position the Midheaven (alternatively, **Medium Coeli**; the center of the heavens, "the MC").

As the Sun travels in a clockwise direction, crossing the Descendant to go below the horizon, daytime becomes night. When the Sun has reached the point where it is in complete 180-degree opposition to the Midheaven (approximately noon), it is midnight. We call this position (the "half past" position in clock reference), the **Nadir**, which means the

---

1 The compass directions on the horoscope will seem confusing to most beginners. We usually assume the northerly direction as facing upward, but in the horoscope, the northern area is the *lower* part of the wheel. Because of the plane of the Sun's ecliptic and the tilt of the Earth, the uppermost point is to the south for those people who live in the northern hemisphere, the farthest point north of the equator reached by the Sun—a technical measurement called "Declination," oriented to the poles of the Earth.

lowest point (alternatively, the **Immum Coeli**; the Bottom of the Heavens, "the IC"). When we draw a vertical line from the Midheaven to the Nadir, it defines the horoscope's left and right divisions (East and West). The name we give to this line is the **Meridian** axis, the Midheaven axis.

These four points—**Ascendant-Descendant, Midheaven-Nadir**—define the horoscope's strongest personal points because they symbolize the points of our day when temporal awareness changes—sunrise, noon, sunset, midnight. **They are the strongest points in any horoscope.** They are like extremely sensitive antennae points organizing signals of life. **These four points are the ANGLES of the Horoscope.** (We will see that the Midheaven is established by the time of birth and the Ascendant is established by the place of our birth. The two axes together orient who we are in time and space.)

Every horoscope is divided into twelve areas that you now know are the Houses. Each radial dividing line is called a **Cusp**. The cusp is the beginning point of a House. The cusps of the Ascendant, Midheaven, Descendant, and Nadir are called Angles, as we have seen. The Angles and the Houses they describe (1, 4, 7, and 10), again, are **the strongest areas of any horoscope**. Any planet that is particularly close to an Angle at birth will represent a behavioral archetype that is easily and conspicuously projected outward. It bears repeating that the Angles are like giant antennae that **transmit and receive qualities to and from the world**.

The further divisions of the wheel give us the interior House cusps. These divisions, based on complex mathematics that divide up space and time, help us to measure the transition between the Angles. (The computer does the computations for us. All we have to do is select the House system of choice).

There are at least thirty ways (systems) of dividing up time and space to define the interior Houses. The most commonly used are named Placidus, or Placidian (after sixteenth-century monk Placidus de Tito) and Koch (after twentieth-century mathematician Walter Koch). The system of analysis that we are using recognizes the Placidian system. **In all House systems, the important Ascendant and Midheaven axes (the four angular key points) are always the same.** Choosing one system or an-other comes down to quibbling discussions about interior House cusps, which, in the end, are just not so important or significant in their small variance from one system to another.

With the construction of the Angles and the interior Houses, the horoscope structure is complete: twelve Houses, each representing an important area of life experience.

Astrologer Marc Edmund Jones, in *Astrology: How And Why It Works* (1969), suggested an inspired metaphor through which to appreciate the sweep of meaning of the birth horoscope: he described an infant at birth, stepping into life with outspread arms forming the horizon; his spine setting the Midheaven axis; and the scope of his embrace collecting the experience of his life. It is an extraordinarily helpful image. Know it, see it, and reflect upon it!

Deeper into Houses

The horoscope captures a moment in time (the Midheaven) and anchors it to a geographic point of observation (the Ascendant). As the Earth rotates on its axis, we see in the sky the Sun rising in the East, along with the planets, which move at different speeds and are spaced out in different positions relative one to another. The Sun culminates at the Midheaven and then begins to set at the Descendant. Now, remember always that, in the horoscope, **East is positioned on the horizon line at the left**; and the Sun appears to rise up there at the left, in the East, and travels in a clockwise movement, left around to right.

Now, in the horoscope, as we begin to introduce the Signs, the Sun, and the planets into the drawing, we have to appreciate a relativity factor among three things: the motion of the Earth as it turns on its axis; the apparent motion of the Sun, and the real movement of planets around the Sun; and all of this occurring throughout a stationary projection of the signs of the zodiac used to mark out zones in the heavens as our reference points.

We will be placing the signs of the zodiac into the horoscope drawing soon, and they will flow in their never-changing order, in a counterclockwise motion. [More about this later.] This captures the relativity problem: while in the sky we see the Sun and planets rising over the horizon in a clockwise motion, in the horoscope drawing we will see the Sun and the planets dependent for location upon the Signs of the zodiac aligned in a counterclockwise motion.

After the perception of this scheme clears in your mind, it will never be a problem again in your work. It takes a little time to sink in, and we will go over it again later. We need to be aware of it now though as we prepare the infrastructure of time and space in the horoscope drawing.

This process of turning, of rising, of developing takes place inexorably every twenty-four-hour period; the tilt of the Earth establishes our seasons in relation to the Sun; and the orbit of Earth around the Sun establishes our cycle of years.

The birth horoscope is a picture of **a specific moment in time** (that time when the baby first breathes on its own), when a "snapshot" is taken of the heavens. **This snapshot becomes the horoscope**, a frozen imprint of the heavens upon the newborn. Each horoscope has a particular degree of a particular Sign that is rising at the horizon at the time of

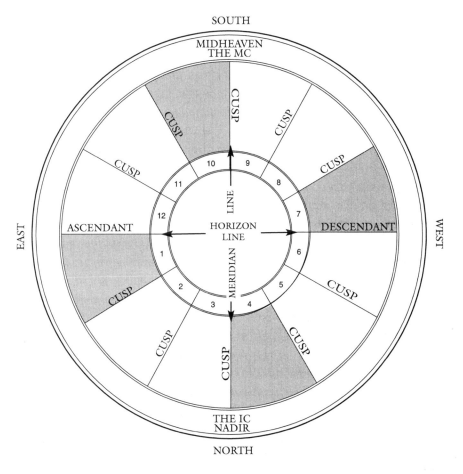

Figure 1
Parts of the Horoscope

birth. **This Sign establishes the order of how the rest of the Signs are placed upon the other eleven House cusps,** in counterclockwise fashion, in the unchanging order you have learned. There is no perceptual problem here; it is as easy and regular as can be, and it is all presented very nicely for you by your computer.

Interpretive Orientation to the Houses

The Houses of the horoscope represent zones of life experience such as marriage, career, and health; self-worth, loving, cooperation, and much more. In astrology, we recognize that the twelve Houses capture the whole of life experience. The first step to learning what the Houses symbolize is to understand that the Houses all get their basic meanings **from the Signs that are placed upon them in the natural distribution (flow order) of the Signs and Houses** (see Fig. 2, p. 47): we see Aries on the first cusp, the Ascendant. Since Aries is the first Sign of the Zodiac, it is associated to the first House. Taurus is the 2nd Sign and is therefore associated to the 2nd House, etc!

First, let us review the angles: The Ascendant is located at the point on the east of the horizon. Because it is represented in the natural distribution of Signs, by Aries, the beginning of Spring (in the Northern hemisphere), the time of year when plants are thrusting through the cold winter ground reaching for the Sun, **the 1st House also takes on connotations of birth and the projection of Self for growth.** *The Sign that is upon the 1st House cusp—in a particular freeze-frame moment of birth—is vital in determining the style of the person's self-projection. This becomes further modified by any planets within the 1st House.*

The 4th House, the north point, the Nadir (or Immum Coeli, remember, "the bottom of the heavens," IC for short), symbolizes the beginning of another season and so it marks an important point of *new beginnings in the horoscope. It represents endings, beginnings, the early home development and one parent in particular, who may have played a particularly important role within that development.*

The 7th House marks the beginning of Fall. The Sun becomes weaker, suggesting a symbolic weakening of the ego. There is now concern with other people, with relationships and the merging with others in many ways, through their resources, their thoughts, even losing oneself to the other person(s), etc. The ego subsides in order to learn to share and interact with others. The 7th House represents *relationships of all kinds (including business partnerships), marriage, the spouse, the public at large.*

The 10th House—the south point or *Medium Coeli*; the middle of the heavens, MC for short) marks yet another important focus of change. It symbolizes the profession, career, and another parent from the one symbolized in the fourth House.

These four Angular Houses—I, IV, VII, and X (often referred to by Roman numerals)—are critical points for analytical orientation.

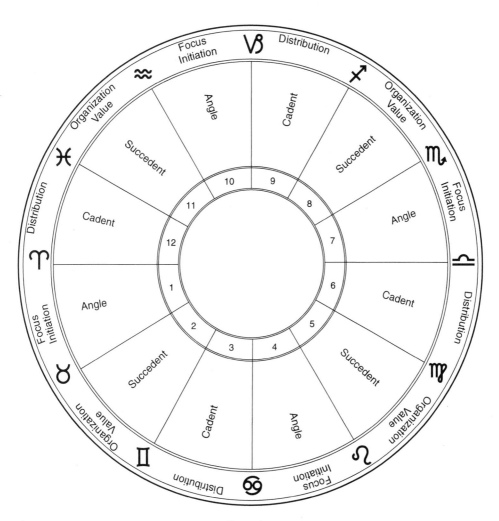

Figure 2
Natural Distribution of Signs

In a larger view now, we can see the first six Houses telling the story of self-development, projected from the Ascendant (birth, identity formation) through development in the early home and the parents (keyed initially at the fourth cusp, the 4th House, House IV and reaching up further through the 5th and 6th Houses to come above the horizon into the 7th House. The complementary six Houses, then, issue from the 7th House; these are the Houses above the horizon, which are concerned with ego awareness among others, from society's vantage point.

Now, for the Interior Houses: The Interior Houses: 2, 5, 8, 11, are called Succedent Houses because they succeed, they follow, the Angular Houses. The Signs that are on these Houses in the natural distribution of Signs are Taurus, Leo, Scorpio, and Aquarius. We know that these Signs are **Fixed Signs; they give their symbolic meanings to the Succedent Houses by organizing security and various factors that have to do with worth, value, and love.**

The Signs falling on the **Cadent Houses**: 3, 6, 9, 12, in the natural distribution of Signs, are called **Mutable Signs** (changeable). They are Gemini, Virgo, Sagittarius, and Pisces. **They give their symbolic meanings to the Cadent Houses** (Cadent comes from the Latin word, *cadere*, which means "to fall"). Cadent Houses are falling away from the Succedent Houses to pave the way for a new focus and initiation in the next Angular House). Cadent Houses reflect **the sense of distribution of what has been focused and initiated in the preceding Angular House and organized and given value in the Succedent House**. This development is taken forward, is transmitted to a new level of focus and initiation by the Cadent House, **falling into the next Angle.**

The Basic Meanings of the Houses

1st House (an Angle): Identity formation, self-projection; I, me, Self. The Sign upon this House cusp, the Ascendant—which is determined by where on Earth you are born (your horizon point at the moment of birth)—represents archetypally how a person shows himself/herself to the world, wants to be seen by others. **The planet ruling the Sign on the first cusp is also extremely significant in interpretation** and we will study that soon.

2nd House: The psychodynamic of Self-worth; personal resources, money.

3rd House: Communication; point of view, mindset, state of mind, short travel, brothers and sisters, neighbors.

4th House: Early home development; the home; one parent; endings and new starts.

5th House: The psychodynamic of giving love (also part of the sexual profile); creativity; children; teaching; theatricality.

6th House: Employment; the work environment; cooperation; service extended to others; part of health considerations.

Once you learn the first six Houses, you basically know the second six, except that their application for orientation refers to other people, not so pointedly to the Self. For example, the first House is a "me" House that refers to self-projection. The opposite House to it, the 7th, refers to the other person (the spouse, business partner, etc.), not to the Self. Where the 2nd House refers to my self-worth or my material resources, the 8th House refers to the self-worth of others and their resources.

7th House (an Angle): Relationships; marriage; the spouse; partnership; reception by others.

8th House: Others' resources, self-worth, and values; experiences and matters relating to death; sex (along with the 5th); occult interests; taxes; inheritance; crisis; and healing.

9th House: Education; internationalism; long journeys; academia; religion; metaphysics; law; publishing.

10th House (an Angle): Career, profession; job; another parent; public honor or scandal.

11th House: The psychodynamic of love received; friendship (the kind of people who are chosen for friends); clubs, hopes, goals, salaries (the rewards from others).

12th House: Self-undoing; confinement; large organizations, societal cooperation; critical illness; the sense of the self being blanketed somehow; jail, prison, hospital, spirituality (along with the 9th), the occult.

The Wheel of Houses Tells the Story of Life

In the 1st House (an Angle), we have an emergence, a birth of the Self. A newborn thrusts out of the womb into a new environment.

In the 2nd House, the newborn begins to touch itself. It realizes that there is a Self to touch! The Self takes form and realizes its own substance. Values are formed.

In the 3rd House, the newborn begins to say its first words, to begin the process of communication and thought. A point of view is formed in relationship to how one sees the Self. Interaction with brothers, sisters, or the immediate environment in general begins to make an impact. The first stages of growth are complete.

In the 4th House—an Angle—the child gains full recognition of its home. The parents become role models, perhaps one in particular. The influence of the home prepares the child for further development and preparation for relationship with the world.

Moving into the 5th House, the child begins to use what it has learned at home as the model for the first extension of Self, in loving, creative ways—dysfunction at home, for example, usually results in difficulties giving love in later life. One's relationship to one's own children becomes heightened in relationship to one's experience with one's own parents. Sexual awareness comes into focus as part of extending the Self.

In the 6th House there is a reaction to what was established in the 5th House. The love and creativity of the 5th House are used to communicate the Self onto a new level (in the relationships of the 7th House). The first experiences with work and worker relationships envelop the Self in the 6th House. If all that has been experienced so far becomes too frustrating, sickness can invade the body, there can be breakdown: "I'm sick of all this!" The 6th House is a place of refining, of preparation for relationships, of learning cooperation with others.

The 7th House—an Angle—is another important point of new focus. The Self is now involved in relationships with others, especially through marriage or business dealings. One emerges above the horizon into the public. The Self is given over to others for their reflection back to oneself.

Once one has begun to interact with others, there is the necessity to learn about their values; we evaluate our own sense of self-worth by acknowledging the worth and/or values of others in the 8th House.

Experiences with death and various other crises enlarge and deepen the personal viewpoint. All of this becomes explained in the 9th House through education, world experience, publications, and the laws of society. The ideas of the Self have been worked out in the previous Houses. One's viewpoints join the viewpoints of others in various ways. Higher learning prepares one for a career.

The Angular Houses all reflect different ways of concretizing Self: birth (Ascendant); home security and new beginning (4th House); relationship (7th House); and now, in the 10th House, there is entrance into the career arena, into one's profession. Regarding the "other parent," shown

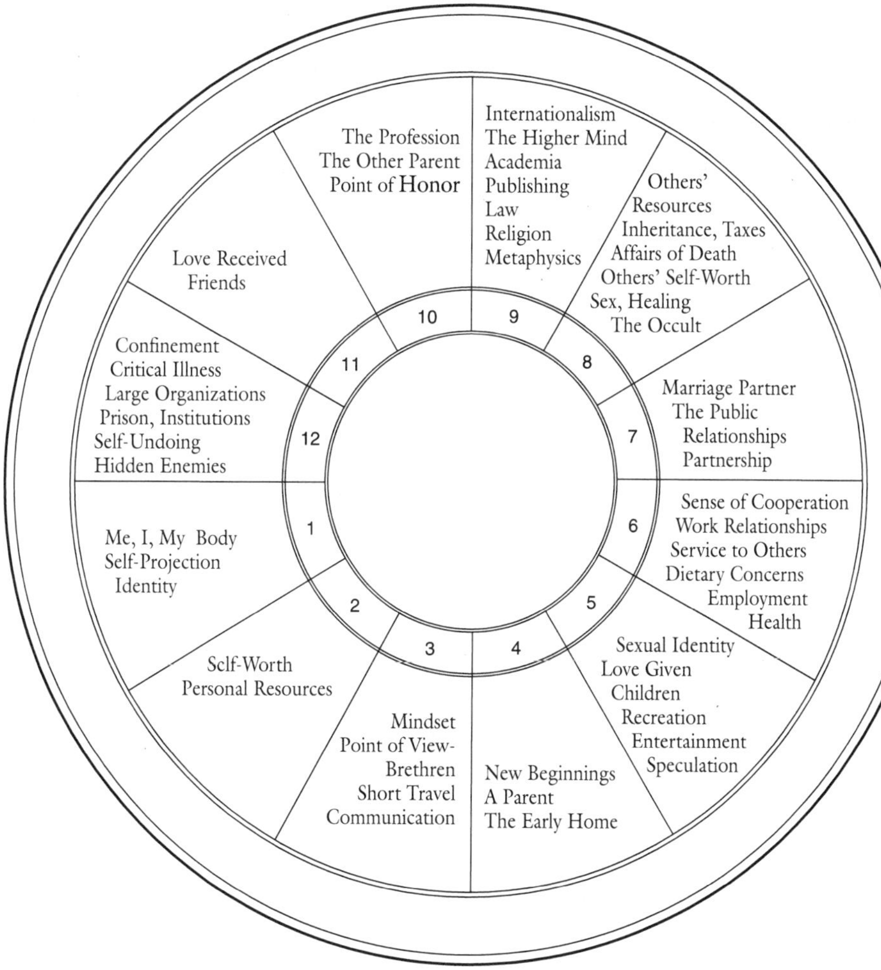

Figure 3
The Wheel of Houses

in the 10th, there are unresolvable arguments over which parent is "found in" the 4th or 10th House. We will never know, for sure, which parent to associate with which House. As a professional astrologer, you will eventually learn to allow your client to offer that determination by simply providing or reacting to parental descriptions and relating them to these Houses. The client will quickly help you make the proper assessment.

In the 10th House, one's circle becomes larger through the profession. Rewards and honors are made possible publicly. The 11th House structures and consolidates that which was earned in the 10th House. There are larger goals. There are income concerns from the profession. New friends and others give love and accolades. After one is on top of the world, things gradually subside. There is always the end of a cycle for the beginning of another, and we find the sense of the end of the cycle in the 12th House. There is nothing left to be done now and one accepts the reality of completion; the ego has given itself over to renewal. One learns to cooperate with society or pay the price by going to jail, being ignored or there is systemic or somatic breakdown to ill health, in tandem with the aging process. Allowing full recognition of this factor leads into a new cycle again in the 1st House: the refreshed, reborn Ascendant.

We have presented much information in this chapter. Our texture of synthesis has grown greatly. We began with the behavioral faculty of a planet. We learned that its placement within a Sign tells us how that behavioral faculty needs to express itself in order to reach optimum fulfillment. And now, with our study of the Houses, we can locate the area of life involving the planet in its Sign, the House experiences labeled by the Sign on the House cusp and articulated by the planet in the House (or ruling the Sign on the cusp, as we shall see). We have already taken a giant step of understanding into the art of astrology!

Now: Your First Horoscope!

You know that the Sun rises above the horizon, creating sunrise (on the left) in the East, is at the top of the horoscope—the Midheaven (MC)—at 12:00 noon, and sets below the horizon at sunset. The Sun crosses the bottom of the horoscope (the IC) at midnight. **As the Sun travels from Angle to Angle, it enters into and stays in each House for approximately two hours** (at average latitudes). **You can use this time reference easily to check the accuracy of a horoscope!**

The Sun appears to traverse each House, clockwise, for approximately two Hours as follows[2]:

House 1: 4 A.M.–6 A.M.
House 12: 6 A.M.–8 A.M.
House 11: 8 A.M.–10 A.M.
House 10: 10 A.M.–12 P.M.
House 9: 12 P.M.–2 P.M. (12–14 hours)
House 8: 2 P.M.–4 P.M. (14–16 hours)
House 7: 4 P.M.–6 P.M. (16–18 hours)
House 6: 6 P.M.–8 P.M. (18–20 hours)
House 5: 8 P.M.–10 P.M. (20–22 hours)
House 4: 10 P.M.–12 A.M. (22–24 hours)
House 3: 12 A.M.–2 A.M. (00–02 hours)
House 2: 2 A.M.–4 A.M. (02–04 hours)

If you were to see a horoscope with a birth time of 10 A.M. and you see that the Sun is in the third House, it is a sign that a serious error of data entry has been made; The Sun is below the horizon! If you were to see a horoscope with a time of 9:15 P.M. and the Sun in that horoscope is located in the twelfth House, it tells you that an error has been made. It's easy. Remember to use the Sun position as a check for errors in the work-up of the birth time.

This example horoscope belongs to United States President Bill Clinton.[3] (Fig. 4, p. 55). Remember: in our natural distribution of Houses, Aries was on the cusp of the first House. Yet in Mr. Clinton's horoscope, **Libra is upon this cusp.**

Here's why: the planets and Signs are constantly orbiting, rising above the horizon at the Ascendant and peaking at the Midheaven, like a giant spinning wheel. At the moment of birth, POW!, we stop the universe and record a snapshot of that moment, to mark the positions of that moment. **Whatever Sign that is rising at the birth location at the birth time then shows itself as the rising Sign, the Ascendant. The degree and minute of this Sign are placed at the Ascendant position, on the outer rim of the horoscope.**

---

2 Actually, the Earth revolves on its axis and the Sun *appears* to move; to capture this motion in the relativity perception, the Houses (the Earth) revolve in a counterclockwise motion "underneath" the Sun and planets.

3 Data: August 19, 1946; 8:51 A.M. CST; Hope, Arkansas; 93W35 33N40.

Clinton's horoscope shows 5 degrees and 31 minutes of Libra as the Ascendant. You should see that number as the "doorway entrance to that 1st House." It is its address; its purpose is to tell you where to place any planets that happened to be in Libra.

The computer has computed the Ascendant and Midheaven positions and the rest of the House cusps. All the Signs are placed around the wheel **in order** accordingly, as you have learned, but **reflecting a new starting point at the individual's place of birth!** See for yourself: starting at Libra, counterclockwise, you then see Scorpio on the cusp of the 2nd House, then Sagittarius on the 3rd, then what's next? Capricorn, right, on the 4th; then Aquarius, etc. Aries, the sign opposite Libra is, of course, opposite Libra there in the horoscope (as in every horoscope); in this horoscope it is on the 7th cusp because Libra is on the 1st!

The natural distribution of Signs is imaginary, a poetical starting place for understanding. We have used it as a teaching concept. **Do not expect every horoscope to look like the natural distribution horoscope.** Remember, we are working with the zodiac as a big spinning wheel, with the Signs always in the same order but, at the moment of birth, that wheel is stopped somewhere special, somewhere individual, defining the Ascendant, the individual's starting point for the series of Signs.

[We have spent time with clockwise motion but now, conspicuously, the flow of Signs in counterclockwise motion will take over. Why do the Signs flow in counterclockwise motion? Here is our relativity problem again. Remember, the Earth revolves on its own axis, once every day, **from west to east.** This motion makes the Sun appear to rise in the east and set in the west. If you hold your fist stationary in front of your face, keeping your eyes on your fist (the Sun), and slowly move your head from right to left, the fist (the Sun) will appear to move from your left to the right. If to your right, where the Sun rises, is the East, then North is above your head. Your head's motion (the Earth's) gives apparent motion to your fist (the Sun), "rising" in what we call the east. Relativity changes the direction when the motion is assigned to the Sun rather than to the Earth. See! I promised that you would understand this gradually!]

Man's entire directional orientation is based upon the *apparent* motion of the Sun from East to West. During the Sun's apparent motion, it appears to pass *overhead*, in the position we call north. In transferring this orientation to a two-dimensional drawing (a map), we place East on the right, North at the top, and West to the left.

We describe clock time by rotation in the opposite direction, from the left, over the top to the right. This motion is based upon the Earth's rotation on its axis and not upon the motion attributed to the Sun. "Clockwise" refers to the Earth's motion from west to east (the "clock" is on the Earth); "counterclockwise" refers to the Sun's apparent motion from east to west.

Let's repeat that: the Sun does not move. The earth rotates on its axis. This rotation gives apparent motion to the Sun, in the reverse direction. Humankind's clock reflects the Earth's rotation. The Sun's apparent motion is counter to our human clock motion.

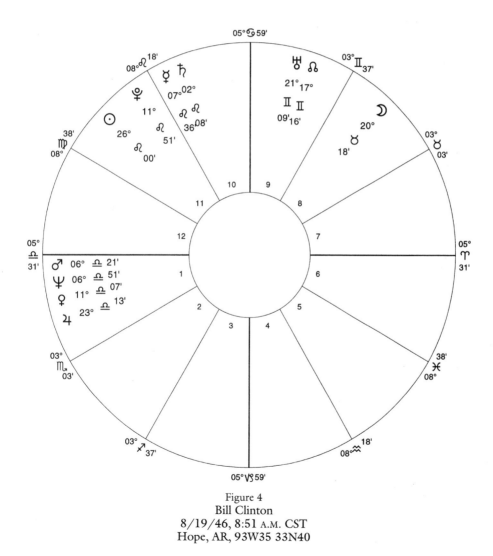

Figure 4
Bill Clinton
8/19/46, 8:51 A.M. CST
Hope, AR, 93W35 33N40

As the Sun appears to go along its path, it is measured in longitude by reference to our stationary projections of the zodiac. The Signs, marking the vault of the heavens, have been ordered in a certain succession for millennia, from Aries and Taurus throughout the whole circle to Pisces. Linked to the apparent motion of the Sun, the Signs flow similarly in counterclockwise direction. [That is about all we will need to discuss on this issue! Thanks for hanging in there!]

Now, in Clinton's horoscope, notice Mars in its position at 6♎21. If Mars were at 2 degrees of Libra, **it would be placed in the 12th House because its degree would be lower than the degree number upon the entrance of the House.** This is a vitally important observation. Think counterclockwise, the way the Sun and planets really "move"on paper.

The position of Clinton's eleventh cusp is 8 degrees of Leo. Mercury's position is 7♌. It is placed then in the *10th* House because its lower degree number does not entitle it to enter the 11th House, but the Sun, located at 26♌ is entitled to enter this House because its number is in a higher degree than the cusp mark of the House.

Signs Are Not Houses — Houses Are Not Signs

Another major point of confusion for beginners has to do with the **difference** between Signs and Houses. **Each Sign contains 30 degrees** and will have a certain degree shown as the entrance or doorway to a House. The areas called Houses, in turn, may contain any number of degrees.[4] For example, in Clinton's horoscope, the 12th House cusp's doorway entrance is 8♍38. Some of Virgo is in the 11th House (8 degrees +) and some of it (21 degrees +) is in the 12th. *There is an overlapping taking place*. The Ascendant at 5♎ tells us that four degrees+ of Libra are in the 12th and the rest of Libra is in the 1st. So the size of the 12th House is approximately 22 degrees of Virgo (to use up the 30 degrees in the Sign, starting from the cusp notation of 8), plus about 5 degrees in Libra, for a total of 27 degrees.

You see that President Clinton has Libra on his Ascendant. This suggests a style of presenting himself to others (remember, the 1st House represents Self-projection) that is charming, attractive, and oriented to be popular (recall all Libra descriptions). Now, here, in his individual horo-

---

4 Unless you are using the Equal House system.

scope, this personally descriptive fact is **emphasized strongly since Clinton has FOUR planets in Libra within the 1st House, all with a need to fulfill their individual behavioral faculties in LIBRAN terms through the avenue of self-projection.**

When the wheel of the zodiac was stopped at the moment of Clinton's birth, from the vantage point of his place of birth (the longitude and latitude), these several planets in Libra were *just about to rise*, as we say. They are at the Ascendant. They are on and in an Angle. They are very powerfully, impressively situated, and they show up that way in Clinton's personality.

Notice that Mars and Neptune are in the same degree. What happens when Mars and Neptune get together? Mars is going to stir up all that is Neptune, and Neptune is always something other than it seems, mysterious, often aesthetic or even spiritual, depending upon other horoscope factors. **Might such a combination produce a strong sense of charisma?** Sure it would! Mars and Neptune contacts always seem to relate to charisma. (That Mars-Neptune charisma was what magnetized Charles Manson for his followers in their mass-murder spree; actor Marcello Mastroianni was famous for his suave charisma; and so was murderer-suicide gigolo Andrew Cunanan.) There is definitely here the suspicion of something below the surface, something other than it seems working in the core of Clinton's identity.

Clinton's Sun is in Leo. His life energy is centered in the need for recognition and ego triumph (and you just feel how that energy thrust is reinforced by the Mars-Neptune charisma). Now, where does this life energy place itself for maximum fulfillment? Its placement in the **11th House** shows that there will be a strong need for love, recognition, appreciation; perhaps a focus on goal orientation, upon a considerably illuminated network of friends, **all 11th House dimensions.**

These are the beginnings of synthesis in astrology. With every chapter of our study we are adding a bit more to the synthesis process. You are learning to analyze a horoscope with more and more confidence and sophistication!

Summary

1. The circle that describes the ring of any horoscope is called the ecliptic. It represents the apparent path of the Sun and is the imaginary path along which planetary movement occurs.

2. The Horizon, the ground that you stand on, is represented by the horizontal line that separates the wheel into upper and lower divisions. The left-most point of the Horizon line is East. It is where planets rise above the horizon for visibility. This point is called the Ascendant. The Ascendant is Self.

3. The right-most point of the horizon line, opposing the Ascendant, is the Descendant, the West. The Descendant is Others.

4. The uppermost point of the wheel (the 12:00 noon position) is called the Midheaven (or MC). The point exactly opposite to it is called the Nadir (alternately, the Immum Coeli or IC). The line described by the Midheaven and Nadir axis, separating the wheel into left and right halves, is called the Meridian line.

5. The Ascendant, Descendant, Midheaven, and Nadir are the horoscope's strongest points. They are called Angles.

6. The twelve areas of a horoscope are called Houses. Houses represent zones of life experience whose basic meanings come from the Signs placed upon them in the natural distribution of Signs. Each House is separated by a radial line called a Cusp.

7. The Angular Houses: I, IV, VII, X, represent focus and initiation; the Succedent Houses: II, V, VIII, XI, represent the organization of security and various factors that have to do with worth, value, and love; the Cadent Houses: III, VI, IX, XII, distribute what has been initiated and organized to transmit to a new level of focus and initiation.

8. The Sun's House position can be used to check for data entry errors regarding the time of birth.

9. The degree labels on each House cusp are "mail addresses" telling us (the computer) where a planet should be delivered (placed).

10. Houses and Signs are not the same. Signs contain thirty degrees, Houses may contain practically any number of degrees.

Test Yourself

(See test answers, p. 233.)

1. Using a blank wheel, write what each House symbolizes. Write them in pairs. Begin with the 1st House–7th House, 2nd House–8th House, etc. [Remember, Noel Tyl's answers to this test are in the Appendix, p. 233.]

2. What are the radial lines separating the Houses called?

3. What is the purpose of the numbers shown on the outer rim of the horoscope at the beginning of each House?

4. What is a House?

5. What is the name of the horizontal line that separates the wheel into upper and lower halves? What does it symbolize?

6. Can the Sun be in the 3rd House if the time of birth is 1:18 P.M.? Explain your answer.

7. When the Sun is in the 10th House, it is near an important Angle that we call _____.

8. Houses II-V-VIII-XI are called _____ Houses.

9. What is the name of the line that separates the wheel into left and right halves?

10. Is there a difference between a Sign and a House? Explain your answer.

11. What is the Ecliptic?

12. Just tell yourself you do appreciate the clockwise/counterclockwise relationship that the Signs have to the wheel of Houses!

13. Why is the Descendant so named?

14. What is the essential function of Cadent Houses?

15. The "bottom of the heavens" is called _____.

16. The need to think and communicate in a critically refined manner in creative matters is suggested by which planet-Sign-House combination?

17. Marriage to an older, wiser person is suggested by which planet-House combination?

18. True or false—Planets travel in a counterclockwise motion in the horoscope.

19. Which planets-Signs-Houses combination is suggested by the following: the energy to identify with intangibles within the mindset expresses itself in a personality form that needs to be popular within career concerns.

20. What are the most important areas of the horoscope?

Chapter 4

• • •

Your Computer and Your Horoscope

I BEGAN MY STUDY OF ASTROLOGY AT THE RIPE old age of thirteen. The year was 1967. At that time astrologers lacked the advantage of astrological software; in fact, the personal computer was still a dream for the future. For an astrologer, there was no choice but to do all computations manually! Printed blank horoscope wheels could be purchased from special interest book-stores that carried astrology books, and the rest of the task consisted of patient, hard work.

Constructing a horoscope required an Ephemeris, a book called *Tables of Houses*, another reference book called *Tables of Diurnal Motion*, a pencil with a big eraser, and lots of patience. Although, with patience, one finally learned the process with some proficiency, it was still tedious, laborious, and fraught with the potential for error.

Astrological software and computer technology have progressed rapidly over the past twenty years. Computers are now quite affordable, and there is a broad array of professional as well as amateur software programs for astrologers. While these developments have helped professional astrologers who have already honed their craft by manual computation, beginners are at a disadvantage. **They do not learn the details and reasons of time correction and horoscope construction, thus limiting their knowledge and qualifications.**

In our course of study, it is important to know and understand exactly what the computer is doing when it constructs a horoscope. After the computer has printed a horoscope, we need to know what it is we are looking at and how we should use it effectively. This is the only way to achieve a thorough basis for learning: it will allow you to bloom in skill, securely and all the sooner.

Procedures

No matter what level or kind of software you use for astrology, there are certain basic precepts being used universally, certain basic bits of information that are used by the computer to construct a horoscope.

For starters, your input obviously begins with the entering of a **name, date of birth, time of birth, city and state of birth or city and country of birth, the longitude and latitude of the birth place, and very importantly, the world/national time zone of the place of birth.** One can enter all of this data *without any knowledge of astrology*, and get the same result as a professional astrologer does, but your knowing what happens to this data and how the items relate to each other adds significance and meaning to a routine process. The computer's purpose is to help your mind, not just save you time.

What Time Is It, Anyway?

The time of birth is all-important in our astrology because it records the imprint of the beginning of life, that moment when the child is separated from dependency upon the mother to begin breathing on its own. An understanding of time, locationally and philosophically speaking, is therefore a vital prerequisite in our astrology. The first thing of importance is to understand the concept of time on Earth and time in the sky. We must know why, when it is 12:00 noon in New York City, it is *not* 12:00 noon in Johannesburg, South Africa or in Tokyo, Japan.

Time differs all over the world, of course, but it was not always that way. Long ago, before clocks, time was conditioned only by the passage of day and night, by the visual appreciation of the Sun in the sky and the phases of the Moon. But as the world became more populated and more aware, especially with regard to transportation and communication, as communication linked places further and further apart, the commonality of time in the world became less and less realistic, less and less efficient. A new concept of time had to be developed; this management of time is a key focal consideration for what the computer does to create a horoscope.

Sidereal Time

The central tool for our astrology is the heavens. Without the planets in the heavens, we have no archetypes to be reflected below, as they are symbolized above; we have to know where they are at any given moment, past and future; we must harness exact positions through calculation of speed and time. On Earth, we use our own clock time, but the heavens use their own time, which is called *Sidereal* (star) Time, the time that orders our planetary system orbiting the Sun.

To bring the times together, *we have to convert our time on Earth to Sidereal Time in the heavens.* This is the first dramatic step the computer takes in processing birth information.

Sidereal Time differs from Earth's clock time in this way: Sidereal Time flows through its own *twenty-four* hours **in approximately one Earth year.** Sidereal Time begins at 0 hours, 0 minutes, and 0 seconds every year on March 21, approximately (precisely when the Sun enters the sign of Aries).

Longitude

After the computer has converted Earth time to Sidereal Time, it has to make a correction to that time for the exact longitude of the birthplace. Here is the engrossing principle of the conversion: **The Sun appears to travel 1 degree on the ecliptic,** the apparent arc completely around the Earth, **every four minutes of our clock time,** completing the 360 degree circle in 1,440 minutes (4m x 360) or 24 hours (1440/60). Scientists use this apparent Sun movement in order to standardize time throughout world geography.

Maps show clearly our capture of the Sun's movement with vertical lines drawn from north to south **every 15 degrees around the Earth.**

The distance from one longitude line to another measures 15 degrees of the Grand Circle; it is the distance covered by the Sun in sixty minutes of time (4 x 15 degrees). **This is how the Earth is divided into what we call time zones.** To process the birth information, the computer makes calculation adjustments to bring the Sun from the birth location (measured in longitude and latitude) to the closest time zone longitude line. This is the second part of what the computer does.

Time measurement must begin somewhere on our globe. In the mid-seventeenth century, serious work with time was being conducted in England: astronomical tables needed correction to improve the safety and efficiency of rapidly expanding ocean navigation. A center for this work was established by Charles II in 1675, at the Royal Observatory at Greenwich, England. For the Earth, Greenwich is still the beginning point for time reference and geographic longitude measurement. We refer to the time in Greenwich as Greenwich Mean Time (GMT).

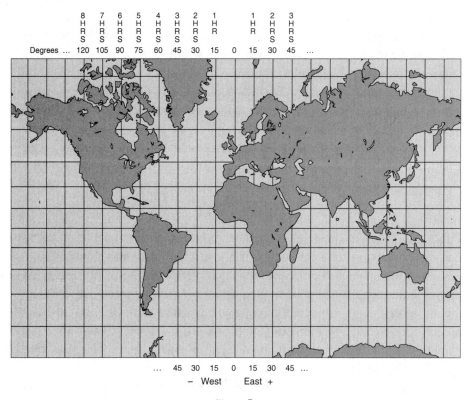

Figure 5
Beginning at Greenwich, England, time zones chart the hours; 15 degrees longitude = 1 hour.

Now, every 15 degrees west of Greenwich equates to a *subtraction* (–) of one hour of clock time from the time in Greenwich, England. New York City is located at 75 degrees of west longitude: 75 divided by 15 equals 5 (the number of time zones); thus **when the time in Greenwich is 12 noon, it is 7 A.M. in New York City, five hours earlier.**

Every 15 degrees *east* of Greenwich equates to an *addition* (+) of one hour of clock time. Johannesburg, South Africa is located at 28 degrees of east longitude. 28 divided by 15 equals 1.86, which we round off to 2 (*time zones*) This places Johannesburg next to the closest time zone— Eastern European Time 2 hours east of Greenwich, and an *addition* of time. Thus, when it is 12:00 noon in Greenwich, England, it is 2:00 P.M. (1400) in Johannesburg, South Africa.

Countries in many of the world's time zones change their clocks during their Spring season to establish Daylight Saving Time. It is accomplished by **advancing** the clock time (usually at 2 A.M.) one hour. (Think: "Spring forward.") This is a vitally important consideration to be aware of in the construction of a horoscope, as the horoscope will be in error by 60 minutes if Daylight Saving Time was in effect at that location at the time of birth, and was not being included in the calculation of the horoscope! Fortunately, the advent of World Atlas software for astrologers lets us know when and where Daylight Saving Time was everywhere and anywhere.

The clocks observing Daylight Saving Time (DST) normally return to Standard Time (ST) in early Autumn. (Think, "Fall Back.")

Now, here is the time in your learning program to get to know your computer and your astrological program. Practice entering data so that you can do it easily, knowing just what each line of data means and what your computer is going to do with each line. Go over the process again and again in your mind; you will then feel more at home with the data; you will be in command of the process.

Use Bill Clinton's horoscope data from the last chapter to check your work; you should get exactly the same cuspal arrangement and planetary positions from your computer.

Study the ins and outs of your program, the data entry particulars, the abbreviations in the Atlas notations, the times when DST was employed (see how the computer adjusts this time to Standard Time); understand what your eyes are seeing on the data entry portion of the screen. Get comfortable with the process.

Summary

1. The details of time correction and horoscope construction are necessary prerequisites for an astrologer.

2. The data input required by astrological software to print a horoscope includes: name, date of birth, city and state of birth or city and country of birth, the longitude and latitude of the birth place, and the time zone of the place of birth.

3. Time is measured in the heavens using Sidereal Time, which flows through its own 24-hour period in approximately one Earth year. The first important step in calculating a horoscope is to convert Earth time to Sidereal Time.

4. **The Sun travels one degree upon the ecliptic every four minutes of clock time.** All geographical maps capture the Sun's movement with vertical lines drawn from north to south every 15 degrees of Earth's Grand Circle, beginning at Greenwich, England. To process birth information, the computer makes calculation adjustments to bring the Sun from the birth location to the closest time zone longitude line.

5. Every 15 degrees west of Greenwich equates to a subtraction of one hour of clock time. Every 15 degrees east of Greenwich equates to an addition of one hour of clock time.

6. Countries in many of the world's time zones change their clocks during their Spring season to establish Daylight Saving Time. It is accomplished by advancing the clock time (usually at 2 A.M.) one hour, and then readjusting (falling back) in the autumn.

Test Yourself

(See test answers, p. 235.)

1. What is the name of the place that is used as the reference point for time standardization?

2. To calculate a horoscope, there is a necessary conversion of two different kinds of time. Explain.

3. The Sun appears to travel _____ degrees of arc, every _____ minutes of clock time.

4. What happens to many of the world's time zones during their Spring season?

5. Why is the time in Los Angeles, California 8 hours earlier than the time in Greenwich, England?

6. Every 15 degrees _____ of Greenwich equates to an addition of _____.

7. How is the Sun's apparent movement shown on maps?

8. Why is the time of birth so important in the calculation of a horoscope?

9. What information is necessary to calculate a horoscope?

10. A birth location at 43 degrees of east longitude equates to how many hours of clock time from the standard reference place for clock time measurement?

Chapter 5

• • •

Introduction to Aspects

WE HAVE LEARNED THAT **PLANETS ARE SYM-
bols of needs and the behavioral faculties to fulfill
them.** These needs and behavioral faculties are conditioned by the planets' placement in a Sign; this conditioning (synthesis) individualizes psychological needs and
defines behavior further.

In Chapter 3, we extended our process of synthesis
through the study of Houses. We learned to find the primary area (zone) of life experience where specific needs
work toward fulfillment.

Now, **we must assess the level of tension or ease put
upon that process of need fulfillment.** Psychologists
call this tension "need press." Our developmental tensions—our need presses—originate internally in the *inner*
environment (the body and its maintenance, the spirit and
its discovery) and in the *outer* environment (the world in
which we live, the interactions with others).

Our feelings of health, welfare, and happiness in life
are centered upon the fulfillment of needs. The points of
tension that we encounter represent specific areas for

development and growth. In astrology, we measure that developmental tension through the measurement of **aspects**.

An aspect is the longitudinal distance relationship, in degrees, measured between planetary positions in a horoscope. It is a geometric angle between planets or between planets and Angles (the cusps of the 1st, 4th, 7th, and 10th Houses).

Through the early centuries of observation of the heavens, it was noted that certain distance relationships between planets synthesized their individual characteristics dynamically and paralleled powerful reactions on Earth. Other distance relationships paralleled lesser reactions, or no reaction at all.

To order this development of planetary relationships, we use the most easily observable Moon-Sun relationship—the lunation cycle—as a model.

Early astrologers observed that people who were born when the Moon and Sun were together in the heavens, in nearness of degree (we call this the New Moon), frequently seemed to be people who had a sense about them of being newly formed, of slow emergence, of tentativeness and, fascinatingly, often were the people who eventually gave birth to new ideas in the world. The parallel here was that the New Moon (the reigning need symbol of the personality: the personality's form) received little light from the Sun, but as it continued in development it would gain light, see it all, and then reflect it fully.

This closeness of degree is called **conjunction**. The symbol of a conjunction is ☌.

In Full Moon births, the Moon is exactly across from the Sun in the heavens—180 degrees away (one-half the circle). People who were/are born at the time of a Full Moon, when the Moon is in full awareness of the Sun's light, seem to have a keen awareness of their relationship to others. There is objectivity. They "see the light!" This awareness relationship is given the name **opposition**. The symbol for opposition is ☍.

The New Moon light at conjunction increases to the Full Moon, but halfway to Full Moon, the emerging, developing Moon reaches a halfway point, 90 degrees from the New Moon position. Then, after the Full Moon's occurrence, there is a distribution of light until it reaches a point 270 degrees from the original New Moon (90 degrees from Full Moon and 90 degrees to go to the next New Moon). These two positions, 90 and 270 degrees, midpoints between New and Full Moon (conjunction and opposition) and Full and New Moon (opposition and conjunction), are called **squares**. The symbol for a square is □.

Squares are points of extreme dynamic activity, developmental tension, and change. These four points—conjunction, opening square, opposition, closing square within the lunation cycle model—easily bring to mind the orientation we have studied with reference to the Angles of the horoscope. Let this recollection feel like a "Grand Cross concept."

Squares and Oppositions (and obviously, conjunctions) link Signs of the same mode! And since the Signs are of the *same* mode, there is **an inherent tension that has to be worked out.** For example, there is Aries' ego thrust (Sign in the Cardinal mode) *square* Cancer's emotional security demand (another Sign in a Cardinal mode); or, there is the Taurean insistence to keep things as they are, *square* the Aquarian insistence to innovate and create progress for a better tomorrow (two Signs in the Fixed mode). There is Capricorn opposite Cancer: practicality and emotions fighting together for the center of the stage!

Imagine two people living together with such competing or conflicting energies and needs: it is easy to see that *something* would have to be done (adjusted) for things to work out effectively or one person would be fulfilled only at the other's expense. This is the dynamic process that happens between needs and behavioral faculties when planets are **in a square aspect** within the horoscope. *They are in a developmentally tense relationship.* We use the word *developmental* because **growth and development come from the process of resolving the inherent tension of a square** (see Fig. 6, p. 72).

On the 360-degree circle (in the lunation cycle model), there are points before and after the New and Full Moons (conjunction and opposition), when, in quadrants, there is a beginning of full illumination or distribution of the light of full illumination. Including the New Moon point, these three points form an equilateral triangle, **which is the same triangle concept connecting the three Signs of each element family!** (see Fig. 7, p. 72).

This triangular relationship is given the name **trine**. Just as squares reflect the numerological base of 4 (360/4 = 90, the sense of cross purposes), trines reflect the numerological base of 3 (360/3 = 120, a balance and harmony). The symbol for a trine is △. It is an aspect that measures 120 degrees.

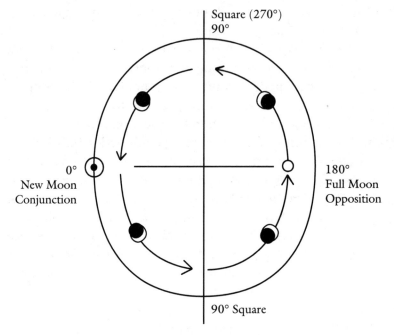

Figure 6
Squares and Oppositions

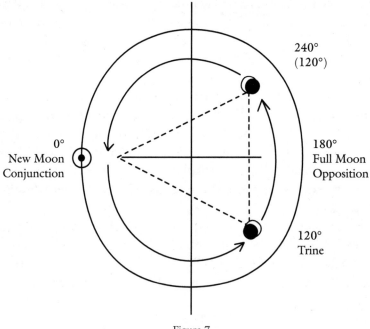

Figure 7
The Trine

In 95% of the trines that you will see between planets, or between a planet and an Angle, the symbols involved will be in **Signs of the same element!** For example, if the Moon is at 15 degrees Aries, finding a trine to it is simply a question of knowing that Aries is a *Fire* Sign; you then look at the other Fire Signs (in an orderly sequence, counterclockwise, i.e., to Leo and then to Sagittarius) to see if there is a planet at or close to 15 degrees. If there is, you will then know *without counting* that a trine exists between the Moon and the other planet!

Planets involved in a trine, being in the same element, capture the sense of support, easy flow, and smoothness between/among them. A secondary supportive aspect emanates easily from our appreciation of the trine: by subdividing a trine into two 60 degree aspects, we establish the sextile. The symbol for a sextile is ⚹.

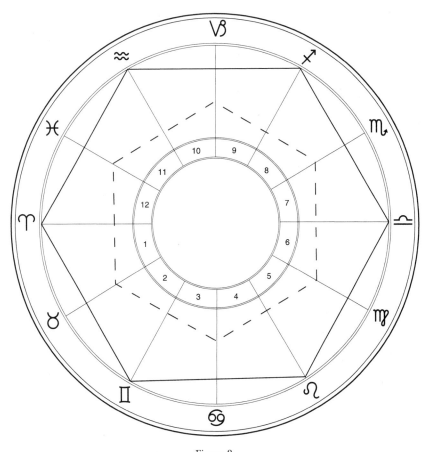

Figure 8
Sextiles

Learning the aspects named thus far: conjunction, sextile, square, trine, opposition [☌ ⚹ ◻ △ ☍]—is easy when you know and understand that they are based on divisions of the circle. Any two or more planets or planet and point (like the Ascendant or Midheaven) that are joined around the same longitudinal position are in conjunction. Conjunctions are easily seen in the horoscope *with the eye*. Oppositions are also easy to see with the eye because you can see their 180-degree relationship to each other within the circle, just as you can see that the "6" is in exact opposition to the "12" on a clock dial. And, remember: you have learned the Signs in pairs of opposites (as well as in orderly counter-clockwise flow).

These five aspects—conjunction, sextile, square, trine, and opposition—are the major aspects used in astrology. They are named after the brilliant Egyptian astronomer, geometer, and geographer, Claudius Ptolemy. When you hear the term "Ptolemaic Aspects," it is a reference to the aspects we have studied thus far: conjunction (☌), sextile (⚹), square (◻), trine (△), and opposition (☍).[6] Please understand that our opening model for explanation of aspects used the Moon-Sun relationship — the Lunation Cycle—because it is such an obvious model in the sky; it taught the early astrologers the dynamism of aspects among planets. *Every* planet and Angle in a horoscope can be involved in any aspect between/among each other.

The Master Elements and Modes Chart (Fig. 8, p. 75) is all-important to your learning to read aspects easily. You will have this chart organization in your mind for as long as you practice astrology throughout your life. It must be learned completely, indelibly, and knowingly. We first introduced it on page 37 in our introduction of the Signs, but now it is lifted to *full importance in helping you to organize the reading of aspects.*

As you marry this chart with your mind, know that planets (and points) similarly positioned in Signs of the same element (reading across) are going to be in trine aspect to one another; that planets (and points) similarly positioned in Signs of the same mode are going to be in conjunction, square, or opposition to one another. We can not emphasize enough the importance of knowing this chart absolutely.

Our aspects are named in terms of the imagery that is projected by their symbols—the tension of opposition shows in the face-off between

---

6   There are further divisions of the circle, additional aspects, that will be explored as our study advances.

two opposing circles; the smooth trine is based upon the balance of an equilateral triangle; the sharp square aspect is symbolized as perpendicularly aligned cross-tensions, and the sextile symbol suggests a hexagon approaching, tying together the comfort and unity of the circle.

Master Chart: Elements and Modes

	C	F	M
F	♈	♌	♐
A	♎	♒	♊
W	♋	♏	♓
E	♑	♉	♍

The Concept of Orb

In the example below (Fig. 8), if the ☉ were at 9♌ and, say, ♄ were also at 9♌, the two would be in conjunction, an *exact* conjunction. But aspects are still bona fide when they are *not exact*, but within established ranges, an allowance for **degrees approaching and separating from exactness.** This consideration is called **orb**. If ♄ were placed at 11♌ instead of at 9♌, it would *still* be in conjunction with the ☉ because, when aspecting the Sun or Moon, *we allow a 7-degree orb* for aspect measurement. In other words, any planet or Angle from 2♌ to 16♌ in this example would be in conjunction with the Sun at 9♌.

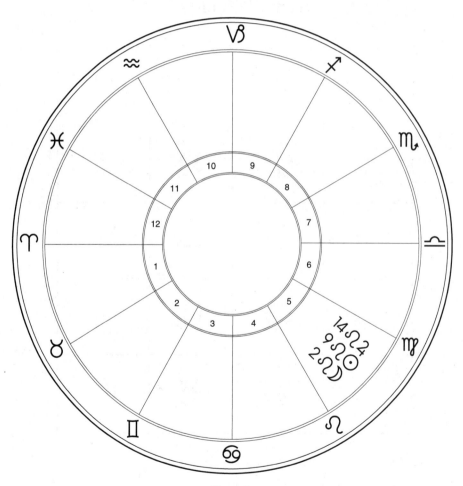

Figure 8
Example of the Concept of Orb

Look further here: the Moon is seven degrees away (behind the Sun) at 2 ♌, but it is still in conjunction because of the 7-degree orb we observe for the Sun and Moon. Jupiter is shown at 14♌. It, too, is in conjunction with the Sun because we allow a 5-degree orb when the aspect involves the Sun or Moon and a planet. Note, however, the Moon and Jupiter (although both are in Leo) are *not* in conjunction in this example; they are too far apart. Think about this and learn it well.

Determining Aspects

Analysis of the horoscope is aspect-dependent. There is no way to gauge the need-fulfillment process so necessary for life development without knowing the aspect relationships between planets and between planets and Angles. It may seem complicated at first, but be patient: there are exceptionally easy guidelines to follow in order to find the aspects in a horoscope.

Degrees

Each Sign contains 30 degrees; in the flow of Signs, the beginning of each Sign is always 30 degrees from the beginning of the next Sign. If you know the degree measurement of the aspect, you simply count the number of Signs appropriate to the distance. We bring Bill Clinton's horoscope forward again from page 55 (Fig. 9, p. 78): Jupiter is at 23♎ in his horoscope. You have learned that sextiles relate between *every other Sign* (2 x 30 = 60). Two Signs before Libra is Leo. Now, look to see if anything is within orb of 23 degrees, *in Leo*. The Sun is at 26♌, within orb; it is *sextile to Jupiter*. (If you were to actually count the degrees, you would count 4 degrees to finish Leo, plus 30 degrees in Virgo(!), plus 23 degrees to Jupiter's position in Libra, for a total of 57 degrees, within orb of the sextile reference of 60 degrees.)

To see if there is a trine to Jupiter, look for similar degrees in the other *Air Signs* (because Jupiter is in Gemini, an Air Sign). Uranus is at 21♊, an Air Sign and within orb of 23 degrees. Jupiter is being trined by Uranus.

No matter what the Ptolemeic aspect is, you *never* have to actually count individual degrees to find it!

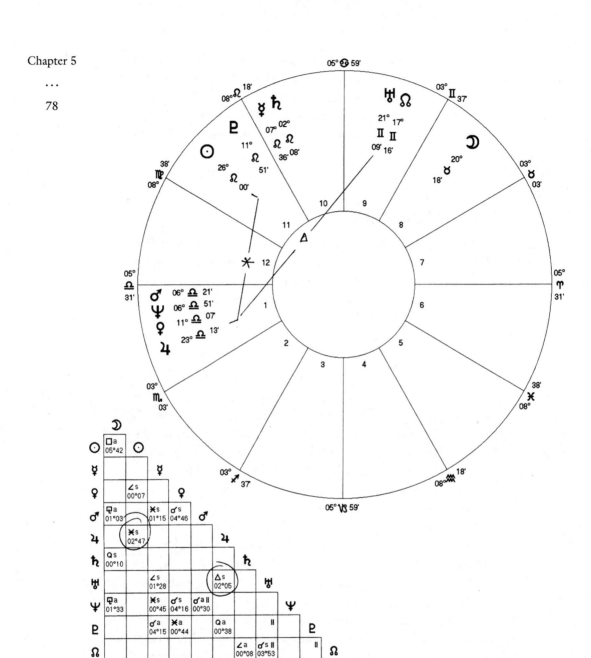

Figure 9
Bill Clinton
8/9/46, 8:51 A.M. CST
Hope AR, 93W35 33N40

Houses

Houses are not Signs and Signs are not Houses. Never measure an aspect using the Houses as reference, since Houses may have any number of degrees in them or ever contain the same Sign on two consecutive cusps.

Interceptions

Because of the irregular curvature of the Earth, as astrological measurements proceed along this curvature from the equator to the poles, the projections into the heavens that establish house cusps become congested. This mathematical congestion, "an accordion effect," when represented in the horoscope drawing, is called "interception." Two or more Signs can find themselves within one House.

Interpretatively (except for extending time for arcs and transits within an intercepted House—our advanced study ahead), interception has no special significance.

For example, in Ann-Margret's horoscope (p. 80), we see planets in Aquarius, Aries, and Taurus, *all in the 12th House!* Mars squares the Moon, Jupiter, and Saturn, all within the same House! Visually speaking, Neptune appears to be in an opposition to the 12th House group *but is actually trining the Moon and Jupiter!* You know that because Neptune is in Virgo (an Earth Sign) and the Moon and Jupiter are in Taurus, *also an Earth Sign.* This example shows why you cannot use Houses to count aspects.

Because Ann-Margret was born in Sweden, so far North, there is a double interception that falls across (within) her 12th–6th House axis. This is a frequent occurrence in extreme northern latitudes. Even the computer has difficulty fitting everything in: you can see Uranus tucked in there too! When you check the aspect grid (the table in the lower left corner, which we have introduced without fanfare) you see that Uranus is in conjunction with Jupiter (within a 2-degree orb) and exactly conjunct the Moon. This would be a powerful zap to the Moon-Jupiter conjunction in Taurus! Interpretatively, this would be an intensification of things Taurean within her reigning need complex, certainly including aesthetic organization of her life. As well, the dimensions of communication, etc., would be brought in through the position of this formidable Moon-centered emphasis *so close to her Gemini Ascendant!* Remember the relative speeds of the planets? This information is important because we read

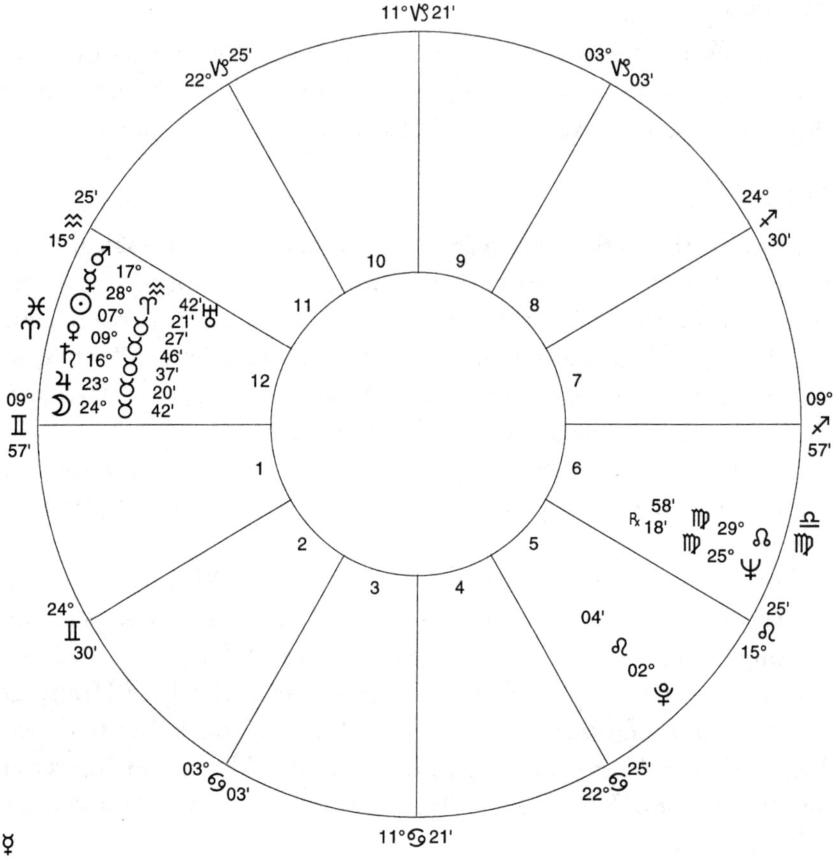

11°♑21'

22°♑25'

03°♑03'

24°
♐
30'

25'
≈≈
15'

17°
28°
07°
09°
16°
23°
24°

42'
21'
27'
46'
37'
20'
42'

♓

09°
♊
57'

09°
♐
57'

24°
♊
30'

58'
℞ 18' ♍ 29°
♍ 25' ♑
♎
♍

04'
♌
02°
♇

25'
♌
15'

03°♋03'

11°♋21'

22°♋25'

10   9
11   8
12   7
1   6
2   5
3   4

	☽												
☉	‖	☉											
☿	⚼a 03°39		☿										
♀	‖	♂s‖ 02°18		♀									
♂					♂								
♃	♂s 01°22			□♃ 05°38		♃							
♄	‖	‖		♂a‖ 06°52	□s 01°04	♂s 06°42	♄						
♅	♂a 00°22			♂a‖ 01°45				♅					
♆	△a 00°36	⯈a 02°50		⯈a 00°32		△a 01°58		△a 00°13	♆				
♇		□s 05°23	□a 03°43							♇			
☊	△a 05°16		⯒a 01°37		⯈s 02°44		⯈s 01°39	△a 04°54	♂a 04°41	⚹s 02°06	☊		
Mc	⯈s 01°39	△s 03°54		△s 01°36			△a 05°16	⯈s 01°17		⯒	Mc		
Asc		⚼s 02°30		⚼s 00°11						⯒s 01°25		Asc	

Figure 10
Ann-Margret
4/28/41, 4:30 A.M. CET
Valsjöbyn, Sweden, 14E08 64N04

aspects interpretatively in terms of the slower-moving planet (intrinsically) being in aspect to the *faster-moving planet*. In other words, the Moon does not aspect Pluto, Pluto makes an aspect ("affects") to the Moon. Mars aspects the Sun, Mercury, or Venus (not vice versa): Pluto aspects everything else because it is the slowest-moving planet! This will become second nature to you, don't worry!

Conjunctions ☌

Conjunctions are seen visually. Simply remain aware of the orb and your eyes will spot the conjunctions. You must also be aware that conjunctions can take place between planets in two different Signs! The ☉ at 28♈ is in conjunction with ♃ at 2♉ because **they are separated by 4 degrees** and we are allowed 7 degrees orb when it comes to the Sun. There is no impenetrable barrier between the Signs, all of which have 30 degrees each. Think that through and learn it well.

Sextiles ⚹

See "Degrees" on page 77. Now, some additional information: We know *we look two Signs ahead or two Signs backward* for a similarity of degree area to discover a sextile. A planet in a Fire Sign is sextile to a planet in an Air Sign and vice versa. A planet in an Earth Sign is sextile to a planet in a Water Sign, and vice versa. As was mentioned in the conjunction section, there will be occasions when, similarly, a sextile aspect takes place between Signs that do not fit the general mold.

For example, ☿ at 2♏ is sextile to ♂29♐, *even though these Signs are adjoining*. Here is why: you know the sextile is a 60-degree aspect. Sixty degrees from ☿ at 2♏ is 2♑. Our planet in question is ♂29♐. There are 3 degrees from 2♑ backward to 29♐, making a 57-degree difference between ☿ and ♂, **thus a sextile**. This is called an out-of-Sign (or over-the-Sign-line) aspect. Your eyes will be alerted to these subtleties very quickly—don't worry!

Squares ☐

Squares are easily seen by looking at Signs of the **same mode** (be on the look out for out-of-Sign relationships as well) because, as we know, Signs of the same mode are 90 degrees apart. A planet in Aries will square a planet in Cancer or Capricorn. A planet in Cancer will square a planet in Aries or Libra (orb allowance considered).

Trines △

Trines are found between planets in the **same element** (consider out-of Sign placements) because Signs of the same element are 120 degrees apart. A planet in Gemini will trine a planet in Libra or Aquarius (orb allowance considered). A planet in Taurus will trine a planet in Virgo or Capricorn, etc.

Oppositions ☍

Oppositions are easily seen visually; we see the "12" and "6" or the "2" and "8" on a clock's face. In Chapter 2 you learned the Signs in pairs of oppositions: Aries-Libra, Taurus-Scorpio, etc. These Signs are in a 180-degree relationship to each other (six Signs away, orb allowance considered).

It bears repeating yet again that the chart on page 75 is the ultimate reference for helping you to see aspects. Make ten copies of it and post them everywhere—on your bathroom mirror, in your car file for red lights, on your desk at work to keep people away from you, on the refrigerator to help you keep the door closed! I kid you not, it is *that* important!

Another example: for practice in measuring aspects, look at my horoscope (Fig. 11, p. 83). Begin with the Moon's aspects and then follow through to the Sun, then Mercury, and on with the other planets through Pluto; that's Moon-Sun, Moon-Mercury, Moon-Venus, on through to Neptune-Pluto.

The Moon and Sun are in adjoining Signs but *not* within orb, so there is no Moon-Sun aspect; Moon-Mercury are two *Signs* apart and within orb, for a sextile.

Next, your eye can see that there is a Moon-Venus conjunction, with seven degrees separating them.

Now: Moon-Mars—quickly assess the degree numbers of these two—the orb is too wide to be in aspect so you immediately dismiss the relationship! Moon-Jupiter is next. Two Signs are separating them and the degree is exact for a sextile. The degree numbers of the Moon and Saturn are too far apart to be in aspect so you immediately dismiss it; similarly with Uranus, Neptune, and Pluto.

Now, continue the same way with the Sun, Mercury, Venus, through Neptune. Make a list of what you discover, and match your list to the aspect grid shown with the horoscope.

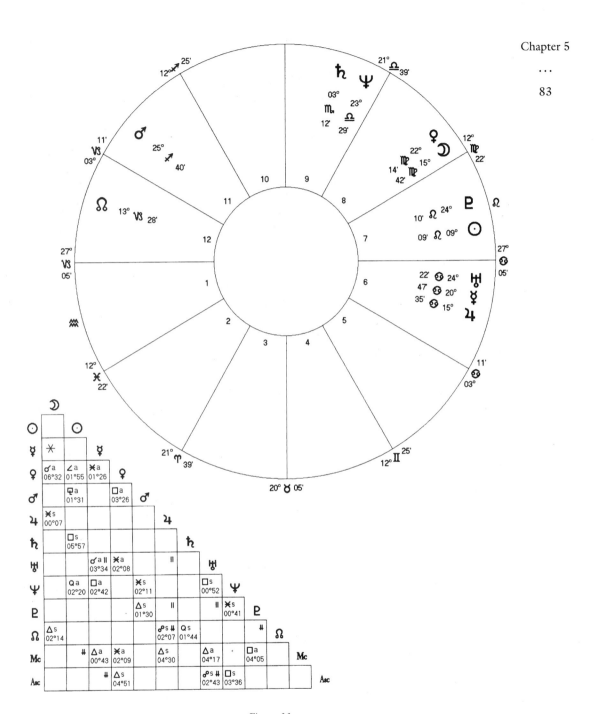

Figure 11
Basil Fearrington
8/1/54, 7:31 P.M. EDT
Philadelphia PA, 75W09 39N57

Interpreting Aspects

The interpretation of aspects is best achieved by learning to "feel" the measurements. Of course, this will come to you through experience. But, for now, in our beginning stage, there *is* a way of synthesis, a method to use, that will soon provide the experience necessary to "feel" aspects.

First of all, the intrinsically slower-moving planet usually alters the expression of the intrinsically faster-moving planet in any aspect together! The relationship between these planets is modified by the actual aspect involved. Each aspect has a basic keyword associated with it. **The conjunction suggests *focus*; the sextile suggests *support*; the square suggests *developmental tension*; the trine suggests *ease*; the opposition suggests *awareness*.**

If a horoscope has ☿□♆, or in manifested effect, ♆□☿, this tells you, first of all, that the symbolism of Mercury is receiving some moderation or alteration from the symbolism of Neptune, and this is being accomplished in a *developmentally tense* way, a way wherein something needs to be worked out and resolved (the square). If there is no resolution, the Neptune faculties, in effect, will operate on Mercury in a way that may be problematic.

Neptune represents, most often, the sense of camouflage and the idea that things are other than they seem. Mercury represents the mind. The *square* between them would indicate that Neptune has got the "upper hand" on Mercury. The mind could be over-influenced by Neptune, probably manifesting in daydreaming, "foggy thinking," avoidance of issues, duplicity, or vagueness in communication. Indeed, this can also suggest the infusion of spirituality or aesthetics into the mind! We will have more about this in later studies.

If Mercury and Neptune are in conjunction ☿☌♆, the influence is similar: the faculty of Neptune is blending with the faculty of Mercury to *create one structure of focus*. If Mercury and Neptune are in opposition ☿☍♆, the mind is usually quite in *awareness of* creative visualization, perhaps inspiration. If Mercury and Neptune are in sextile aspect ☿⚹♆, there is a support between the behavioral faculties of the two planets. If they are in trine aspect ☿△♆, there will be an easy flow between the two and the world of Neptune enriches the processes of the mind (communication, etc.).

In analysis, the synthesis process that we are developing recognizes *the behavioral faculty of the outer planet as **conditioner***; and the behavioral faculty of the inner planet as ***reactor.***

Examples

♂☌♅: Applied energy is in awareness of intensity, individuation, eccentricity. You can easily see the accident potential here because the energy wants to do what it does individualistically, obstreperously, and perhaps with sudden outbursts! Uranus (the conditioner) zaps Mars (the reactor in this aspect)!

☽△♀: The reigning need of the personality is in an easy flow with the need (ability) to relate a certain way, manifesting to one degree or another a dynamic of an attractive personality.

♀☌♄: Necessary controls and the need to relate to others a certain way are focused together. There are probably control factors upon relationships or in romance.

☉□♂: The need to apply energy in a certain way is in a developmentally tense relationship with the core life energy. This pairing would manifest positively as leadership or negatively as temperamental explosions, even to heart problems.

♂✶♄: The need to apply energy in a certain way is supported by necessary controls, manifesting in efficiency. If these planets were in Aries and Libra (an opposition), aggression and restraint would be at odds.

With experience, we get certain feels for certain special hard aspects. These are: □☌☍:

☉□☽: Expect parental upheaval around the time of conception, birth, or very early in life. [The male and female symbols—father and mother—are at odds or face a major problem.] What does this set up in the earliest home atmosphere? (John Kennedy, Jr. is a perfect example.)

☉ in hard aspect with ♄: Nature of ambition; early home tensions involving the father; difficulty with men in a female horoscope. Might there be difficulty in accepting, dealing with authority? (Oprah Winfrey)

☉ with ♇: One's "hand grenade" of potential (empowerment of life-energy thrust) is smothered by a "blanket"; The Self can't get out from under. (Prince Charles: ☉□♇)

☽♄: Ambition; emotional frustration; strategic gambits galore. (Steven Spielberg)

The Major (Ptolemaic) Aspects

Aspect	Symbol	What It Means
Conjunction	♂	The conjunction symbolizes two planets in the same longitudinal measurement position within orb of each other. Interpretatively, the conjunction suggests a focus of the symbolisms of the two or more planets at the same position. The conjunction is a 0-degree aspect measurement reference, with its orb allowance depending on the planets involved. It is a dynamic, "hard" aspect.
Sextile	⚹	The sextile symbolizes planets in a 60 degree longitudinal relationship to each other. Interpretatively, the sextile suggests a supportive relationship between the two or more planets. The sextile is a "soft" aspect that does not usually stimulate changes in terms of the planets involved; it supports the status quo.
Square	□	The square symbolizes planets in a 90 degree longitudinal relationship to each other. Interpretatively, the square suggests great tension between the symbolisms of the planets involved. This tension provides enormous strength to achieve and grow within the behavioral faculties suggested by the planets involved. The square is a dynamic, "hard" aspect, usually indicative of a strong inner concern, the sense of attack, often self-induced anxiety.

Aspect	Symbol	What It Means
(Square cont'd)		

The square is dramatically important in development; much can be said about the square being indispensable. Growth requires tension.

Trine △ The trine symbolizes planets in a 120-degree longitudinal relationship to each other. Interpretatively, the trine suggests a free-flowing sense of ease between the symbolisms of the planets involved. The trine is a "soft" aspect that tends to keep things as they are rather than manifest a necessity to make changes. The trine indicates a strong state of equilibrium. The principle weakness of a trine is passivity and laziness, usually an over-protection of the status quo.

Opposition ☍ The opposition symbolizes planets in a 180-degree longitudinal relationship to each other. Interpretatively, the opposition suggests an intense tie between two (or more) planets and/or a tug of war. The opposition is a dynamic, "hard" aspect that usually involves other people, others' authority (someone else's individuality), and other challenging concepts.

☽♇: In a female horoscope particularly, there is the strong suggestion of mother fixations, possibly of mother-daughter conflicts and competition between them; also present in male horoscopes as a probable smothering maternal influence or a painful absence of maternal caring. (Charles Manson)

♂♃: Being ahead of one's time; energy running expansively; speeding along. (David Copperfield)

♂♄: Potential of bad judgment; braking when one should accelerate and vice versa; stop-and-start. (Ernest Hemingway)

♂♆: Magnetism; charisma. (Bill Clinton)

♂♇: In the conjunction, energy is focused with a strong perspective; in the square, energy has difficulty applying itself with the ways of the world, producing rebelliousness; in the opposition, the perspective of energy application is so aware of its application in the world that it can overdo or self-destruct: there is the potential for militaristic coercion, brusqueness, meanness. (General Norman Schwarzkopf)

♃♄: The need to prove a point; a strong sense of rightness about things; sometimes law and order. (Psychedelic researcher Timothy Leary, Cher)

♃♇: Tremendous resourcefulness and success potential. (Bill Gates, chairman of Microsoft)

♄♅: Pressure to resolve the old and the new, the conventional and the avant garde, the conservative and the liberal, eventually to leave the Saturn environment behind. (Barbara Streisand)

♄♆: Ambition focused through intuition or ambition going to sleep. (Betty Ford)

♄♇: Control and empowerment come together, creating either a very difficult situation or the tendency toward record-breaking achievement through ambition and prominence breaking down for stronger renewal. (Arnold Schwarzenegger)

Idealism

Idealism is suggested in the horoscope most reliably as follows: *any combination of* ☉☿♀, as pairs or as a group in conjunction; contacts of these innermost planets with ♆, especially the conjunction, square, or opposition; in addition these Neptune contacts can point to a strong sense of aesthetics, art, and creativity. To a different (usually lesser) degree, the same applies to contacts between the innermost planets and Jupiter.

Realism Aspects

It is important to know and remember that when the Sun or Moon make important hard aspects (☌ ☐ ☍) with the planets Saturn through Pluto (the outer planets), there is the suggestion of demanding conditions in life development **through controls** (♄), **intensifications** (♅), **bewilderment** (♆), or **power struggle** (♇). These demanding conditions and situations determine growth.

When these outer-planet aspects occur with the Sun or Moon in a horoscope, the person takes on the significance of these aspects **at the core of his or her life orientation.** The Sun's life-energy flow is probably affected, and the Moon's drive to fulfill the reigning need of the personality is probably affected. **These become enduring life considerations.**

The measurements of planets in aspect with the points of the Ascendant or Midheaven will be added to our study soon. They are very important, but we know that learning all this in stages is best. Be patient!

Summary

1. An aspect is the measured longitudinal distance relationship, in degrees, between planetary positions (including the Angles) in a horoscope.

2. Aspects describe the level of tension or ease put upon the process of need fulfillment.

3. The determining factor in measuring developmental tension is through the measurement of aspects.

4. As the base of astrological synthesis, there are five major aspects, called "Ptolemaic," after the Egyptian scholar, Claudius Ptolemy. Each aspect conditions development between positions in a specific way: conjunction (0-degree measurement suggesting focus), sextile (60-degree measurement suggesting support), square (90-degree measurement suggesting developmental tension), trine (120-degree measurement suggesting ease), and opposition (180-degree
measurement suggesting awareness).

5. Signs of the *same mode* are linked by squares and oppositions.

6. Signs of the *same element* are linked by trines.

7. Sextiles are easily seen by counting two Signs ahead or backward from a given position with similarity of degree reference.

8. There is an allowance for degrees approaching and separating from exactness. This is called orb. We allow a 7-degree orb for the Sun and Moon, 5-degree orb for the planets.

9. The intrinsically slower-moving planet always makes the aspect to and alters the expression of the intrinsically faster moving planet with which it is in aspect.

10. Idealism is suggested in the horoscope by any combination of ☉☿♀ in aspect as pairs or as a group and through Neptune contacts; as well as contacts with Jupiter.

11. Hard aspects from the outer planets to the Sun or Moon are the aspects of realism. They suggest demanding circumstances that are at the core of a person's life orientation.

Test Yourself

(See test answers, p. 236.)

1. Is there an aspect relationship between ☉29♉ and ♆4♎? Explain your answer.

2. What are the hard aspects?

3. The aspects named after Ptolemy are, in order of arc size:

4. What is the name for the degree allowance given to an aspect when it is approaching or separating from exactness?

5. What is the easiest way to see sextiles in a horoscope?

6. The trine aspect measures _____ degrees.

7. What does ☉□♅ suggest?

8. What is the easiest way to see squares in a horoscope?

9. Are the Midheaven and Ascendant included in aspect measurements?

10. The aspect with the key concept of "awareness" is _____.

11. What does ☽△♄ suggest?

12. What are the names of the soft aspects?

13. Most horoscopes have hard and soft aspects. Upon which do we focus more in the horoscope and why?

14. The mind in developmental tension with necessary controls suggests what aspect?

15. The term "blanket over a hand grenade" refers to

    _____.

16. A focus of individualism at one's core life energy suggests what aspect?

17. What is the key to interpreting an aspect?

18. ♃□♆ suggests _____. What other aspects are similar in effect?

19. Using each Ptolemeic aspect, explain the suggested manifestations of Venus and Mars in aspect.

20. In the ♄□♇ relationship, which planet's expression is being altered?

Note

The computer is now listing the aspects on the page with the horoscope wheel in a **grid** (see Fig. 11, p. 84). We have quietly introduced the "aspect grid" in our last examples so that you could begin to figure it out for yourself; and you did, didn't you!!?

Note that the grid contains the measurement of orb, along with each specific aspect! The aspect will not appear unless it meets the definition of orb you have stored in your computer, but the notation of orb comes in handy in advanced work.

And finally—**the reward is in sight!** When you understand the building of aspect relationships, the measurement concepts abbreviated in the ways we have shared—when you know these thoroughly—not only will your eyes just "eat up" all the relationships very quickly and surely, but you will be able to simply scan the aspect grid and absorb it all in about 30 seconds! I promise!

Chapter 6

• • •

Special Aspect Structures

ASPECTS FREQUENTLY OCCUR IN SPECIAL PAT-
terns. These patterns can give us important information
for our interpretations of the horoscope.

You know now that planets connected by **two Signs of
the same element are in trine relationship to each
other.** There will be many horoscopes that you will see in
which planets in **ALL THREE Signs of the same element are connected by trine aspects.** For example,
☽15♑ △ ♀16♉ △ ♂16♍. This grand configuration
found throughout all the Signs of the same element
(remember the orb consideration, as well) is called a
Grand Trine.

The Grand Trine

The next horoscope example (Fig. 12, p. 94) shows a
Grand Trine in the Air element: Mercury is trined by
both Uranus and Neptune. In a Grand Trine, three
modes of an essential element combine, overlap, and
blend conspicuously at the center of identity. One set of

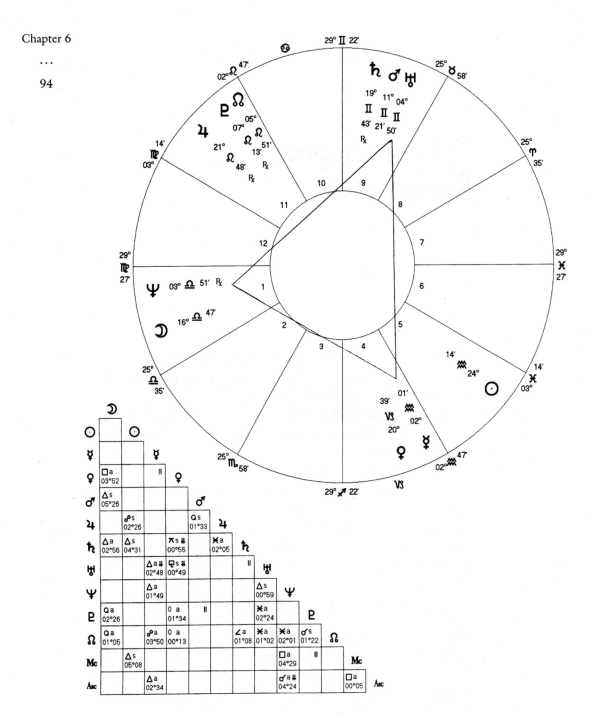

Figure 12
Male

need energies flows smoothly into yet another set of need energies which flows smoothly into another set of need energies, creating **routinized holistic responses.** A sense of **completeness** is formed within the identity that manifests as **defensiveness,** as **self-sufficiency in terms of the element so conspicuously emphasized.** And because of this, **the Grand Trine is self-isolating in its manifestation**; *It tends to work against relationship.* **In analysis, see the Grand Trine as an entire structure, not one of three or more separate parts. As a powerful defense mechanism in development, it is a key observation for interpretation.**

The **Fire Grand Trine** gives the sense of a closed circuit of **inspirational or motivational self-sufficiency,** which is another way of saying that a person is motivated from within rather than from anyone else's leadership. *It works against the fear of being ignored.*

In an **Air Grand Trine,** there is the suggestion of a closed circuit of **intellectual and/or social self-sufficiency,** usually accompanying a threat to the identity or self-worth profile in development. One becomes easily delighted with one's own pleasure or one's own thoughts or accomplishments, *a frequent countermeasure to inferiority feelings.*

In a **Water Grand Trine,** there is the sense of a closed circuit of emotional self-sufficiency, usually as *a defense against the fear of being hurt emotionally (again).*

In an **Earth Grand Trine,** there is the sense of a closed circuit of practical self-sufficiency resulting in the sense of not asking for anyone's help. Things are frequently overdone to prove a point. *"I can do it myself, thank you!"*

A Grand Trine will almost always have within it at least one of the outer planets, as well as the Sun and/or Moon. When the Grand Trine *does not* involve the Sun or Moon, it becomes a counterstructure to the major core as suggested through the Sun and Moon blend (which we will study intensely soon). It is as though the person has **two themes of developmental focus in life at the same time.** One may be obviously happy and easy to get along with in one sector of life, but raise extreme defenses (change personalities!) when pressed to enter into social activity (Air Grand Trine, without Sun or Moon) or emotional relationship (Water Grand Trine, without Sun or Moon).

Anytime there is a square or opposition to any point within the **Grand Trine,** that planet and its House position become very important as a way into or out of the defensive organization of the Grand Trine.

In the same way that we have out-of-Sign aspects, we have *apparent* Grand Trines in which two planets in trine aspect to each other are *also in trine aspect to the Midheaven or to the Ascendant*. The suggestion here is the **inclination** to the closed-circuit defenses. The horoscope of Jackie Kennedy-Onassis (Fig. 13, p. 97) is a perfect example: the Moon and Saturn are both trine to the Midheaven and Neptune, creating *an apparent Fire* Grand Trine. There is a Venus opposition with Saturn, showing the way into and out of her Grand Trine to be through relationships and issues involving control factors within her *relationships as they have to do with her self-worth—very deep, real issues in her life development.* [Note: Saturn is in the 2nd House of Self-worth; Venus is the ruler of Taurus on the cusp of the 7th House—so it refers to that House, the House of others in relationship, and Venus is placed in the 8th House, others' monies, resources. We are going to learn that there is a thin line between money and love.]

The T-Square

The T-Square is an opposition axis that is given strong developmental tension potential by/in terms of a planet or planets squaring that opposition axis. The T-Square represents a dominating reservoir of energy. It embodies a prime resource in personality development.

Visualize this example T-Square: ♀15♉ ☍ ♂13♏, with ♄16♌, square both planets, i.e., the opposition axis. In interpretation, *define the opposition axis first* and then give it further definition in terms of the squaring planet. In the example above, Venus opposing Mars suggests an awareness of passion within individual expression. Saturn squaring this axis will introduce dimensions of control or discomfort upon the passion. It is almost as if Venus and Mars, as an intimate couple, enter into someone's home who is decidedly Saturnian. Instead of being able to express their relationship freely, they have to do it within the enforced limitations established by the host. Contrarily, if the squaring planet were Jupiter, the sense of intimacy and passion would be expanded, increasing all the potentials of the Venus/Mars pairing.

Visualize this example T-Square: ☉23♑ ☍ ☽20♋, □ ♅18♈ □ the axis. In interpretation, this Sun-Moon blend suggests a tug-of-war between practicality (Capricorn) and emotions (Cancer). The square to

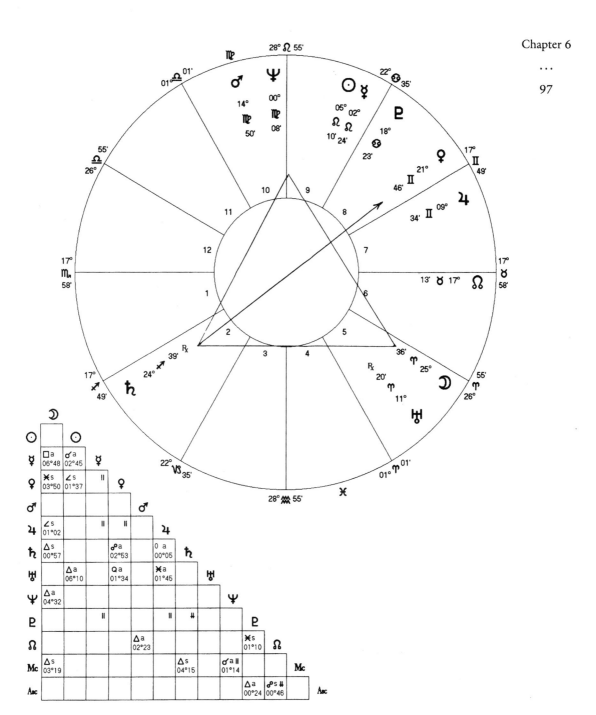

Figure 13
Jackie Kennedy-Onassis
7/28/29, 2:30 P.M. EDT
Southampton NY, 72W23 40N53

the opposition axis from Uranus intensifies the situation, threatening upset, relationship split (Sun-Moon, male-female). If the squaring planet were Saturn in Libra, there would be controls or conservative factors at work that would tone down the drives, resolving the business and feeling interaction differently, but probably, the resolution would be reasonably enforced, more easily accepted, in this example, since Saturn is in Libra (Libra: fairness, calm, balance). Think that through, remembering the ♄♎ archetype.

When the T-Square takes place in **Cardinal Signs**, the energy is more active, outgoing, and enterprising, as it is when it takes place in **Angular Houses** (surely including important dimensions connected with identity, parental tension, or relationships). In **Fixed Signs** there is a deeply tenacious, rooted, hard-to-change dimension that is also prevalent when it takes place in Succedent Houses (surely including self-worth concerns, concerns about others' resources). In Cadent Signs, energy is reactive to external stimuli; a mindset is established for responses to the world.

The Grand Cross

When the open arm of a T-Square pattern is filled in at birth, is tenanted by another planet, the structure ceases to be a T-Square and becomes a *Grand Cross*. A Grand Cross is *a developmentally tense interaction, a crossing of two opposition axes.*

In effect, the Grand Cross shows energies and needs focused strongly in two separate but often complementary directions, two areas of concern in life. These energy drives and life concerns are usually related somehow, since in most cases, by House tenancy, the four corners of the Angular, Succedent, or Cadent Cross of Houses will become activated. Since the oppositions cross each other in "square fashion," the behaviors manifested are often in the form of indecision, because energies are usually working at cross purposes to each other.

In Angular Houses, the Grand Cross suggests concerns about parental issues in the early homelife; about relationship concerns and personal projection to others; about in-laws, the parents of the spouse.

In Succedent Houses, love issues are brought to the foreground: self-worth, giving love, the reaction to others' values, our expectations of love, how we want others to react to us—all of these are given strong developmental tension. There are issues also of establishing personal value, creativity, putting oneself forward speculatively, and earning rewards from the job.

A Grand Cross located in the Cadent Houses focuses in the mindset, the point of view, one's education, and the way we cooperate with others. **The way we look at things affects our health.** This is a very important dynamic of the Cadent Grand Cross.

Crazed cult leader and murderer Charles Manson's horoscope is shown on page 100 (Fig. 14) with its Grand Cross. Mercury receives an out-of-Sign opposition from Uranus (the exact opposition would be at 2♉. Uranus needs 2 degrees to get to 0♉ and two more to arrive at 2♉. It is an opposition with a four degree orb). The Moon is opposed by Pluto, just one degree outside of our orb allowance (tolerable within such a grand aspect configuration). The Moon is square with Mercury (as well as Jupiter) and Uranus. Pluto squares Mercury and Uranus. This is the Grand Cross construct.

Interpretatively, this Grand Cross should be quite clear for you: just look at the tension on the horizon line, which we know is *identity formation* from the Self (at the Ascendant) and with/through others (at the Descendant). The Mercury (the mind) is being zapped by Uranus in the opposition; and we can point out (what we will be studying intensely soon) that Mercury refers to the self-worth development here because it rules Gemini, the sign on the cusp of the 2nd. Gemini is also on the cusp of the 3rd House because of an interception in the 12th–6th axis—see it there? So the tension from Uranus (as conditioner) to Mercury (as reactor) is going to involve references not only to self-worth but also to the mindset, since that is a basic meaning of the 3rd House.

Now, we know that Aquarius is the Sign of rebellion, innovation, making a difference somehow, even humanitarianism, even tyranny. With the Moon in Aquarius, we know these concepts will dominate as Manson's reigning need. This is especially strong since the Moon is *angular* (the 10th House) so high in the chart.

Now this Moon is intensely confronted, if you will, by Pluto in the opposition aspect across the Sign-line. All this action takes place in the 10th and 4th House axis, where we see the parental situation in the early home. This tells us so much, and we have learned besides that the Moon-Pluto relationship in a horoscope is going to introduce very strongly concerns about the mother.

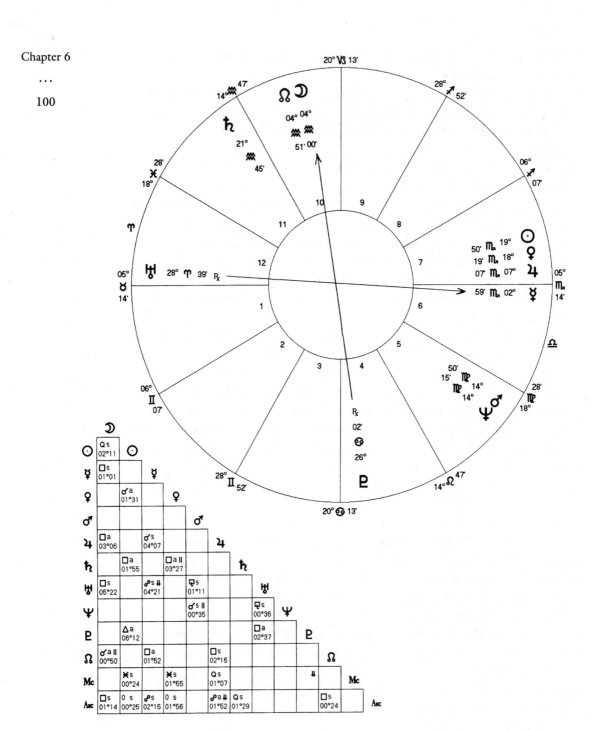

Figure 14
Charles Manson
11/12/34, 4:40 P.M. EST
Cincinnati OH, 84W27 39N09

We can note further that Pluto is the ruler of Scorpio. Therefore, all this tension in the early home will somehow be played out, be related to dynamics of relationship *since Scorpio is on the 7th cusp!* Pluto refers to the 7th from its position in the 4th within the awareness opposition with the Moon. Note as well that the Moon rules Cancer, the sign on the 4th House holding Pluto. Here is yet another reinforcement of the early home situation that must have been very, very difficult for young Charles. Remember: Cancer connotes emotional security, security in the early home; here the reference is clearly related to the parental axis, many times over through the symbols.

So within Manson's Grand Cross we have identity development tensions tied painfully to early home-parental concerns involving self-worth and mindset, all this being played out in relationships. That all of this has a Scorpionic twist (control, even matters of death or messianic dimensions of grandeur) is not at all surprising with Mercury, Sun, Venus, and Jupiter all in Scorpio.

Then, there is the charisma indication of Mars-Neptune, a kind of personal magic that supported exertion of Manson's will (Mars, energy application), even in the rebellious retaliation upon society for all his own individual developmental pains.

Finally, note Saturn in the 11th House, the House of love needed, expected, yearned for. There are controls operating here; there is a tremendous need for love stirring up the whole situation, isn't there? Notice that Saturn is square to Venus (two Fixed Signs), and Venus is the ruler of the Ascendant Sign, Taurus! Saturn, in turn rules the MC, Capricorn, part of the parental axis! It is important to know that Manson attributed his murderous spree to a frustration with and rejection by the recording industry in which he felt he belonged as a performer; the Moon in the 10th, Saturn ruling the 10th, the 10th House symbolizing the profession.

We could go on and on here. The horoscope is saying the same thing over and over and over again. And you will learn soon that all horoscopes do: they establish a first impression and then development issues from that impression throughout all areas of experience and throughout all time of development.

Now, sit back and realize how much you have learned. There is nothing here you can not follow!

You have just done quite a formidable bit of synthesis and interpretation. Congratulations!

Summary

1. Single aspects frequently form special patterns within the horoscope, and these patterns suggest important information about the identity.

2. Planets connected by all three Signs of the same element (orbs considered) form a configuration called Grand Trine.

3. The Grand Trine is a key defense mechanism that suggests self-sufficiency and separation from relationship in terms of the element it is in.

4. The Fire Grand Trine suggests a closed circuit of inspirational or motivational self-sufficiency.

5. The Air Grand Trine suggests a closed circuit of intellectual or social self-sufficiency.

6. The Water Grand Trine suggests a closed circuit of emotional self-sufficiency.

7. The Earth Grand Trine suggests a closed circuit of practical self-sufficiency.

8. When a Grand Trine does not involve the Sun or Moon, it becomes a counterstructure to the major core, as suggested through the Sun-Moon blend.

9. A square or opposition to any point within a Grand Trine suggests a way into and/or out of the defensive organization of the Grand Trine.

10. "Apparent" Grand Trines occur when two planets in trine aspect to each other are also in trine aspect to the Midheaven or to the Ascendant. Behavior inclines to the routinization so often seen within Grand Trine situations.

11. The T-Square is an opposition axis given strong developmental tension potential by, or in terms of a planet squaring that axis. It is a reservoir of energy.

12. To interpret a T-Square, define the opposition axis first and then give it definition in terms of the squaring planet.

13. The Grand Cross is a developmentally tense crossing of two opposition axis that shows energies and needs focused strongly in two separate directions, creating indecision in behavior, and thus frustration.

Test Yourself

(See test answers, p. 237.)

1. What is a Grand Trine?

2. Describe the behavioral manifestation of a Grand Trine. What does it suggest?

3. Describe the behavioral manifestation of a Grand Trine in each element.

4. What do you look for as a way into and/or out of the Grand Trine, and why is there a need to look for a way into and/or out of it?

5. You see that a horoscope with a Grand Trine has an opposition to a point within it made by Saturn in the 10th House. What does this suggest to you?

6. Do all Grand Trines involve three planets? Explain your answer.

7. What is a T-Square?

8. How is a T-Square interpreted?

9. What does the following suggest: ♂ ☌ ♃, □ ♇?

10. In any T-Square, what is suggested when Saturn is the squaring planet?

11. What is a Grand Cross?

12. How does a Grand Cross differ from a T-Square?

13. What is the basic behavioral manifestation suggested by a Grand Cross?

14. Describe some of the suggested concerns found in an Angular Grand Cross.

15. Describe some of the suggested concerns found in a Succedent Grand Cross.

16. Describe some of the suggested concerns found in a Cadent Grand Cross.

17. What is the difference between a T-Square in Cardinal Signs and a T-Square in Fixed Signs?

18. The Air Grand Trine is frequently seen in horoscopes with which planet retrograde? Why?

19. Do the following positions describe a Grand Trine: ☉28♈, ☽2 ♍, ♂1♑?

20. What is suggested in a horoscope that has a Water Grand Trine that doesn't include the Sun or Moon and also has a T-Square involving ☉♈ ☍ ☽♎, □ ♅♋?

Chapter 7

• • •

Houses and Rulership Networks

EVERYTHING WE DO IN LIFE IS MOTIVATED and driven by needs. We use our personalized core life energy ☉ to fulfill the all-encompassing reigning need of our personality ☽; we need to think and communicate in a certain way to be fulfilled ☿; we need to relate to others socially and intimately in certain ways in order not to be alone ♀; we have a need to apply energy in a certain way ♂; we have reward needs ♃, needs to administer ambition ♄, needs to be individual ♅, to visualize creatively ♆, and we need to establish a perspective for our personal empowerment ♇.

The Grand Crosses

We know that the Moon represents the reigning basic, vital need of the personality, using the Sun's energy, and the rest of the planets in their Signs represent subsidiary needs that work to help the fulfillment of the reigning need, just as departments of a corporation all aid in the overall development of the corporation. The horoscope is our gift from above, the best tool available to us to guide our awareness of self and the directions of development.

Within the horoscope itself, we can clearly see three vital areas of concern, all of which contain the most vital psychodynamic dimensions of the human experience. These areas of concern are seen within the Grand Crosses of Houses in the horoscope: **Angular** (1st, 4th, 7th, and 10th Houses), **Succedent** (2nd, 5th, 8th, and 11th Houses), and **Cadent** (3rd, 6th, 9th, and 12th Houses). It is through these Grand Crosses of Houses that we discover more dimensions of life development.

All Houses in a given Grand Cross—that is, **all the areas of human life experience in a given Grand Cross—are square to each other.** Each is in high developmental tension with the other three in the Grand Cross. They are that way because the universe has made it so in order for development to take place! In reality, this is how life progresses. *Progress requires tension.*

The Angular Grand Cross

The Angular Grand Cross has as its base House, the 1st House. The core concerns of the 1st House are identity development and self-projection. The 4th and 10th Houses form the parental axis, as you know well by now. Note that the **1st House is always square to the 4th and 10th Houses,** telling us that the way we need to project and develop identity MUST be fashioned by developmental tension with our parents. That is what parents are for! This reality is vital and enduringly important.

It is through the relationship with our parents that we learn lessons of life and eventually the definition of what we will and will not model or emulate. Whatever one becomes through the role model at home is then projected to society in relationships *through the 7th House,* another arm of the Angular Grand Cross. The astrologer's objective in relation to the Angular Grand Cross is to determine *to what degree* **the development of self-projection has been affected by interaction with the parents and then to determine exactly how this *has spilled over into relationship concerns.*** Whom do you know who has married "a parent" to resolve unfinished business from earlier times? Amazing, isn't it!

The Succedent Grand Cross

In our study of the Houses, we learned that the Succedent Houses organize for value that which was initiated in the Angular House preceding it.

In these Houses, our core concerns have to do with self-worth development and the giving and receiving of love (which includes sex). The 2nd House is the House symbolizing self-worth development; the 8th House is the House symbolizing the dimensions of others' worth; the 5th House symbolizes the idea of giving love in many ways; the 11th House symbolizes dimensions of receiving love from others (even the salary for one's work is a recognition factor from others that fits into the 11th House).

The 2nd House is always square to the 5th–11th House axis. This fact points up a fundamental truth that **there is a powerful interdependence between how one feels about oneself and one's ability to give or receive love**, including sexual intimacy! When the self-worth profile suffers in development, self-doubts muffle the ability to give of oneself easily and intimately, often creating difficulty in accepting love offered by others. When this self-worth profile breaks down, the exchange of various kinds of resources with others (the 8th House) suffers: one finds it difficult to accept and/or give compliments; dealing with others secure in their worth can become extremely difficult and problematic. Relationships can not get started; or established relationships break down over and over and over again *for the same reasons!*

If the Succedent Grand Cross of Houses is comfortable and without too much tension, or the problems have been solved, the self-worth development will allow for a smooth exchange of resources with others and the fulfilling exchange of love with others. In analysis of the Grand Crosses, the concern is always **to *what degree* tensions in the specific areas have been internalized by the individual and become integral to routinized behavior.** This kind of perspective is essential in conversation with the client during the consultation.

The Cadent Grand Cross

The Angular Houses focus and initiate. The Succedent Houses organize values that have to do with worth and love. Now, in the Cadent Grand Cross, we are concerned with matters that have to do with learning, processing information, education, establishing a point of view, and cooperation with others experiencing the same developmental challenges.

The 3rd House symbolizes what and how we think, communicate, and deal with information about our identity. The mental outlook (mindset) of the 3rd House colors the way we look at everything.

The 6th and 12th Houses symbolize the zones of experience that have to do with the cooperation demanded of us in work situations and within the institutional standards of society, respectively.

The 3rd House is always square to the 6th/12th House axis and, of course, it always opposes the 9th House. This tells us that there MUST be tension between the way we think and what others have to say—what they have to share educationally—for us to adjust our personal perspective in order to learn more, in order to fit in where we need to fit in.

When problematic, Cadent Grand Cross Houses show concerns that have to do with how personal opinion can be destructive (even a lack of humor or rigidity of view); how a lack of cooperation with others, *on their terms*, invites social breakdown, even illness; how an interruption in education lowers the personal resources, the accreditation necessary for optimum advancement opportunities, and how a negative image (viewpoint) of oneself becomes destructive, an anathema to progress.

When there is little or no tension among these Houses, learning, education, the processing of information, cooperative liaisons, etc., will all tend to be most helpful and fulfilling for the person, or these areas will be routined in dullness, acceptance, and passivity.

The Empty Houses

In our discussion of the Grand Crosses of Houses (above), you have learned about the focal elements of tensions that formulate life development, the zones of life experience wherein tensions manifest. We can pinpoint these tensions even further.

The word and concept of **significator** will help us! It means, "that which indicates." *A significator is the planet ruling the sign on the cusp of the House, or the most prominent planet in the House* (in Charles Manson's horoscope (p. 100), Venus is the significator of the 1st House because it rules Taurus on the 1st House cusp. Mercury is the significator of the 2nd House because it rules Gemini on the cusp. The main significator of the 7th House is Pluto because it rules Scorpio on the cusp. The Sun, Venus, and Jupiter are cosignificators of the 7th House.) The use of significators in the horoscope *leads the horoscope into the various concerns of a Grand Cross of Houses; the use of significators routes developmental tension throughout the Houses of the horoscope.*

We know that when a planet is involved in developmental tension (conjunction, square, or opposition) within the horoscope, the core concerns of the House where the planet is located become illuminated and must be discussed in the consultation setting. Now, we take that further: when the Angular Grand Cross significators are under tension, **no matter where they are located in the horoscope,** you know for sure to **expect developmental tension regarding parental issues, relationship issues, and identity development (self-projection).**

For example, the horoscope shown next belongs to actor Leonardo "Titanic" DiCaprio (Fig. 15, p. 110). It reveals the Moon and Saturn in square aspect, an aspect that often symbolizes strong ambition, among other things. *But as significators,* **the Moon rules Cancer on the *10th House* and Saturn rules Capricorn on the 4th House.** What this says is that since the "rulers" of these two (parental) Houses (the significators of these two Houses) are in a developmentally tense relationship with each other, **you should expect a high degree of parental tension in this person's life.**

Now, this tension may have been tied to DiCaprio's motivation to become a great actor! [Note: indeed, when we see more and more parts of any horoscope accumulated in analysis, it could well be suggested that such a Moon-Saturn square was too debilitating for ambition to get off the ground, i.e., the parental situation in this case overpowering personal drive. Again, reading aspects suggests a developmental condition; full analysis then suggests the degree of intensification; and consultation dialogue brings reality to the symbolic profile being developed.]

Significators in Developmental Tension

When the significator of the 1st House is involved in tension, expect concerns having to do with identity development and self-projection.

When the significator of the 2nd House is under tension, expect concerns with self-worth that will surely relate to the House of the aspecting planet *or the Houses that these planets rule.* For example, you see in this horoscope that *Pisces* is on the cusp of the 7th House. Within that horoscope, Mercury in the 11th House opposes Neptune in the 5th

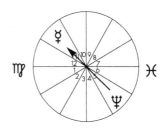

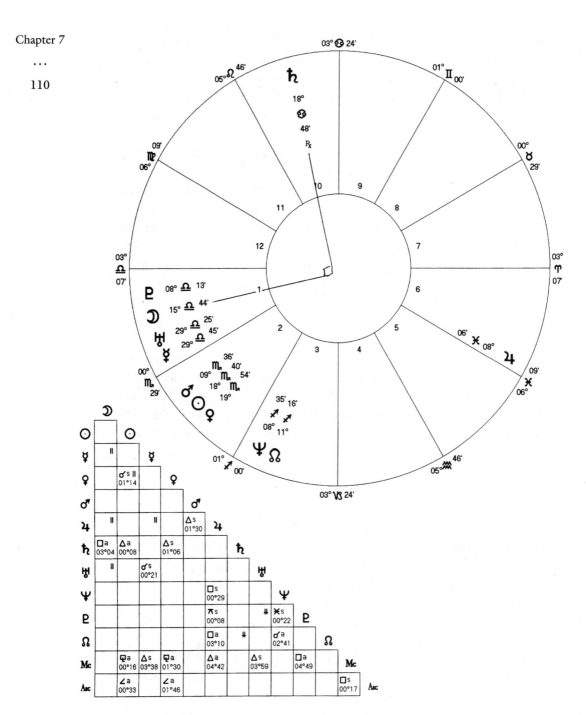

Figure 15
Leonardo DiCaprio
11/11/74, 2:47 A.M. PST
Los Angeles CA, 118W15 34N03

House. Pisces is on the 7th House cusp and Virgo is on the 1st House cusp. Mercury opposed Neptune shows a mind that is very aware of creative visualization. That could be daydreaming or idealism *in terms of giving and receiving love* (because it is taking place in the 5–11 axis of giving and receiving love).

With Virgo on the 1st House cusp and Pisces on the 7th, we know that this idealism about giving and receiving love will also include concerns (confusion) about identity and relationships.

So, these concerns are all tied together; a confusion or bewilderment about what constitutes an ideal relationship. Does this ward off relationships generally? Is the person too hard to please? Are self-worth concerns being projected onto relationships and undermining them? Is a defensive position being formed in terms of an ideal that is impractical?

When the significator of the 3rd House is involved in developmental tension, expect problems that have to do with communication, often in familial networks among brothers and sisters. Also, we see the frame of mind developed by all the early life experiences.

The significators of the 4–10 axis point to parental tension, as we have already seen many times.

When the significator of the 5th House is involved in developmental tension, expect problems with the giving of love, which can easily include issues of trust, possible sexual dysfunction of some kind, sometime in life development, especially if this significator relates at all to a significator of the 2nd House and/or the 8th. There could also be suggested concerns with children, a 5th House matter.

When the significator of the 6th House is involved in developmental tension, the concerns are with the dynamics of cooperation, working together with others, often specifically the work environment. For example, when the Moon is in the 6th, we expect the reigning need to be focused within 6th House dynamics, i.e., the "workaholic" position. Would this extremism be overcompensatory? If so, of what? Would work be warding off relationship, or trying to prove a point about a wounded self-worth profile (shown by other aspects)?

When the significator of the 7th House is in developmental tension, issues having to do with establishing and maintaining relationships are undeniably heightened.

When the significator of the 8th House is in developmental tension, dealing with the values and self-worth parameters of others is a core concern, and this easily includes concerns of sexual relationships.

When the significator of the 9th House is under developmental tension, the higher education will almost always be found to have been interrupted (not necessarily terminated). What caused the interruption? No family encouragement? A precipitous marriage to escape family conditions?

The significators of the 10–4 axis point to parental tension, as we have already seen many times.

When the significator of the 11th House is under developmental tension, issues having to do with one's feeling of being lovable, of being able to attract others, are core concerns in life. Is this why compliments are not believed or trusted? Does this work against relationship? Can one give a compliment (love) when one can not receive love easily? What does that suggest about behavior modeling in the early home environment (look further into the Angular Grand Cross of Houses!)?

When the significator of the 12th House is under developmental tension, cooperation dynamics are highlighted in terms of what society expects, often to blanketing the person's own stand. This is a zone of possible unfulfilled hopes ($♀$ in 12, for example—what goes wrong with love dynamics?), of deep anger ($♂$ in 12, what is the anger about?).

Whew! We are closing in on the high art of Analysis in Astrology. It's exciting, isn't it! Again, congratulations on how much you have learned!!

With experience, you will find that the zones of experience that are indicated by the three Crosses tend to spill over into each other; that's a reality! Parental tension found in the Angular Grand Cross will almost always also include tension with the self-worth dynamic that spills over into relationship issues that spill back over into issues having to do with the giving and receiving of love, resulting in a less than optimum way of viewing the Self. The spill-over effect will be revealed through rulership dynamics, the significator networks.

On the next page (Fig. 16, p. 113) is another example for study: you have given your computer the data for this horoscope. Now, you begin to study the printout. **Remember**: for now, you begin first to *locate the hard aspects.*

In this case, the Moon in Cancer in the 11th House, ruling the 11th, is square the Sun, Mercury, Mars, and Jupiter. The reigning need of the personality is to establish and maintain emotional security at all costs clearly including the vital concerns of receiving love, accolades, and holding onto friendships.

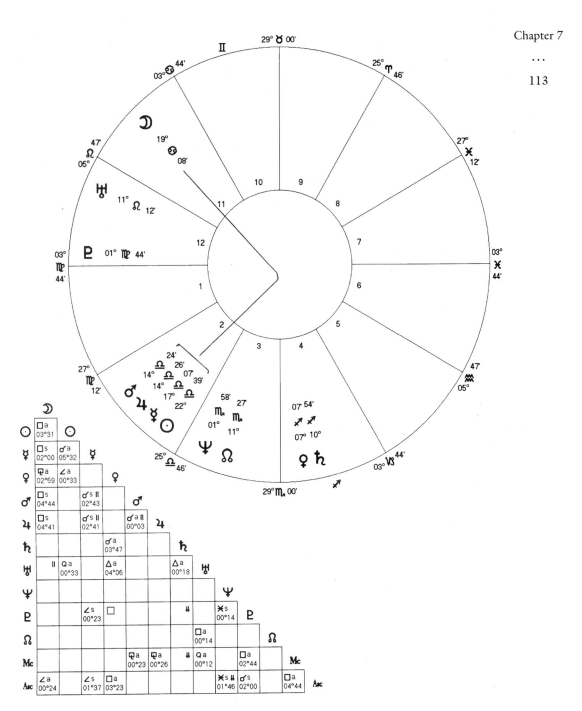

Figure 16
Female

This security-seeking Moon is squared by four planets in the 2nd House. This suggests strongly that there is developmental tension between the zones of experience symbolized by the 2nd and 11th Houses, where the cluster, a "stellium," and the Moon are, respectively. This means that we are looking at developmental tension related to self-worth concerns and to feeling lovable, feeling attractive (unloveable, unattractive).

Through significator dynamics, other concerns are brought into this core deduction: the planets in the 2nd House cluster "bring in" the 9th House (education, through Mars), the 4th House (parental tension, through Jupiter), the 10th House (the other parent, through Mercury), the Ascendant (identity development, also through Mercury), and the 2nd House (self-worth, again through Mercury ruling the 2nd and the whole cluster being in the 2nd). **Just the tension (square) with the Moon alone involves six Houses!** And within this is the telling Moon square Sun, almost always an indicator of parental upheaval early in life, especially if the aspect orb is very small.

Additionally, the eye immediately sees Saturn conjunct Venus in the 4th House, *squared by Pluto*. This suggests parental tension that results in difficult factors relating to this woman's romantic or social ways: Venus and Pluto rule the 4–10 parental axis! Parental difficulty is confirmed and, with Libra on the cusp of the 3rd House, the way she views herself is also included within this aspect (her prevailing point of view), confirmed and corroborated by Neptune's presence in the 3rd House! Additionally, Saturn rules the 5th House! There are certainly confined feelings, threats to emotional security within her that suggest **a difficulty enjoying intimacy.** Venus trines Uranus, ruler of the 6th . . . she is able to cooperate effectively with others in the workplace, but we can deduce **how this probably overcompensates for the breakdown in relationship comfort!**

The woman who lives this horoscope is an attractive mother of two, is well respected, well liked, quite intelligent, and has fantastic communications skills. The tensions that we have outlined in her horoscope are in her life, for sure. However, her life is still productive, with its share of ups and downs as we all have. She lives her life through and in spite of the concerns we have outlined.

You can see from this example how important these significator dynamics are, and how they lead you into the core psychodynamic concerns symbolized by the Grand Crosses of Houses.

Summary

1. The Grand Crosses of Houses contain the most vital psycho-dynamic dimensions of the human experience.

2. The Angular Grand Cross of Houses (Houses 1, 4, 7, 10) refers to identity development, parental tension, and relationships.

3. The Succedent Grand Cross of Houses (Houses 2, 5, 8, 11) refers to dimensions of self-worth and others' worth, and the giving and receiving of love.

4. The Cadent Grand Cross of Houses (Houses 3, 6, 9, 12) refers to dimensions of communication, the point of view, cooperation at work and within society's institutional standards, education, and the expectations of others.

5. **Significator dynamics** lead the astrologer into various concerns of the Grand Cross of Houses; developmental tension among the Houses is routed throughout the horoscope. A significator is the planet ruling the Sign on the cusp of the House or it is the most prominent planet in the House.

6. When the significator of a House is in an aspect of high developmental tension, the Houses that it is in and rule are highlighted in analysis; they are brought into synthesis importantly.

Test Yourself

(See test answers, p. 239.)

1. How many Grand Crosses of Houses are there?

2. What are the names of the Grand Cross of Houses?

3. Listing each "Cross" separately, list the tensions to which each House of each Cross refers.

4. What is a significator?

5. Pisces is on the cusp of the 7th House. What is its significator?

6. The 4th and 10th House significators are in a developmentally tense aspect relationship. What does this suggest?

7. If the sense of self-worth is tense, the _____ of the ____ House is under developmental tension.

8. What is the significance of the fact that the 1st House is always square to the 4–10 House axis?

9. What is the significance of the fact that the 2nd House is always square to the 5–11 axis?

10. What is the significance of the fact that the 3rd House is always square to the 6–12 axis?

11. A horoscope shows the following: Cancer is on the 7th House cusp. Saturn is in the 2nd House in conjunction with the Moon. What does this suggest? Be careful! See each planet as a "significator."

12. Uranus is conjunct the Sun in the 6th House. Leo is on the Ascendant. What does this suggest?

13. The significator of the 2nd House is in trine aspect with the significator of the 7th House. What does this suggest?

14. What is the base House of the Angular Grand Cross of Houses?

15. What is the base House of the Succedent Grand Cross of Houses?

16. What is the base House of the Cadent Grand Cross of Houses?

17. Tension between the zones of experience found in the 3rd and 6th Houses suggests _____.

Chapter 8

•••

Exploring Parental Tensions: The Phenomenon of Retrogradation

PLANETARY RETROGRADATION REFERS TO THE *apparent backward movement of a planet* in its orbit. The planet appears to "slow down" in its motion during certain sections of its eliptical orbit around the Sun. This phenomenon of backward movement is an illusion caused by the fact that sometimes—in relation to the planet in its orbit—the Earth is revolving (spinning) past the direct sightline to the orbiting planet. We view and locate the planet against a stationary backdrop of the zodiac. Getting ahead in our sightline "through" the planet to the zodiac backdrop can give us readings that go backward in the zodiac (note the symbol ℞ for retrogradation).

In the diagram on the next page (Fig. 17, p. 118), you see the Earth spinning on its axis and the planet continuing on its orbit in counterclockwise motions. Relative changes in their respective positions can cause the planet in our line-of-sight reference to the stationary Zodiac to appear to go backward.

Before a change between retrograde and direct motion, the planets have a theoretical *stationary period*, just before and after a shift of apparent motion, during which the longitude appears not to change. This short period, this stationary position is called the planet's **station** (shown with the letter **S** in the Ephemeris listing): the planet *makes a station* and *turns direct or retrograde* (*SD* or *SR*). In prediction work, stationary periods can represent powerful turning points in time when the stationary positions conjoin key planetary positions in the natal horoscope.

In practice, we see retrogradation as a **counterpoint**, a second level of meaning given to the planet's significances—two levels exist side by side interpretatively, a second agenda. In analytical practice, the Sign and House placement of the retrograde planet must be given consideration, of course, *as well as the House that the retrograde planet rules.* (Don't even

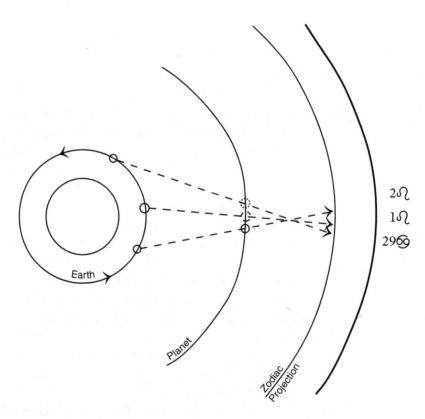

Figure 17
Retrogradation creates the appearance of backward movement in planetary cycles.

think of overlooking the planets' role as significator! We have worked hard to learn that.) Either one of these Houses is subject to *counterpoint experiences*, experiences that sometimes demand overcompensation or result in weakness of the Houses concerned.

The Sun and Moon are never retrograde. Retrogradation of Uranus, Neptune, and Pluto do not often significantly apply to the individual horoscope, except when ruling an Angle (especially the Ascendant) and in special patterns we will study soon. **Mercury retrograde** is extremely important: it suggests a thought counterpoint within one's reality. Thoughts are internalized and reprocessed for new meaning in personal terms. There can be conspicuous subjectivity in the way a person sees things (O. J. Simpson). Why is that? **Venus retrograde** suggests a withdrawal counterpoint with social, romantic, sexual, or emotional expression (Robert DeNiro). Why? Where does the tendency come from developmentally? **Mars retrograde** tends to keep energy inside, directing it inward instead of outward, for censorship, consideration, adjustment, and/or timidity (Betty Ford). Why? How did things get that way? **Jupiter retrograde** suggests a muted enthusiasm, a contentment with being alone (Dustin Hoffman). To serve what purpose?

When the ruler of the Ascendant is retrograde, we are alerted to a counterpoint (often a difficulty) in identity development and we immediately look to the parental axis, the self-worth concerns, relationships, etc., for corroboration and amplification. That's the pattern we have come to know quite well.

Saturn Retrograde

Astrologer Noel Tyl is the theoretician and analyst who brought astrology into the psychological mainstream. In the 1970s, he introduced psychological need theory to astrological symbolism, developed the psychodynamic interrelationship paradigm of the Houses, and discovered dramatic parental references within the symbolisms of Saturn retrograde and the Lunar Nodal Axis (next in our study). His research has been extremely important to keep astrology in pace with the times. His discoveries place astrology securely in the forefront of humanistic studies and give astrologers extraordinary tools with which to understand and improve life development.

Saturn symbolizes the concept of controls that are necessary in our lives to guide orderly development, the controls that are designed for the efficiency of the life process itself. We have controls for traffic so that cars may move on the road more efficiently. When someone goes against the traffic controls, accidents occur. We have social controls, health-related controls, relationship controls, even the controls exerted by Nature upon the Earth. If the Sun were to come too close to Earth, we would all burn to death; if the Earth were not tilted on its axis, we would not have seasons, respite from the heat, or rescue from the cold. The universal order has placed dramatic controls upon the Sun-Earth relationship!

With necessary controls—somehow, in the scheme of things, floods, earthquakes, lightning strikes, even epidemics and war work their purpose—our world operates, moving forward in time enduringly. Without these controls, balance could not endure. In our personal sphere, without controls, there would be little concern beyond our selves, for others. Without law, life would be chaos. Control factors are *necessary*, and they are symbolized by Saturn, time itself. In astrological analysis, the question is to what degree, just how deeply, is control absorbed in the individual life? Is it assimilated productively? Is it understood developmentally? Is it inhibiting, confining, even debilitating?

Saturn is our horoscope's chief symbol for the father; it reflects the awesome importance of the father figure in the early home, leading, supporting, providing the necessary controls for efficient family development, especially through his children. Paternal authority administered in a firm but loving way, and in accordance with the needs of a child, is absolutely vital for the psychological health and productivity of a child. When this leadership is *not* present in the life of a child, problems develop that implode upon the child's self-worth, the sense of feeling loveable, confidence, etc.

When Saturn is found to be retrograde in the horoscope, there is a strong probability of an interruption or disturbance or veiling in the father-child relationship; the father will surely not have fulfilled the child's needs for loving leadership and support (complicated greatly in the case of a male child through gender reflection, of a female child through mate modeling). Saturn retrograde almost invariably suggests that the father himself (or the father figure in the home) is not completely formed within the individual's life. This can result from the father's having been weak and passive, tyrannical, having traveled a great deal and been away from home, or taken out of the picture early by separation, divorce, or death. For these reasons, the individual may not have had an opportunity to absorb *constructively* the influence and guidance of paternal authority, to aid the development of pride and to endorse self-esteem. Sadly, so very often, the child never hears "I love you" from the father.

The father is somehow involved with his own traffic pattern, his own problems. The relationship with the mother is insecure or threatening. There are preoccupations that take the father away from the child's developmental pattern. Do the father's problems come from his relationship dynamics with *his* father? Are generational practices and even national cultural influences handed down to play roles in this dynamic development with the present-day child?

Within patterns of behavior, feelings of inferiority can develop to haunt the individual deeply, and this stimulates overcompensatory, often superiority counterreactions within life expression, especially in the zone of experience (House) where Saturn is placed, and/or in affairs of the House that Saturn rules in the horoscope.

For example, if Saturn retrograde is placed in the 10th House and rules the 7th House, you would expect overcompensatory activity with one's career pursuits (as an adult) or within the parameters of relationships. Quite simply, the 10th and/or 7th House man or woman may marry a father figure or father model to continue work for resolution of the early home difficulties (lacks).

If Saturn retrograde is in the 3rd House and rules the 2nd, there would be a close connection between the father concerns regarding the mindset emerging through the sense of self-worth or itself conditioning the self-worth profile.

Please commit the following paragraph to memory; practice speaking it aloud so it is natural to you, and so that you may inflect it vocally properly when beginning an analytical discussion:

When Saturn is retrograde in the horoscope: *There is a legacy of inferiority feelings taken on in the early homelife through relationship with the father figure, usually the father, who was taken out of the picture early; or was there but absent or passive, or was so tyrannical . . . one or any combination of these . . . so as not to have given the guidance of authoritative love.*

The above paragraph is taken verbatim from Noel Tyl texts. It is powerful. As you begin to get closer and closer to discussing horoscopes with people who live them, this key insight, when it presents itself, must be managed very carefully in discussion. It should be offered as a suggestion of condition, as a beginning of explorative conversation, backed up by other measurements and a keen sensitivity to family development dynamics and remediation techniques.

Marilyn Monroe's life story is well known and documented. Born as Norma Jean Baker, her early home life was difficult for many reasons that began with the absence of her father (there was never any home stability due to her being reared in foster homes). Marilyn was born as the result of an affair her mother had while married. This man, Stanley Gifford, deserted Marilyn's mother when he learned of the pregnancy. In her later life, Marilyn attempted to make contact with Gifford, only to have her efforts ignored, even rebuffed. The pain of this father situation resulted in Marilyn's extreme vulnerability to attention from others, especially from men (father-figure men), as she tried to capture what was never found in her early home development. The search to find the love that was never received from her father motivated Marilyn to behavior that led to numerous relationships, affairs, and marriages. We can infer that preoccupation with this problem took precedence in her development over cultivation and deployment of her talents.

We see the potential for all this, for the kind of inferiority feelings Marilyn had, through the Saturn retrograde symbolism in her horoscope (Fig. 18, p. 123) placed in the 4th House square her Moon (placed in the 7th, relationships, and ruling the 12th, the idea of blanketing, of self-undoing).

Chelsea Clinton, daughter of Bill Clinton, has Saturn retrograde in her horoscope! Unlike Marilyn Monroe, Chelsea's father has been quite a force in her life, but what kind of a force? The President's many sexual affairs while married, his public denials of these affairs followed by revelations of his having lied about the denials, and his world-wide reputation as a womanizer certainly lay the groundwork for defensive behavior in the adult Chelsea, all as a result of internalized feelings resulting from her father's activities. We are going to take a look at Chelsea Clinton's horoscope, in detail, in an upcoming chapter of this book.

Others with Saturn retrograde whose lives you may want to research on your own include Muhammad Ali, Marlon Brando, Betty Ford,

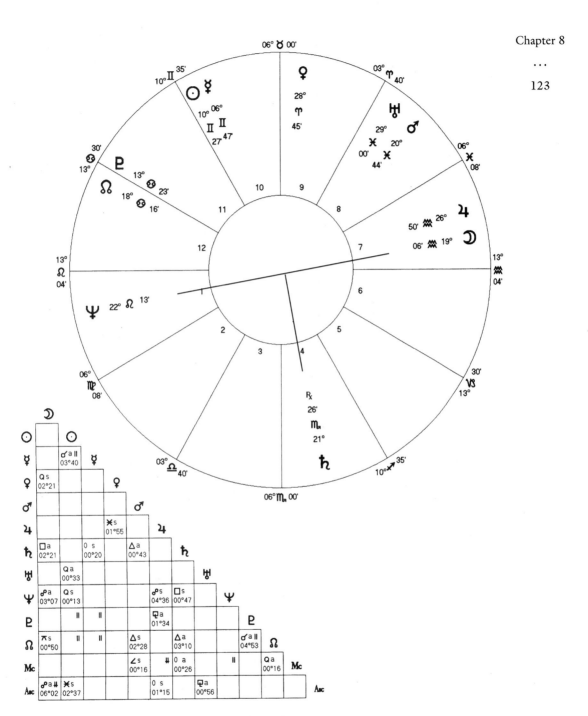

Figure 18
Marilyn Monroe
6/1/26, 9:30 A.M. PST
Los Angeles CA, 118W15 34N03

Ernest Hemingway, Dustin Hoffman, Jesse Jackson, Jackie Kennedy-Onassis, Madonna, Richard Nixon, Princess Diana, Norman Schwarzkopf—all extraordinary examples of the power of the Saturn retrograde phenomenon. In many of these cases, the phenomenon operated as extreme motivation to right things, and, therefore, to achieve much.

The Lunar Nodal Axis

Where the Moon's orbit crosses the apparent path of the Sun (the ecliptic), two crossing points are formed: the Moon moves northward across the ecliptic and the Moon moves southward across the ecliptic. The northern crossing is named the North Node. Its symbol in the horoscope is ☊ (the loop is to the North). The southern crossing is named the South Node. Its symbol is ☋ (the loop is to the South). The Moon's Nodes are always in exact opposition to each other, so when you see the North Node in the horoscope, you automatically know where the South Node is. This is why the South Node need not be shown in the horoscope. We refer to the Nodes as an axis—the Nodal Axis. In our computer and analytical work, we are using the "Mean Node" measurement.[1]

In astrological tradition, the Moon's North Node has been thought to represent, by Sign and House, the place where the greatest level of growth can and should take place. The South Node, by Sign and House, was said to represent the place of comfort, a place that one retreats to under duress. These definitions have been a source of consistent contention and confusion with astrologers, and will not be explored in our course.

Modern psychodynamic astrology—again, thanks to the imagination and work of Noel Tyl—now recognizes the link between the Moon's maternal/feminine symbolism and the symbolism of fecundation as the Moon's orbit crosses the ecliptic of the Sun (the paternal/masculine symbolism). *Whenever a planet or Angle closely conjoins or squares the Nodal Axis, there will almost always be a strong maternal influence coloring the life, especially in terms of the behavioral faculty of that planet*

---

1 Ephemerides and computer programs give the option of "True Node," a compelling reference indeed. The True Node introduces retrograde and direction motions to measurement of the Nodal axis. It appears unnecessarily complicated. The Mean and True positions can be slightly different but, again, not critically. It is safe to say that the vast majority of astrologers in the world use the Mean Node. Additional note: planets have nodes as well, but this is still a research frontier in astrology.

and/or the House ruled by that planet. For example, ☿♓, ruling the 7th tightly square the Nodal Axis, suggests strongly a maternal influence upon the person's mind (probably inhibiting or debilitating) about a marriage partner (for example, early dating prohibitions, intrusion about the ideal relationship, etc.).

You will note the frequency of Nodal conjunctions or squares coinciding with the occurrence of Saturn Retrograde in a horoscope; both measurements will frequently occur in the same horoscope. This suggests the mother adopting a paternal role (often by the husband's default, or to rescue the situation) or, in the case where Saturn retrograde itself is conjoined with or square the Nodal axis, the mother herself is the sole authority of the family.

The suggested **orb is 2.5 degrees**: the tighter the orb, the surer is the deduction. With experience, you will learn intuitively when the orb can be expanded. For example, in a horoscope with Saturn retrograde and also significator tension involving the parental axis, a three or even four-degree orb can be considered to capture the reality of early home conditions.

In summary, the occurrence of Saturn Retrograde in a horoscope is of prime importance in suggesting paternal difficulty. Look to the significator of each parental House for corroboration. Then, look at the 2nd House significator(s) to assess *tension with self-worth development.* Tension will usually spill over into affairs of the 7th House through its significator. Parental tensions in the early home threaten and undermine relationship concerns of many kinds.

The horoscope shown on the next page (Fig. 19, p. 126) exhibits Saturn retrograde. We know that there is high probability of a legacy of inferiority feelings regarding an undeveloped father figure, a relationship that was out of the picture somehow. That Saturn is in the 8th House suggests counterpoint experiences that will reflect in the way the person relates to the worth, values, and resources of others.

Saturn here is conjunct Uranus. Saturn rules the 9th House and immediately we can anticipate that the education is interrupted, because the 9th House significator (Saturn) is under tension through the conjunction with Uranus, and *Saturn also rules the 10th, part of the parental axis.* This is a clear indication of parental tension in the life coming from the father, relating somehow to probable interrupted education. (The urge to bolt from the home situation?)

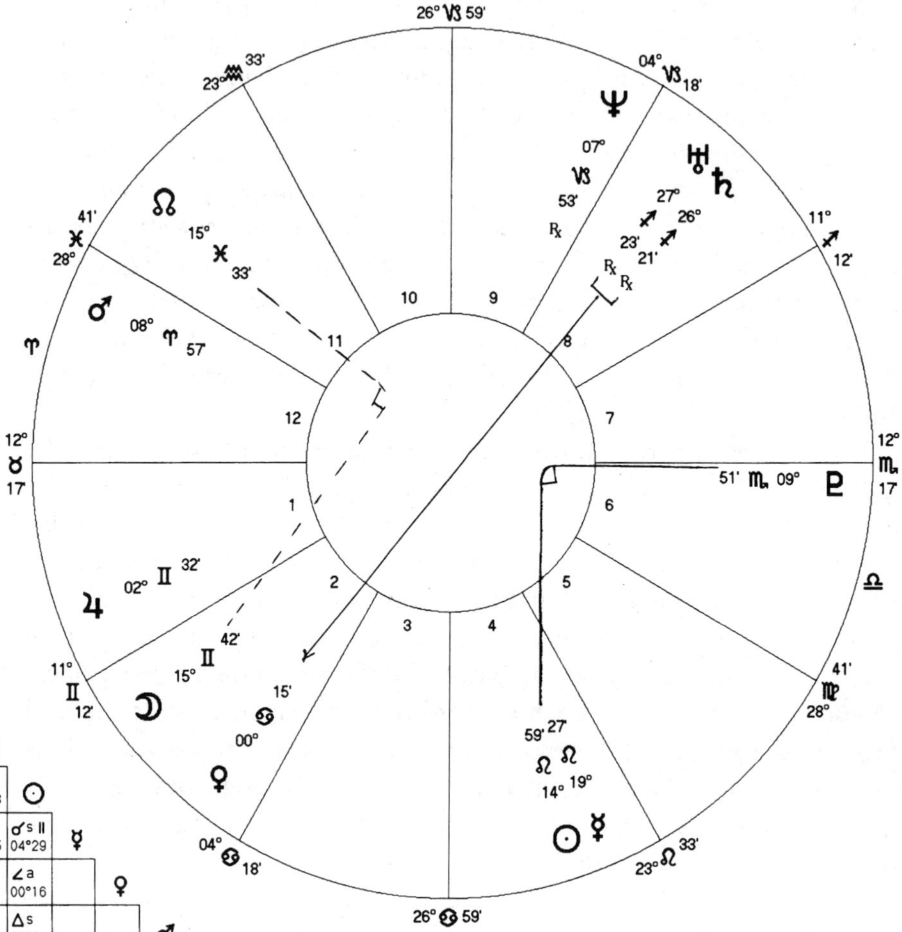

Figure 19
Male

We immediately check the other arm of the parental axis and find the Sun there *square Pluto*. (This person's "hand grenade" is *covered by some kind of blanket. Finding what the blanket is would be a key point within a consultation*, and we already know it will involve the father.) There will be a strong need for personal power and importance (echoing the Leo energy profile of the Sun) but it will have difficulty in externalization because of a problem in the home. With the Sun and Pluto ruling the 5th and 7th Houses, respectively, this difficulty expressing self-empowerment will also probably involve giving love, managing sex, and/or concerns with his own children, as well as deep relationship concerns.

That's not all! The ruler of the 4th House, the Moon, is exactly square the Nodal Axis! There is a strong maternal influence, indeed, and note the *idealized* hope framed through her in the early home (Mercury conjunct the Sun in the 4th House)!

Venus, cosignificator of the 2nd House (placed there) **opposes the Saturn-Uranus conjunction** (over the Sign line)! As is usually the case when Saturn is retrograde, we have a self-worth dimension that requires attention, especially since *Venus is the significator of the Ascendant* (and under tension, signifying difficult identity development).

Notice again in this horoscope that dimensions of the same profile are repeated and referred to, over and over again, through successive measurements. This is almost always the case in analysis. The first impression sticks!

There is more here for analysis, but let's advance carefully; so much indeed has already been detected. This horoscope belongs to Justin Simpson, son of ex-football star—turned actor—turned alleged murderer, O. J. Simpson!

As an adult, we can see that Justin Simpson will live emotionally in the memory of his slain mother, while he continues to have to deal with the question that everyone asks, "Did his father do it?"

Summary

1. Retrograde motion refers to the apparent backward movement of a planet in its orbit caused by its apparent slowing down during sections of its eliptical orbit, as our vantage point on the Earth appears to accelerate through axial rotation.

2. Before a change between retrograde and direct motion, the planets have a *stationary moment,* just before and after a shift of apparent motion, during which the longitude appears not to change. This stationary position is called the planet's Station.

3. In practice, we see retrogradation as a counterpoint, a second level of meaning given to the planet's significance—two levels exist side by side, "a second agenda." In practice, the Sign and House placement of the retrograde planet must be given consideration, of course, as well as the House ruled by the retrograde planet. Either one of these Houses is subject to the counterpoint experiences, experiences that sometimes demand overcompensation or result in weakness of the Houses concerned.

4. The symbol for retrogradation is ℞. The Sun and Moon are never retrograde.

5. When Saturn is retrograde in the horoscope, a legacy of inferiority feelings is strongly suggested. The profile is developed in the early home life through the relationship with the authority figure in the home, usually the father figure, who was taken out of the picture early, was there but absent or passive, or was so tyrannical—one or any combination of these—who did not give the guidance of authoritative love.

5. Where the Moon's orbit crosses the apparent path of the Sun (the ecliptic), two crossing points are formed: the Moon moves northward across the ecliptic and the Moon moves southward across the ecliptic. The northern crossing is named the North Node. Its symbol in the horoscope is ☊ (the loop is to the North). The southern crossing is named the South Node. Its symbol is ☋ (the loop is to the South). They are always in exact opposition to each other.

7. Whenever a planet or Angle closely conjoins or squares the Nodal Axis, there will almost always be a strong maternal influence coloring the life, especially in terms of the behavioral faculty of that planet and/or the House ruled by that planet.

Test Yourself

(See test answers, p. 237.)

1. Explain retrogradation.

2. What is a planet's "Station?"

3. What is the association of "counterpoint" with retrogradation?

4. Can the Sun or Moon have retrograde motion?

5. When is the retrogradation of Uranus, Neptune, or Pluto significant?

6. What does Mercury retrograde suggest?

7. What does Venus retrograde suggest?

8. What does Mars retrograde suggest?

9. What does Jupiter retrograde suggest?

10. What does Saturn retrograde suggest? Why?

11. What is the Lunar Nodal Axis?

12. Are the Nodes in any special relationship to one another?

13. What is the interpretive significance of the Lunar Nodal Axis? Why?

14. With Capricorn on the cusp of the 7th House, what is suggested by Saturn retrograde?

15. Venus is the ruler of the Ascendant in a horoscope and it is retrograde and in the 5th House. What does this suggest?

16. Why might you find in the same horoscope with Saturn retrograde in hard aspect to the Lunar Nodal Axis?

17. What is suggested by the Moon's close conjunction with the Nodal Axis?

18. What is suggested by Uranus square the Nodal Axis?

19. Discuss the expected "spill-over" effect of Saturn retrograde.

20. What is the suggested orb of influence regarding Nodal Axis aspects?

Chapter 9

• • •

Hemisphere Emphasis: The Endurance of the First Impression

THINK OF THE TIMES IN YOUR LIFE WHEN THE first impression of a person, place, or thing was confirmed strongly thereafter. It happens so often: experience of the first impression is corroborated.

First impressions carry enormous value profiles with them: you will form a different opinion of someone speeding in a red Ferrari than of a funeral director driving slowly in a black limousine. Whatever the case may be, the first impression is often a long-lasting impression, *an image in the mind that conditions further judgment for some time to come.*

In a horoscope, planets may group together conspicuously, emphasizing one area of the horoscope emphatically. Perhaps there is a kind of grouping wherein one planet stands alone in juxtaposition to the others. When there *is* such an occurrence, **the horoscope is trying to tell us something, to give us the beginning elements, a first impression for analytical insight.**

Every horoscope is divided into four hemispheres: Southern (Houses 7–12), Northern (1–6), Eastern

(10–4), and Western (4–9). **Each hemisphere has a horoscope Angle at its midpoint that conditions the manifestation of that hemisphere.** In the *East*, that point is the Ascendant; in the *West*, that point is the Descendant; in the *South*, that point is the Midheaven; in the *North*, that point is the Nadir. When the majority of planets are clustered in a particular hemisphere, behavioral faculties and need-centers group around a particular point of awareness that is directly related to the Angle of that hemisphere.

With an Eastern emphasis, the life emphasis is conditioned by ego justification, by parameters of (self) defensiveness (our analytical instincts are keyed to ask, "About what?") (Examples: Ross Perot, Cher, O. J. Simpson, Arnold Schwarzenegger).

With a Western emphasis, the life is conditioned around ego projection to others, perhaps to the extent of leaving the Self behind (why might a person do that?) (Jackie Onassis, Princess Diana).

In a Southern emphasis, there is an emphasis somehow on being pushed around, controlled, or victimized by experiences in the world, swept away by events (why is there no anchor?) (John F. Kennedy, Marilyn Monroe).

In a Northern emphasis, there is the issue of unfinished business in the early home (what is at the core of this?) (Barbara Streisand, Michael Jackson).

Additional observations connected with hemisphere emphasis: in the East, there is the sense of one being able to "captain one's own ship." That is, the person has the ability to initiate his or her own progress in life for good or for bad. The sense of self-initiative can be strong, but the orientation is decidely defensive.

In the West, there is the necessity to interact with others. The sense of having personal power to initiate life-changes is less commonly experienced than in an eastern hemisphere emphasis. Frequently, in the West, the individual life seems to be a pawn of fate, of chance, somehow. Things "happen" to the individual. The life is subjected more to what is offered by others through interaction than it is through one's own initiative.

In the Northern emphasis, with the majority of planets below the horizon, needs have difficulty rising up above the early developmental battlefield! There can be an inclination to a great sense of privacy as well as subjectivity.

In the Southern emphasis, where visibility is a focal point, there will be more of a tendency toward extroversion and/or objectivity than is found with the northern hemisphere emphasis. When push comes to shove, the stability and anchor are often lacking.

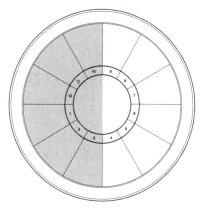

Eastern Hemisphere Emphasis

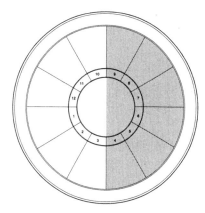

Western Hemisphere Emphasis

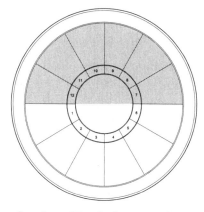

Southern Hemisphere Emphasis

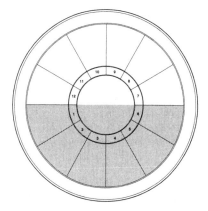

Northern Hemisphere Emphasis

Figure 21

Special Groupings

When you see that a **group of retrograde planets** gather in one hemisphere alone, you **look to the *opposite* hemisphere**; this is the contrapuntal reference from the retrograde grouping.

Look at Princess Diana's horoscope (Fig. 21, p. 135). All planets to the East are retrograde, calling our attention strongly to the opposite hemisphere, the Western hemisphere. The emphasis in this hemisphere suggests giving the self away to others. *This is your first impression. Let it guide you into further analysis.*

We also see Saturn retrograde. You know that this suggests a legacy of inferiority feelings from an absent or unfulfilling relationship with the father. This corroborates your first impression, doesn't it? Sure, it does.

Quickly, we see that Jupiter is retrograde as well, and it is squared by Neptune! Jupiter is the ruler of the Ascendant, so we can expect a difficulty in development of the identity; all this is other than it seems (Neptune), something is under or behind the effort to put forth an enthusiastic, bright image.

Now check the parental axis for even more corroboration: Venus is square Uranus and Mars is conjunct Pluto! There it all is, **and it has all been guided by the first impression.**

Note the counterpoint suggested through Mercury retrograde, ruling (signifying) the 7th House of marriage and placed there in idealistic conjunction with the Sun! Is the retrograde statement tantamount to crucial disappointment in these 7th House affairs? To more than one marriage?

When all planets *except one* are grouped together in a hemisphere, the single planet alone (called a *singleton*) in the hemisphere assumes an added importance in terms of what it symbolizes by Sign, House, etc., or simply by the behavioral faculty of that planet (see my horoscope for the singleton Mars, Fig. 11, p. 83; Mars in Sagittarius, certainly the energy application resource for a teacher!).

In the horoscope of Prince Charles (Fig. 22, p. 136), we see a decided Northern hemisphere emphasis. Uranus is with the Moon above the horizon, but it is retrograde, and this sets off the Moon as a singleton. The Moon is conjunct the Lunar Nodal axis, suggesting a powerful maternal influence. Your first impression of this horoscope is that there is "unfinished business" from the early development with a strong maternal influence.[2]

---

2 Here is an example where we instinctively extend our orb allowance for the Nodal axis from 2 degrees out a bit to 3.5. The singleton Moon is very strong here, needing to keep things as they are, or ideally as they should be; the elevation of the Moon, its singleton nature, its "answer" to the deductions from the Sun square Pluto all beg for this inclusion of the Nodal axis. Experience tells us that it is there. And, after all, we are talking about quite a demanding life situation here, the horoscope reality of the Prince of Wales! Our consciousness must be augmented to include more potentials.

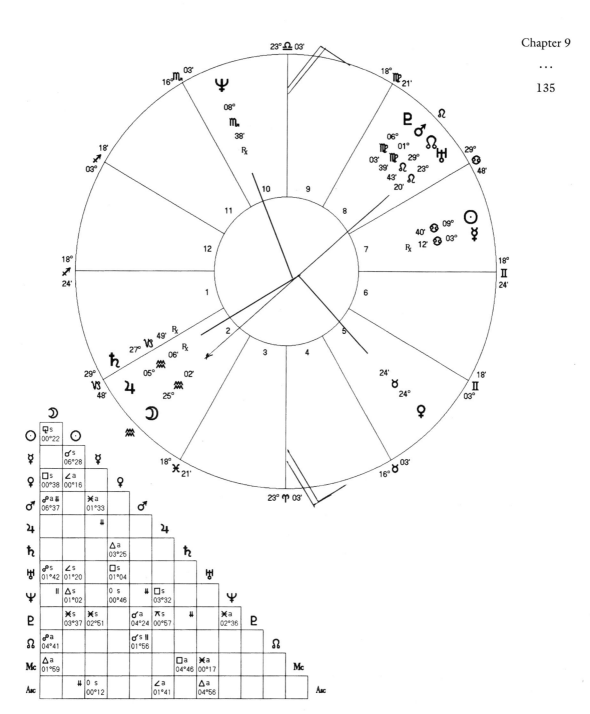

Figure 21
Princess Diana
7/1/61, 7:45 P.M. GMD
Sandringham, Eng., 000E30 52N50

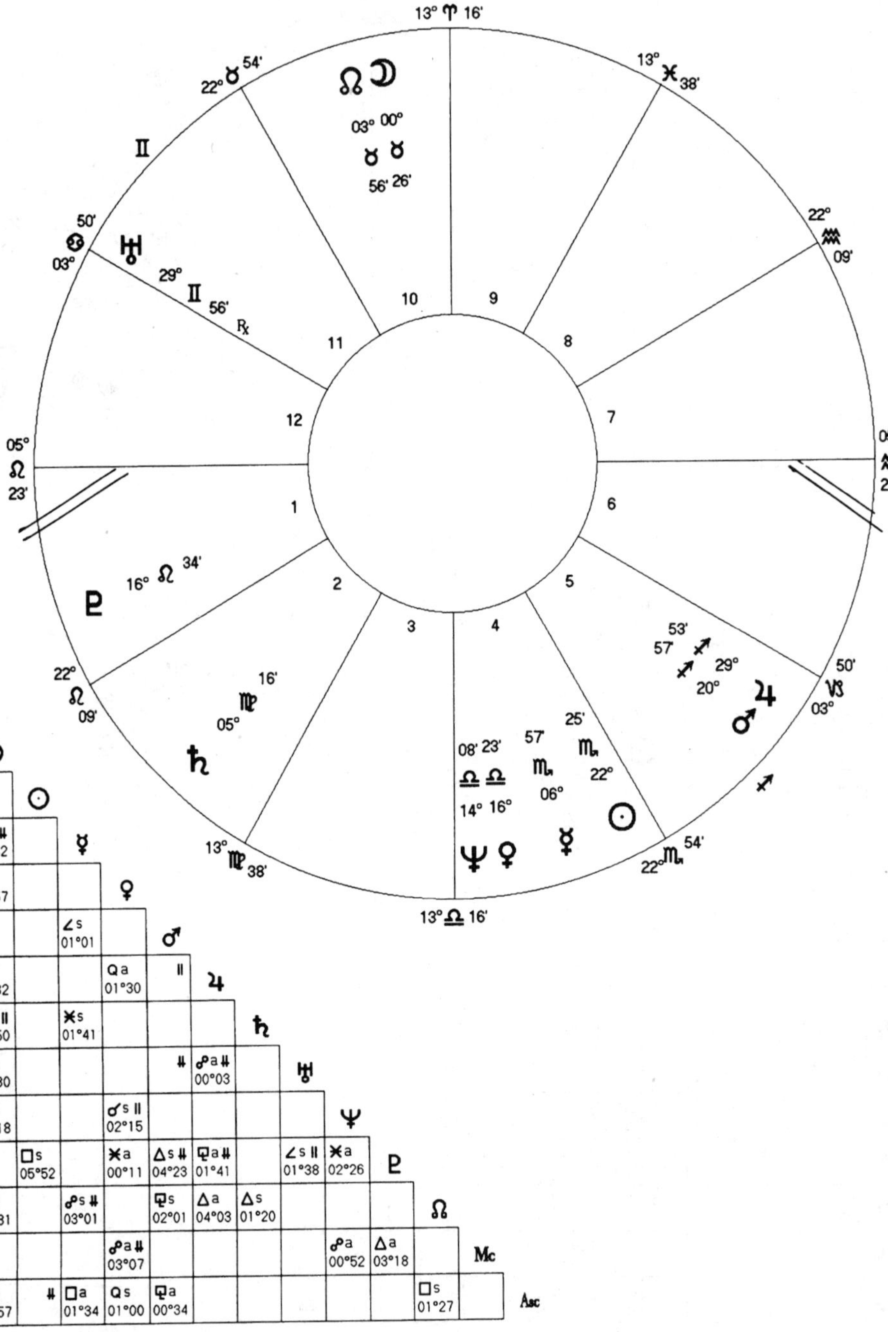

Figure 22
Prince Charles
11/14/48, 9:14 P.M. GMT
London, Eng., 00W10 51N30

We see the accentuation of the 4th House. The Sun is squared by Pluto: Prince Charles has a "blanket over his grenade," something holding down his desire for personal empowerment. The Sun rules the Ascendant, so this "blanket over his grenade" is key to his identity development. You then look further and see that Venus, significator of the 4th House, is conjunct Neptune, further corroborating the unfinished business in the home. And indeed, the elevated Moon on the Nodal Axis and in the parental axis signals the mother relationship as the key; *she* is the "blanket." Charles must toe the line.

We see again how powerful the first impression of the horoscope is in guiding us analytically further into the horoscope.

The Bucket Formation

When a horoscope shows a specific hemisphere emphasis, one planet will frequently be found in a hemisphere by itself, as a singleton, facing the others in the busy hemisphere. This formation is sometimes called a "Bucket" formation. Through this image, the singleton planet, which is the handle of the bucket, controls and dominates the action. Imagine an extremely heavily loaded bucket that must be moved from one location to another. You can barely lift it, *except* if it has a strong handle. In most bucket formations, the singelton planet makes an opposition aspect to the middle of the opposing group.

For example, please refer back to Marilyn Monroe's horoscope (p. 123). From what we have learned about Marilyn so far, we can not be surprised to see that the retrograde Saturn in her horoscope is also the handle to a "bucket" formation. The control factors placed upon her as a result of the absence of her father and the instability of her early years simply dominated her life in every way, propelling her into a life of being pushed around, exploited, and victimized (remember: southern hemisphere emphasis!). This is a perfect example of the strength of the pervasive influences we find in the "bucket" formation.

Jacqueline Kennedy-Onassis' horoscope (Fig. 13, p. 97) has a western/southern hemisphere emphasis (yes, *combinations of hemisphere emphasis* should be considered) with Saturn retrograde as the bucket handle. Immediately, you know that there are self-worth anxieties that are tied to an unfulfilled relationship with the father.

There is an apparent Fire Grand Trine structure involving the Moon, Saturn, and Midheaven (including Neptune). Venus is in opposition with Saturn, as the way into and out of the tendency to motivational self-sufficiency. As we have seen, this suggests that the need to relate is in constant awareness of the self-worth issue concerning the father. Without resolution, this factor threatens to control or confine her relationships. Venus also symbolizes material goods, monies, shiny objects like jewelry, etc.

John F. (Jack) Kennedy was a man very much like Jackie's father (Jack Bouvier, who was divorced from her mother and died prematurely), especially when it came to womanizing. In a very real sense, Jackie married her father when she married Jack Kennedy, and it was through him—the circumstances of the tragic assassination—that she was thrust into the public eye. *It was through the association with her famous husband and the circumstances of his life that she became prominent* (western hemisphere emphasis).

Jackie's marriage to Aristotle Onassis was a continuation of the manifestation of controls upon relationships that are so strongly suggested in her horoscope. The Venus-Saturn factor seems never to have been resolved. Onassis was certainly a father figure as well, although on a different level than Kennedy.

Madonna is one of the most successful entertainers in the music business. Her horoscope shows a conspicuous eastern hemisphere emphasis. Unlike Jacqueline Kennedy-Onassis, we do not associate Madonna with a marriage, partnership, or any event that "happened to her." An adequate singer/dancer, Madonna left a small city in Michigan to come to New York in search of fame and fortune. Through her own efforts and skills in marketing herself (a 3rd House concern, i.e., communication about the self; Pluto, significator of the 3rd, is conjunct Mercury, ruler of the Ascendant, identity projection), she has been catapulted into a position as one of the most successful music business personalities ever—world renown.

Madonna's horoscope (Fig. 23, p. 139) emphasizes ego protection. Our question becomes: "What is being protected and why?" Saturn is retrograde in the 4th House; Jupiter closely conjoins the Nodal Axis; Pluto is conjunct Mercury, also ruler of the career 10th. Neptune is conjunct Jupiter, ruler of the 4th. This is a solid profile of parental tension, managed in overcompensation by enormous self-assertion through career.

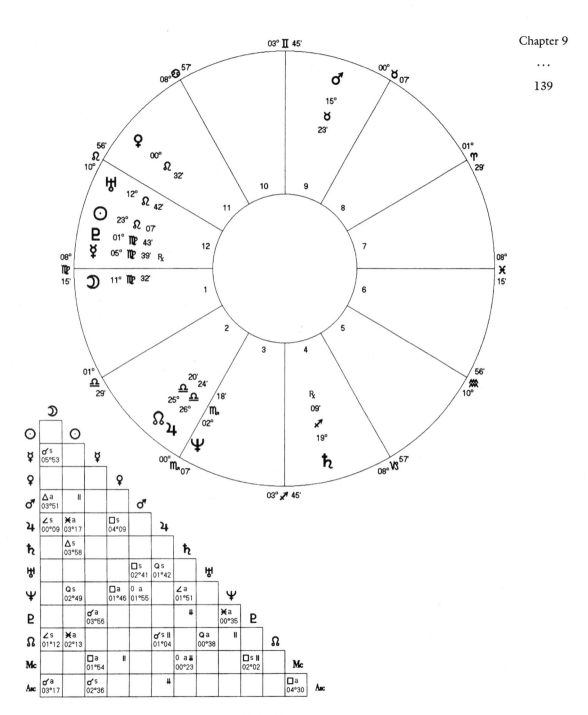

Figure 23
Madonna
8/16/58, 7:05 A.M. EST
Bay City MI, 83W53 43N36

When Madonna (the name she gave herself; Italian for "Holy mother") was seven years old, her mother died of breast cancer. It was a deeply significant, painful event for young Madonna. Her father then married a woman whom Madonna never liked, thus setting the foundation for the ego-defensive, self-protecting behaviors that surely fueled her rise to the top. Please note: Saturn rules the 5th House, part of the sex profile, children, and entertainment! There is overcompensation in this chart for the pain of the home upset through sex, creative entertaining, and birthing, all channeled into professional exposure.

Michael Jackson's horoscope (my rectification of the birth time based on information given to me by Jackson) has a northern hemisphere emphasis (Fig. 24, p. 141). There is unfinished business from the early home life that Jackson would need to resolve; the Sun, ruler of the 4th House, is conjunct Pluto in the 4th; Mercury, within the 4th House is squared by Mars *and is retrograde.* There is parental tension and a concern with identity development because of it.

Michael Jackson's father was a difficult man who allegedly brutalized his children, physically and emotionally. A televised movie about the family, approved by the family, depicted Joseph Jackson as a tyrant, a bully whose children were afraid of him.

In the liner notes of Michael Jackson's album, *History—Past, Present and Future—Book I,* there is a portrait of a young child sitting in a corner, clutching his microphone underneath him and looking very sad. The caption with it says: *"Before you judge me, Try hard to love me, Look within your heart, Then ask 'have you seen my childhood.'"* Northern hemisphere emphasis, indeed!

Over and over again, you have seen how enduring the first impression of a horoscope is when viewed through the lens of the hemisphere emphasis. The first impression endures because it is always corroborated within the horoscope, over and over and over again. When you see a decided hemisphere emphasis, *the goal is to find out why it exists, what fuels it, and what its foundation is.* There is ALWAYS a reason why.

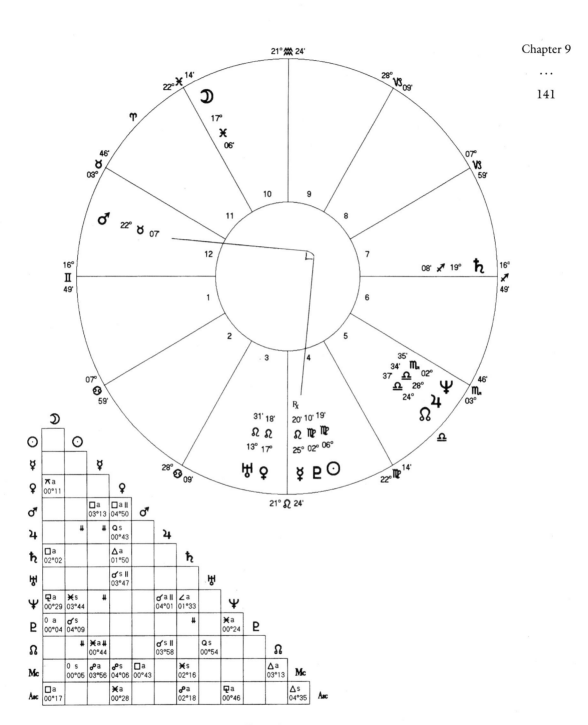

Figure 24
Michael Jackson
8/29/58, 11:53 P.M. CDT
Gary IN, 87W21 41N36

Summary

1. Conspicuous planetary groupings within the horoscope give us the beginnings of analytical insight.

2. Every horoscope is divided into four hemispheres: Southern (Houses 7–12), Northern (Houses 1–6), Eastern (Houses 10–3), and Western (Houses 4–9). The Angle in each hemisphere conditions (anchors) the manifestation of that hemisphere.

3. A Southern hemisphere emphasis suggests an emphasis somehow on being pushed around, controlled, swept up, even victimized by experience.

4. A Northern hemisphere emphasis suggests unfinished business in the early development.

5. An Eastern hemisphere emphasis suggests a life emphasis that is conditioned by ego justification and ego defensiveness.

6. A Western hemisphere emphasis suggests a life development centered around ego projection to others; perhaps leaving the Self behind.

7. When a group of retrograde planets gathers together in one hemisphere alone, attention is called to the *opposite* hemisphere.

8. Often, when a horoscope shows a specific hemisphere emphasis, one planet will frequently be found in a hemisphere by itself, facing the others in the busy hemisphere. This formation is called a "Bucket" formation. Through this image, the singleton planet, which is the handle of the bucket, controls and dominates the action.

Test Yourself

(See test answers, p. 243.)

1. Why is the first impression of a horoscope so important?

2. What do you look for first as the first impression in a horoscope?

3. What is hemisphere emphasis?

4. How do the different hemispheres get their profiles?

5. Explain the manifestation of a Southern hemisphere emphasis.

6. Explain the manifestation of a Northern hemisphere emphasis.

7. When you see a Northern hemisphere emphasis, what else would you expect to see in the horoscope and where would you look for it?

8. Explain the manifestation of an Eastern hemisphere emphasis.

9. Explain the manifestation of a Western hemisphere emphasis.

10. What are some important questions to ask when there is conspicuous hemisphere emphasis in the horoscope?

11. What is a "bucket" formation?

12. How do you analyze a "bucket?"

13. What is a singleton?

14. In a horoscope with an eastern hemisphere emphasis, where might the singleton be located?

15. What is suggested with a horoscope that has a western hemisphere emphasis and a singleton Mars in Sagittarius in the east, positioned in the 11th House and ruling the 3rd House? [Sketch this roughly on paper and think it through.]

16. What is suggested when all planets in a hemisphere are retrograde?

17. What is suggested in a horoscope with an eastern hemisphere emphasis and Saturn retrograde in the 7th House as the bucket handle?

18. What is suggested in a horoscope with a southern hemisphere emphasis and Uranus in Aquarius in the 4th House?

19. Which hemisphere emphasis suggests the necessity to learn interaction with others?

20. Hemisphere emphases can be combined! Explain some possibilities.

Chapter 10

• • •

The Lights of Your Life: The Sun-Moon Blend

WITH THAT FIRST OVERALL IMPRESSION THAT is established when conspicuous hemisphere emphasis presents itself, we must then go to the core of all symbolisms, the Sun-Moon blend. This is the location of the life energy and shows how it is fashioned to drive personality development.

Consider first the physical relationship between the Sun and Moon: **we see the light of the Sun through its reflection upon the Moon.** This is of vital importance to know and understand. In the horoscope, we see the Sun as being representative of a certain kind of fuel, a certain kind of energy that is determined by the Sign it is in. If we stare at the Sun directly, we will be blinded; there is simply too much focused energy, the absolute primal unity (remember the Sun's symbol).

The Moon is the body nearest the Earth, our intimate companion. It is upon the Moon that we see the Sun's light best; it has a special significance for us; we can appreciate the Sun's energy clearly.[1] The Moon gives the

Sun's light manageable form; we call it personality form, the symbol of the reigning need of the individual life.

In reflection of the Sign archetypes, there are twelve generic kinds of energy that can fuel twelve kinds of personality structure. These 144 blends make up our lexicon of Sun-Moon blends.

The concept chart on the next page (reproduced, with permission, from Noel Tyl's work) contains brief descriptions of *how the Sun and Moon operate and blend within the Signs.* **This chart is vitally important! Make copies of it**; place one in your car, on your desk, on the refrigerator, in the bathroom. **You must know this chart cold**. It is an indispensable guide to horoscope analysis.

And it is easy: there are basically just 12 images to learn, one for each Sign, *and you already know them!* The archetype is clearly expressed for each Sign, with *only one adjustment:* **for the Sun, the concept is in terms of energy; for the Moon, the concept is in terms of need. Together in synthesis, the concept is the reigning need using the specific energy for living, expression, for fulfillment.**

The Sun (in the Sun-Moon blend concept chart) is shown in each Sign in terms of the kind of energy it has. The Moon is shown in each Sign in terms of need, the reigning need of the personality.

Using These Concepts

With the Sun in Leo and Moon in Cancer, the basic energy of life is in Leo terms of recognition, ego triumph, etc. This energy is then shown to others through a personality that needs to be emotionally secure, especially in the developmental family. Combining the two gives you this concept: the energy to be recognized is expressed in a personality form that needs emotional and home security. It is easy to see that this is the blend of someone *who uses sensitivity to dramatize his/her self.* The emotions will be well organized and intense. This is usually a comfortable blend for development because both the Sun and Moon are in the Sign each rules.

If the Sun and Moon are in Leo, the personality need profile and the energy that fuels it are one and the same, *emphasizing ego importance and recognition dramatically.*

---

1   Occultists make much of the fact that the Moon, in its nearness to us, has the same apparent disc size as the giant Sun does, so far away. This is dramatically evident during a total eclipse of the Sun, when the Moon passes in front of the Sun in relation to our vantage point on Earth.

Sun/Moon Blends

☉   ☽

♈ Energy to lead, to exert force.   ♈ Need to be important, to be #1

♉ Energy to build and to maintain   ♉ Need to preserve security; to keep things as they are or are supposed to be

♊ Energy to diversify; to communicate   ♊ Need to be bright, clever, scintillating, informed, intense

♋ Energy to create security   ♋ Need to be emotionally secure, especially in the family

♌ Energy to be recognized   ♌ Need to be respected, loved, and honored

♍ Energy to refine, discriminate   ♍ Need to be correct, insightful, exact

♎ Energy to please and gain appreciation   ♎ Need to be appreciated, fair, attractive, popular

♏ Energy to control by knowing; to plumb depths and reach heights   ♏ Need to be in control; to be regarded as deep, significant, reliable, self-sufficient, right

♐ Energy for self-assertion, for what is right; to affect thought   ♐ Need to have one's opinions respected

♑ Energy to organize, strategize, and deploy resources   ♑ Need to administrate progress; to make things happen

♒ Energy to innovate, to intellectualize, to champion all, for/with others   ♒ Need to be socially significant, unusual

♓ Energy to feel, understand, sacrifice   ♓ Need to identify the ideal, understand impressions, work with the intangible

- If the Sun is in Leo and the Moon is in Virgo, the self-dramatic Leo energy is toned down because the personality form that uses it is cerebral, cautious, and more measured (than if the Moon were in Leo).

- Such is the case with the actors Dustin Hoffman and Robert Redford. Both have the ☉♌–☽♍ combination. While they are both top-flight *dramatic* actors, *neither of the two has a* dramatic *personality presentation otherwise*. The measured, cautious personality form, very discriminating and exacting, is obvious in their expression; it tempers the blazing Leo energy strategically.

- Martin Luther King Jr. had ☉♑–☽♓. He used a sensitive, idealistic, compassionate, martyr-like personality profile (all Pisces descriptions), i.e., the reigning need to have these values respected, to get things done (the energy of Capricorn).

- Muhammad Ali has ☉♑–☽♒. He uses/used a social, humanitarian, uniquely fashioned personality image to get things done, to make things happen.

- Let's flip the coin and look at Abraham Lincoln, who had ☉♒–☽♑. He had a "let's get it done" personality that was using social/humanitarian fuel (he freed the slaves, remember).

- Princess Diana had ☉♋–☽♒. She had a humanitarian personality need that was using emotionally-oriented fuel, and all of this coursed through the developmental tensions shown in her horoscope and experienced in her life.

The Sun-Moon blend gives us the basis for anticipation of behavior. **Study the Sun-Moon blend concept chart and see how the words take the Sun's energy and relate it to the expression of the Moon.**

More Considerations to Help

When the Sun-Moon blend is a fire-water or fire-earth combination, for example, you can feel that the personality form in water will generally tone down the fire. Water puts fire out, as does earth. Robert DeNiro has ☉♌–☽♓. Steven Spielberg has ☉♐–☽♏, and we've seen the Hoffman and Redford examples. **The Moon, being exposed to the public,**

leading the way in development, adjusts the energy of the Sun, adapts it to life.

In contrast, when the Sun-Moon blend is a water-fire combination, the personality form will tend to express the sensitivity more vibrantly; the Moon is in the lead, and there is a boil-up potential with the water energy. For example, if the Sun is in Pisces with the Moon in Aries, the sensitive energy will express itself in a personality that is assertive, that needs to be "numero uno." Martial arts actor Chuck Norris is a perfect example of this blend. You can feel his sensitivity, but you see the assertion. Does this make the Aries needs more societally acceptable?

Adjustments to the Sun-Moon Blend

When the Sun or Moon receives hard aspects, especially from Mars or any of the outer planets, *the behavior we anticipate from the Sun-Moon blend will be adjusted in the terms suggested by the planet making the aspect.*

Princess Diana's horoscope (p. 135) shows ☉♋–☽♒. The Sun is trined by Neptune, suggesting a smooth energy flow into Neptune's idealistic realms. The Moon, part of a T-Square structure, is opposed by Uranus. The personality form is intensified; it is given a strong awareness of individualism. We can anticipate extreme innovation in social service because of energy that is sensitive to emotional needs. There can be unconventional courses of action because of the Uranian aspect.

Arnold Schwarzenegger has ☉♌–☽♑. The energy to be recognized is fueling the personality need to get things done, to administrate progress, to make things happen; or, getting things done, making things happen to create personal recognition. Further in analysis, the Sun is conjunct Saturn and Pluto, adding a strong focus of ambition and empowerment to his basic fuel. Neptune squares the Moon, somehow softening the expression of the often-hard Capricorn Moon's personality form. In essence, we have ambitious, empowering fuel that is expressed in a personality form that needs to administrate progress but somehow takes on a "something-is-other-than-it-seems" dimension (films!). Again, is all the self-centered power somehow made easier in social development, more acceptable?

The Role of the Ascendant

After registering the Sun-Moon blend and any adjustments made to it, we then look at the **Ascendant**; it will almost invariably reinforce or add important dimensions to the Sun-Moon blend. Incorporating the Ascendant in analysis is like adding an important herb or spice to something that you are cooking; or introducing another color to the portrait you are painting. In general, the Sun-Moon blend is filtered through the lens of the Ascendant or is refined by it or is rescued by it.

For example, O. J. Simpson has ☉♋–☽♓, with a *Leo Ascendant*. The energy for emotional/home security is expressed in a sensitive personality form, **and all of this is shown to others dramatically, confidently, and with much attention paid to pride and vanity (the Leo Ascendant).** The Sun's *trine* to Jupiter *supports* his basic Sun-fuel, adding to the confidence. However, the Moon is squared by Uranus, intensifying his sensitive personality, especially in terms of his lovability, popularity, etc. Simpson in all his power as a world-famous athlete always appeared personally vulnerable, accessible, and charming. Does this invite sympathy from others? Does the Leo pride issue forth (from the Ascendant, through the Sun) tolerably to rescue the personality (the sensitive Moon) when it is hurt?

Bill Clinton, as we have seen, has ☉♌–☽♉, the energy for recognition expressing itself in a personality form that needs to keep things as they are or make them as he thinks they need to be. This is shown to others through a *Libra Ascendant and four planets in Libra in the 1st House:* attractiveness, charm, needing to be popular, gaining ego recognition through interactions with others, etc. Does this help with effectiveness?

Dustin Hoffman's ☉♌–☽♍ suggests cerebral energies that tone down the Leonian drama. The Sun is squared by Uranus, intensifying the public show. The Moon is veiled in the 8th House and is *in conjunction with Neptune.* His Ascendant is Capricorn, with Jupiter *retrograde* closely conjunct the Ascendant. While Hoffman is easily able to express himself dramatically in public (through his profession), he is withdrawn and introverted in public. The Leo Sun has clouds to shine through, including Saturn ℞, ruler of the Ascendant.

The Sun-Moon blend speaks through every human being at every social level. It is where synthesis of the horoscope begins, after the snapshot of the first impression is taken through hemisphere emphasis.

Summary

1. The Sun shines its energy upon the Moon, and the Moon expresses it as the personality form, the reigning need, determined by the Sign of the Moon's placement.

2. When the Sun or Moon receives hard aspects, especially from Mars or any of the outer planets, the behavior anticipated by the Sun-Moon blend will be adjusted in the terms suggested by the planet making the aspect.

3. The Ascendant invariably reinforces or adds important dimensions to the Sun-Moon blend.

Test Yourself

(See test answers, p. 245.)

1. What astronomical fact regarding the Sun and Moon interaction do we use symbolically in the horoscope?

2. What does the Sun represent in the Sun-Moon blend?

3. What does the Moon represent in the Sun-Moon blend?

4. Describe ☉♋–☽♈.

5. What is the role of the Ascendant in relation to the Sun-Moon blend?

6. What do hard aspects to the Sun and Moon do to the Sun-Moon blend?

7. What does the following suggest: ☉☽♈ ☍ ♆?

8. In the above example, add a Sagittarius Ascendant to your description. How does that adjust things?

9. Which Sun-Moon blend is suggested by this phrase: the energy for emotional and domestic security fuels a personality that needs to keep things as they are?

10 What is suggested when the Sun-Moon blend is a Fire-Water combination?

Chapter 11

• • •

New Measurements
and Full Integration
of Symbology

THE PROCESS OF RECORDING POPULAR MUSIC involves many techniques of enhancement used by musicians and recording engineers. The way a drummer tunes the drums or adjusts the drum machine affects in certain ways what the listener will hear. Keyboard players use a variety of synthesized keyboards that simulate sounds that will inspire certain moods and feelings for the listener. Engineers have a variety of tricks, all designed to project the music in a certain light so that the music is perceived in the *desired* light.

In painting a picture, an artist, also, uses different techniques to give a certain mood to the painting. There are different kinds of brushes and different kinds of strokes that can be used with the brushes. A bit of chalk can be used here instead of a brush and over here we can use a different kind of paint that may have greater presence.

Astrology, too, has its different brush strokes that lead toward analytical enhancement. Some of these tools involve minor aspect measurements and points; they provide astrologers with major meanings.

The Quindecile

Throughout our horoscope studies in this course, as you have grown in sophistication, you surely have noticed in the aspect grid the little aspect symbol of "0," which until now has gone unexplained. This symbol refers to a newly rediscovered aspect in astrology! Use of the aspect is so new, our software companies do not yet have a symbol programmed for it (although one was proposed in April 1999 by astrologer Ricki Reeves and Noel Tyl: ℚ). The "0" in the aspect grid of your charts is a temporary significator of the quindecile.

The quindecile (*quin-deh-chee-lay*) **is an aspect measuring 165 degrees** (we suggest a 2-degree orb). It is easy to find: It looks like an opposition, but it is 15 degrees shy of an exact opposition. It is formed within the 24th harmonic (360 degrees divided by 24 gives 15 degrees, i.e., successive 15 degree aspects: 15, 30, 45, 60, 75, 90, 105, 120, 135, 150, 165, and 180 degrees. Most of these aspects are congruent with already established aspects, but the quindecile stands alone, unmatched in conventional lists derived from other harmonics.

Noel Tyl rediscovered this aspect relationship during his research of the life of Leonardo da Vinci, for his book *Astrology of the Famed*.[1] He found that this aspect corresponds with **disruption, separation, upheaval, obsession, compulsion, a cause celebre in the life that just does not go away.**

To capture and preserve the passion of that sense of significance, Tyl has insisted in his lectures throughout many countries and in his articles and recent books that the aspect name be pronounced in the Italian way rather than in the sterile English way: *quin-deh-chee'-lay* (instead of *quin-dess'-aisle*). No one disagrees with that after they see what the quin-deh-chee-lay connotes!

Leonardo da Vinci

The Moon-Neptune quindecile in Leonardo's horoscope is very helpful to our learning to appreciate the quindecile.

Leonardo da Vinci (Fig. 25, p. 156), born in Vinci, Italy, was a "love child," the result of an affair between a poor girl named Caterina and Ser

---

1 Noel Tyl, *Astrology of the Famed* (St. Paul: Llewellyn Publications, 1996); rectification of the birth dates and times for Cleopatra, St. Francis, Dracula, Leonardo da Vinci, and Beethoven.

Piero da Vinci. Both parents married other people during Leonardo's first year of life.

It was Sigmund Freud who theorized in a prominent study, based on sketchy facts known of Leonardo at that time, that Caterina, who was caring for him in her home, was overly tender with Leonardo, even erotic.

Somewhere between the ages of three and five, Leonardo's tie with his mother was broken. He was then taken to his father's home and cared for by his father's young wife. Working with these family outlines and a very detailed dream Leonardo preserved in his notebooks, Freud suggested that it was during this time that Leonardo developed and repressed his sexual interest in his mother. The way he dealt with the repression was by identifying himself with her, thereby attracting men like himself for homosexual relationships.

At about the age of forty-one, Leonardo brought to live with him in Milan, a very old "mystery" woman, who was called Caterina. Voluminous notes taken during Leonardo's life barely betray his relationship to his mother, but references that do occur obliquely carry clear emotional weight. Many scholars feel that the Mona Lisa is a portrait of Caterina, a small painting Leonardo worked on for eight years and never let out of his possession until his death many years later! And in his other works, analysts point to Leonardo's creation of dramatic mother images (Madonnas), accompanied by symbolic caves (wombs) portrayed in a threatening and foreboding way. The point here is that there is no doubt that there was a mother fixation in Leonardo's life.

These vignetttes about Leonardo da Vinci provide the background for the exact Moon-Neptune quindecile in his horoscope. It suggests a powerful neurosis in his life—a compulsion resulting from the early separation from his mother (the Moon) that manifested itself idealistically through art (Neptune), and never left his consciousness.

There is a second quindecile in Leonard's horoscope between Uranus and the Node; this is yet another link between Leonardo's sense of individuality and the maternal influence.

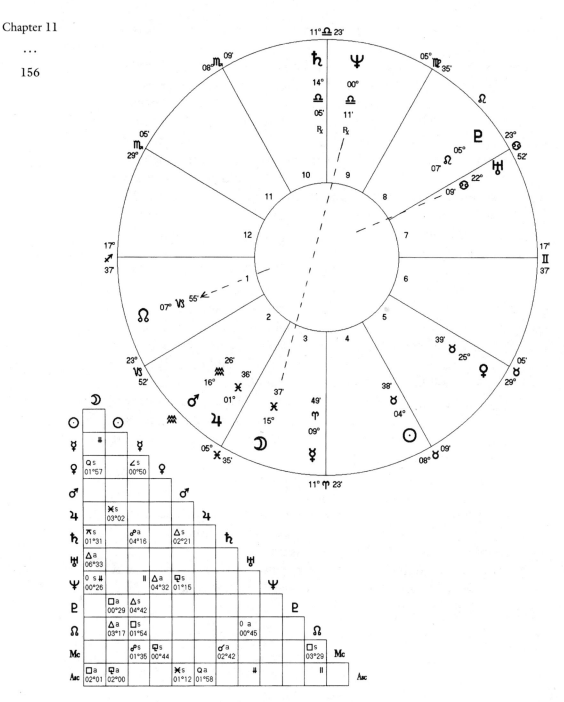

Figure 25
Leonardo da Vinci
4/15/1452, 10:30 P.M. LMT
Vinci, Italy, 10E55 43N47
(Rectification by Noel Tyl)

The Quindecile in Analysis

In analysis we look first for upheaval in the house *holding the intrinsically slower moving planet,* or look to the House(s) ruled/tenanted by the planets in the quindecile aspect. When the quindecile involves the Midheaven, expect an obsession with one's job or career that is heavily relied on for self-evaluation. Quindeciles involving the Ascendant are almost always going to involve a planet in the 6th or 7th House. There is going to be the sense of an obsession or compulsion that involves the identity presentation as it relates to the particular planet, usually in terms of relationship.

For example, Uranus in quindecile aspect to the Ascendant suggests a compulsiveness about individuation of Self. If this Uranus is in the 7th House, the focus on obsession with individuation probably causes "disruption, compulsion, separation, upheaval, or obsession," within relationships. From the 6th House, the Uranian influence would shift to include the dynamics of cooperation and service, especially within the work environment.

Referring again to Marilyn Monroe's horoscope (Fig. 18, p. 123), Mercury in the 10th is quindecile Saturn in the 4th House. This suggests that Marilyn's mind was compulsively tuned to the upset and upheaval in her early life through the love she did not receive from her father. With Mercury ruling the 2nd and 11th Houses, there is a suggestion that this compulsive anxiety includes extending itself to include self-worth and lovableness concerns. Saturn, in turn, is quindecile the Midheaven, suggesting career excess as a way of overcompensation for the tensions that we have learned about, or searching for that father fulfillment through the profession (exposure and contacts).

In addition, Jupiter in the 7th is quindecile the Ascendant, suggesting an overexpansive presentation of Self and/or **disruption, separation, upheaval, and obsession with regard to relationships**.

Prince Charles' horoscope (Fig. 22, p. 136) shows a lower hemisphere emphasis, suggesting unfinished business in the early home (as you have learned). The Moon conjoins the Nodal Axis and is the all-important handle to the "bucket." The Sun, ruler of the Ascendant, is squared by Pluto; Venus rules the 4th House and is conjunct Neptune. This abbreviated profile suggests to us that Prince Charles has a strong desire for (entitlement to) personal power that has been "kept under a blanket" as a result of conditions in the home with a parent. The strength of the

Moon here, in its conjunction with the Nodal Axis, suggests to us that it is his mother that is "the blanket."

Now, we add to this, a strong quindecile between Neptune-Venus and the singleton Moon in the 10th (see it this way: add 15 degrees to Neptune-Venus and you come to an opposition with the Moon). Here we have disruption, separation, upheaval, and obsession with regard to his mother, to feminine ideals, all linked to tensions in the home.

Arnold Schwarzenegger (Fig. 26, p. 159) has five quindecile aspects in his horoscope.[2] The Sun-Moon blend of Leo-Capricorn suggests energies for recognition being fueled into a personality that needs to get things done, to administrate progress, and make things happen. The Moon here, in the 6th House, always suggests the workaholic. This Moon makes quindecile aspects with Mercury (compulsion about learning), the Mars-Uranus conjunction (the energetic assertion and individuation), and the Ascendant (working overtime to present an ambitious image; a compulsion with health matters). In addition, we see that Neptune is quindecile the Midheaven, certainly showing us the career obsession in terms of Neptune (motion pictures). When you factor in the Sun's conjunction with Saturn and Pluto, we can see that this is a man who is very, very driven. Schwarzenegger was born the son of a policeman, won the Mr. Universe title five times (body building), married into the Kennedy family in the United States, rose to be one of the most prominent movie stars in the world, and is as well an extremely successful real estate and business developer.

We know in psychology (and astrology, of course) that any extreme development in life—and Schwarzenegger is an example of extreme development—signals the principle of overcompensatory development. Certainly this insight is valid here: note the conspicuous eastern hemisphere orientation (this man is defensive), notice the threat to relationship comfort through which he would have to grow (Pluto conjunct Saturn, ruler of the 7th), the self-worth anxiety (Saturn-Pluto conjunct the Sun, ruler of the 2nd), and the peregrine Venus in Cancer, ruling the 11th and the 4th (the longing for love security), the Cancer Ascendant ruled by the extraordinarily aspected Moon! In consultation, the astrologer would have much to explore for appreciation of this extraordinary man. It goes on and on, even to the fact that this chart promises

---

2 You will find that roughly 80% of all horoscopes have one or more quindecile aspects.

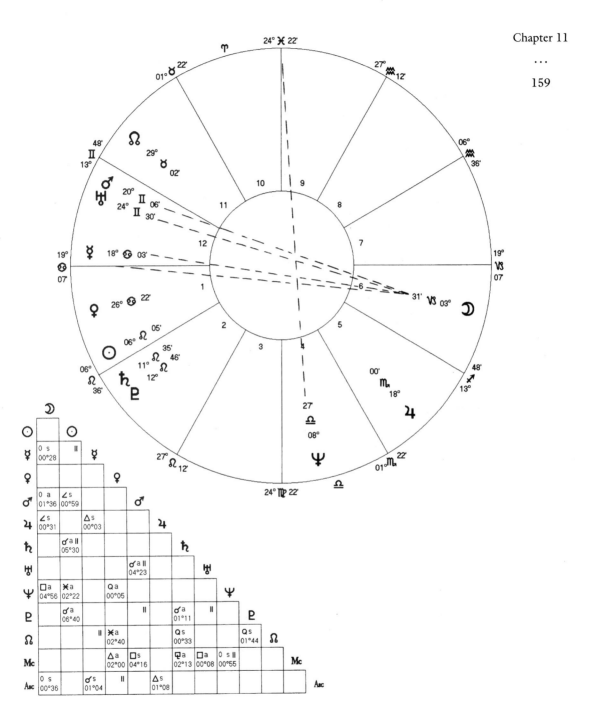

Figure 26
Arnold Schwarzenegger
7/30/47, 4:10 A.M. CED
Graz, Austria, 15E27 47N05

(with advanced study) a heart problem—in such a hero!?—and Schwarzenegger did indeed have open-heart surgery in April 1997.

As you can see, the quindecile adds enormous depth to the astrological portrait. Please be sure to adjust your astrological software to calibrate the powerful quindecile. As we have seen, the quindecile has a most powerful impact. It is a minor measurement with major impact, and we work with a 2-degree orb.

The Aries Point

The Aries Point refers to 0 degrees of Cardinal Signs, all four of them. In technical terms, astronomically speaking, the Aries Point axis of the horoscope is defined by the intersection and widest diversion points of two great circles: the Ecliptic and the Equator. The details of these crossings establish 0 degrees Libra as the cusp of the Ascendant of the Earth. The four quadrants of the Sun's passage are keyed by 0 degrees of all four Cardinal signs.

The Aries Point, 0 degrees of Cardinal Signs (2 degree orb), is sensitive to any involvement when a planet or point is involved with it. When activated, **the planet or point configured with the Aries Point is brought conspicuously forward in personality projection, a public vector is added to the dimension**. It is a distinctly externalized projection, *as if it were on the Ascendant*. In situations where you see the Aries Point being held back in expression, it is probably *taking place at another level of life, displaced or sublimated somehow, or for some reason*. Aries Point is abbreviated "AP."

President Richard Nixon[3] had his 0 *Capricorn* Mercury clearly at the Aries Point: his need to think, communicate, and perceive strategically was certainly projected forward powerfully in his personality (earning him the nickname, "Tricky Dick," and perhaps leading to the election campaign overkill tactics that inspired the Watergate scandal).

Actor Mel Gibson,[4] celebrated (and adored by women) internationally for his talent, his good looks, and charm, has his *Libra* Moon at the Aries Point: the reigning need to be popular, to be thought attractive and enjoyable is thrust forward for all to see.

---

3 January 9, 1913, 21:35 PST, Yorba Linda, California, 117W49 33N53.
4 January 3, 1956, 16:45 EST, New York, New York, 73W56 40N45.

O. J. Simpson has his Venus in *Cancer* configured with the Aries Point: showing the projection of his powerful social popularity, charm, and attractiveness to others, in terms of emotional vulnerability, the domestic image, the child care issues—all complementing his Pisces Moon.

The Aries Point adds a powerful accent in the life portrait. **Whenever you see accentuation of the Aries Point that has *not* shown itself prominently in life, it is an indication that there have been developmental difficulties, typically in the early home life, that have stifled development, that short-circuited this particular development channel somehow.**

The Quintile

The quintile comes from the fifth harmonic: 360 degrees divided by 5 gives 72 degrees (a sextile plus 12 degrees). We can appreciate the quintile by recalling the classical depiction of a man inscribed in the circle with his arms and legs outstretched in contact with the circumference. By drawing straight lines from hand to hand to leg to leg to hand, we square the circle, *we show the developmental energy of the square within the All (the clear orientation of four angular points)*. When we adjust the posture and add the human head, developmental energy is given special intelligence, the potential to manage the energy in special ways. **The quintile suggests *creativity* described by the planets involved, their placement and routings.** (Again, we suggest a 2-degree orb). The symbol for the quintile is Q.

Marilyn Monroe has a Leo Ascendant, making the Sun the all-important ruler for the horoscope (p. 123). Her Sun, in the 11th House, makes quintile aspects to Uranus and Neptune, suggesting a strong accentuation of creativity within her core development, especially since Neptune is in the 1st House. Uranus rules the 7th House, showing the creative dimension within relationships and to the public.

Muhammad Ali has ♀Q♂, rulers of his 3–9 axis (communication, internationalism, spiritual development). Venus is in the 7th House, the public. The young Cassius Clay, before changing his name upon his conversion to Islam, was a particularly creative public communicator, creating storied rhymes as to how he would defeat his opponents! He was a natural communicator, a natural, highly creative publicist.

Dustin Hoffman's horoscope[5] has six quintiles: ☽Q♂, Q♀; ♀Q♆, ♂Q♆, ♃QMC, MCQAsc. This is enormous creativity, displayed publicly through his career.

See the quintile aspect as a sharp accentuation of creativity in the person's life, especially when there are several of them, as is the case with Dustin Hoffman.

Putting It All Together

Isn't it exciting how far we have come, how quickly, in learning astrology! Take a moment and go back to the beginning of this course, read a few of the early pages, and now appreciate the pages you have just been reading! Look at the difference, look at the growth! Congratulations!

The many techniques and concepts you have learned enable you to *anticipate behavior*, to understand the need-fulfillment process, and so much more regarding identity development. Now, let's lift everything up a notch and put it all together.

Here is a list to guide your organization of horoscope preparation. Sure, you can put one step ahead of another, change things around to suit your emerging analytical style, but **the point is to have a procedure**, a way of approaching the horoscope that is the same every time you do it. Your brain becomes grooved with a pattern of observation and deduction and, with repetition, *all of this becomes instinct*. You will be amazed someday soon how quickly your mind will comprehend all the symbols when you settle in to study a new horoscope!

1. Hemisphere emphasis

2. Sun-Moon blend

3. Special aspect structures

4. Idealism aspects

5. Peregrination (introduced below)

6. Mutual reception (introduced below)

7. Significator dynamics

---

5 August 8, 1937, Los Angeles CA, 118W15 34N03.

8. Saturn retrograde

    a. Nodal axis

    b. Parental axis

9. Quindecile

10. Quintile

11. Aries Point

12. Emphasis or absence of an element or mode

If you follow this list as a guideline, your preparation notes for the consultation will give you all the information that is necessary to begin an intelligent conversation with a person, based on his or her horoscope. This is how Noel Tyl, who developed almost all of these concepts, does it; this is how I do it; and it is how so many other successful astrologers have learned to approach their work. It is important to point out as well that astrologers who do *not* have such a collection of techniques, who have not kept up with psychodynamic developments in humanistic study, and who do not have an orderly approach to synthesis, simply remain lost in a maze of measurements, are outdated, and are not fulfilling their personal potentials as analysts.

For our first example, let's look at the horoscope of Chelsea Clinton (Fig. 27, p. 164).

Hemisphere Emphasis

Every planet above the horizon is retrograde, which calls attention to the lower hemisphere. Therefore we know there is the suggestion of **unfinished business in the early development**, something is there (occurred then) that may undermine development. Our mind is alerted to this first impression and we look for it to be corroborated (repeated, explained) often throughout the rest of the horoscope.

Sun-Moon Blend

The Sun-Moon blend shows us a **sensitive, idealistic energy fueling a personality that strongly needs recognition, appreciation, and ego triumph.** Sensitivity, compassion, and idealistic dimensions may be

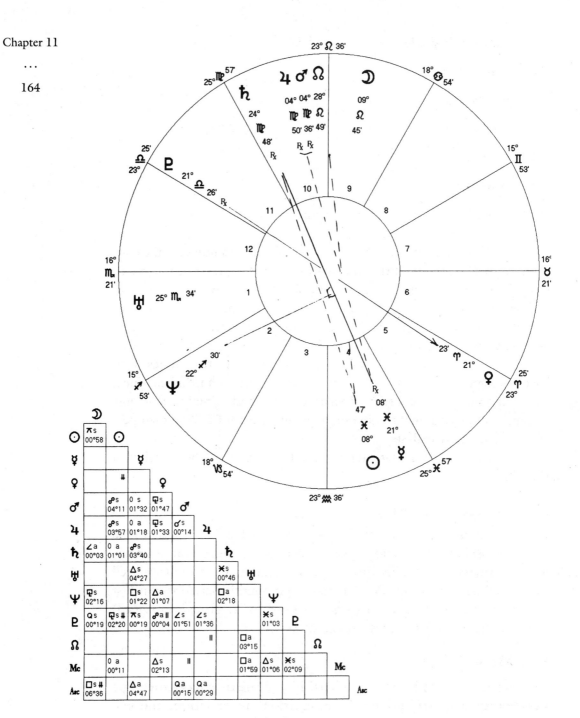

Figure 26
Chelsea Clinton
2/27/80, 11:24 P.M. CST
Little Rock AR, 92W17 34N45

emphasized because of the Sun's oppositions with Mars and Jupiter. But we must note that Mars and Jupiter are retrograde; "the energy will go in before it goes out." Why?

Aspect Structures

There is a T-Square: ♆□ the axis, ☿☌♇♄. This suggests **control factors on the way she needs to think and communicate, all in terms of idealism** (Pisces; Neptune; Sun in Pisces). The relationship among these three planets paints a picture of **mental anxiety, even depression**. With Mercury being retrograde, we expect counterpoint concerns in the thought processes, perhaps uncomfortable subjectivity.

Idealism

We have seen, in step #3, the measurement of idealism thwarted.

Peregrination

The Moon does not make a Ptolemaic aspect in the horoscope; we say that such a planet is peregrine (pear'-a-green); the peregrine planet usually runs away with the personality in some way. Here, the Moon is peregrine, suggesting that a "Queen complex" does/will run away with the horoscope. **The need for recognition, love, honor, and ego triumph are in high gear.** Will this be overcompensation for developmental weaknesses?[6]

Dispositorship and Mutual Reception

This is a very simple concept to reinforce deductions from measurements: a planet that rules the sign another planet is in is called the "dispositor" of the second planet; it "disposes" of the planet. Actually, the word should be "conditions." For example, Chelsea Clinton's Venus is in Aries, therefore it is disposed of by Mars; it is conditioned by Mars; that conditioning registers in the archetype of Aries. Venus in Aries suggests strong, aggressive romantic/social needs, especially pronounced here because Venus is opposed by Pluto, the ruler of her Ascendant, and Venus rules the relationship 7th House! This dimension will work to fulfill her reigning need of the Moon in Leo.

---

6 For a thorough study of peregrination, please see Tyl, *Synthesis & Counseling in Astrology* (St. Paul: Llewellyn Publications, 1994).

Mars is disposed of by Mercury (Mercury rules Virgo where we find Mars), Mercury is disposed by Neptune, Neptune by Jupiter, and Jupiter by Mercury. These routings seem to cluster with a focus on Mercury.

Pluto disposes of Uranus, Venus disposes Pluto, Mars disposes Venus, Mercury disposes Mars, Neptune disposes Mercury, Jupiter-Neptune, Mercury-Jupiter. Again we end up with the importance of Mercury in Pisces, retrograde, opposed (aware of) the crucially important Saturn retrograde (disposed by *Mercury*).

The dynamics of dispositorship help you *feel* the relative importance of planetary symbolism.

When a planet is in its own sign (Bill Clinton's Sun in Leo and Venus in Libra for example), it is called the "final dispositor" of the horoscope, calling attention to its most full-blown manifestation potential. Clinton has two planets this strong: the Sun and Venus; and it shows!

Now, sometimes you will have two planets, each in the sign ruled by the other! This is called "mutual reception." Look at Hillary Clinton's horoscope (Fig. 30, p. 187): she has the Sun in Scorpio and Pluto in Leo, a strong accentuation of individual empowerment (and note that she has Jupiter in Sagittarius, as final dispositor). Lawyer Hillary Clinton has been profiled often as a powerful person indeed; she is known for her strong opinionation.[7]

Significator Dynamics

Returning to Chelsea Clinton's horoscope, the T-Square focuses on Neptune's placement in the 2nd House, ruling the 5th House. **There is the suggestion of an unsureness of self-worth in relationships, to giving love** (Neptune in the 2nd House, ruling the 5th House) **that will spill over into her mindset** (Saturn rules the 3rd House), **the way she feels about herself in terms of being loveable and attractive, as well as how she interacts with the self-worth constructs of others** (Mercury rules the 11th and 8th Houses, and don't forget that Mercury is retrograde, suggesting a counterpoint or weakness in 11th and 8th House terms.).

---

7 Prince Charles (p. 136) has a similar mutual reception and final dispositorship; Bill Gates, the software giant (October 28, 1955 at 10:02 P.M. in Bremerton, Washington) has the Sun-Pluto mutual reception with Jupiter conjunct Pluto in the 2nd House, ruled by the Sun; see how this describes money power? Noel Tyl's horoscope (December 31, 1936 at 3:57 P.M. in Westchester, PA) has mutual reception between Uranus and Venus, which are in tight quintile aspect, suggesting avant garde creativity. See my horoscope (p. 83) for the Moon-Mercury mutual reception, the bond between my mind and emotions.

Pluto opposes Venus exactly. This aspect punctuates what we have already seen regarding giving love by suggesting that **her need to relate is aware of a perspective that is so large as to be unattainable or difficult, at best.** Since Venus and Pluto rule the 7th and 1st Houses, we can see that **her identity development and her relationships are tied into this difficult sexual/relating perspective.** Venus also rules the 12th House, adding **a feeling of a confinement regarding her relational perspective, a blanket placed upon her ability to give love.** Note: Pluto rules the Ascendant and is retrograde! The identity development has blocks in it, for sure.

Saturn, Nodes, Parental Axis

This could have been the *first* thing to catch your eye: Saturn is retrograde, suggesting a legacy of inferiority feelings as a result of **an absent or unfulfilling relationship with the authority figure in the home, probably the father.** We check the Nodal Axis and see Uranus square to it:[8] **a strong maternal influence upon the development of Chelsea's individuation needs.** Added to this profile of parental tension is the reality that the Sun, ruler of the 10th House, is opposed by the Mars-Jupiter conjunction, calling attention again to self-worth considerations (Jupiter rules the 2nd House) and the **dynamic of cooperation** (Mars rules the 6th House).

The Quindecile

Chelsea's Sun is quindecile Saturn retrograde; Mercury is quindecile the Mars-Jupiter conjunction, all accentuating the 4–10 axis (here are the repeat indications of the first impression). This suggests **upheaval and upset concerns in the home,** an echo of what we have seen already. The Sun's quindecile to the Midheaven suggests that Chelsea **will use her career in a compulsive manner as a way to overcompensate for the tensions we have seen thus far with her home development, her father, self-worth, etc.** "I am who I am! Appreciate me!"

The Quintile

With three quintiles, there is the suggestion of **emphasized creative dimensions** within the portrait we are building.

---

8 In horoscopes with accented parental tension, we accept a wider-than-normal orb for the Lunar Nodal Axis as long as it does not exceed four degrees. With experience, you will learn how to instinctively ask about the maternal influence when the orb is wide.

The Aries Point

There are no positions at the Aries Point.

Element, Mode Balances

The horoscope is weak in accentuation of the Air element (only Pluto is in Air), suggesting **a difficulty seeing herself as others do, and perhaps overcompensation or underachievement issues regarding intellectual or socially related concerns.**

What a portrait we have built *by following the guideline steps for analysis!* Here is this sensitive girl with a naturally endowed Princess complex, needing love and recognition. She is highly influenced by her mother and quite fixated on upsets in the home because of her father. And because of this, her self-worth, her mindset, her relationships, and her ability to give love are affected. It appears that Chelsea will be "saved" through her education, as the 9th House is free from tension and its significator is running away with the horoscope (the peregrine Moon). Wow!

Let's look again at Marilyn Monroe's horoscope, repeated on page 169. There is the Southern hemisphere emphasis (procedure point #1)—**this suggests that the person is open to victimization and exploitation through life experience.** *Why?* Furthermore, you notice that Saturn (retrograde!) is the handle to the bucket formation in this horoscope. You now instantly anticipate an early life issue, some tension, probably surrounding the father or home life in general, and that the symbolism of Saturn retrograde is probably what pushed her into a position of victimization and exploitation through life experience.

The Sun in Gemini and Moon in Aquarius (#2), **diversified, communicative, intellectual energy is expressed through a personality that needs to be social, innovative, humanitarian, or unique.** There will be a control factor on this (the adjustment to the Sun-Moon blend) because the Moon is squared by Saturn retrograde. And since the Moon is in the 7th, you **anticipate control factors upon relationships.** This is all shown to others **dramatically** (the Leo Ascendant) and perhaps **mysteriously. She may project something other than what she really is** (Leo Rising with *Neptune in the 1st House*).

There is a T-Square (#3): the Moon-Jupiter opposition with Neptune is squared by Saturn retrograde. First, analyze the opposition and then

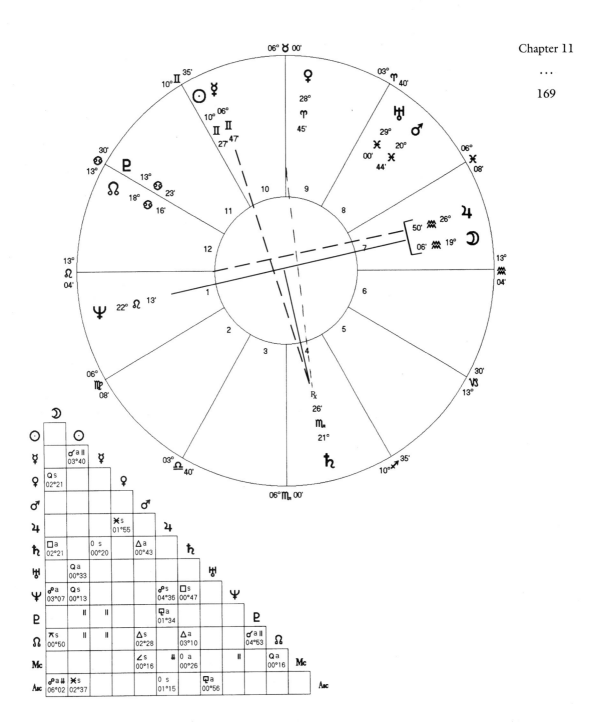

Figure 28
Marilyn Monroe
6/1/26, 9:30 A.M. PST
Los Angeles CA, 118W15 34N03

determine how that is expressed or altered in terms of the squaring planet. Here, we have a control factor placed upon Marilyn's function in relationships and upon her self-projection. Her identity (1st House) and her relationships (7th House) are being controlled (even driven in over-compensation) by the Saturn retrograde symbolism. Once the words flow from your brain into your speech, it's that simple!

Jupiter in opposition to Neptune suggests **idealism** (#4). In that Neptune is in the 1st House, this dimension—the Neptune dimension—is potentially overexpanded into **too much fantasy**, etc. The Sun is conjunct Mercury: **idealism** (so often a defensive projection, a defense mechanism).

Pluto is peregrine (without Ptolemaic aspect, #5), **a measure here of potential prominence** (empowered position). Uranus is also peregrine—**individualism or innovation** (eccentricism) **projected forward to extreme.** In line with what we have developed thus far, you will quickly notice that *Pluto rules the 4th House;* the home indicated again. Uranus rules the 7th House—relationships.

Mercury is clearly the final dispositor of the horoscope (#6), putting repetitive emphasis on Marilyn's mental process, her idealism about attractiveness and attracting love (Mercury conjoins the Sun and rules the 11th).

Significator dynamics: the T-Square (#7) involves Houses 1–7–4, as we know, but by rulership, also includes the 8th House (**the worth of others, their values, their support**), the 6th House (**cooperation with others**), the 12th House (**a blanket or confinement factor** involving what we know about the T-square in this horoscope), and the 5th House (**giving love, sex**).

We have already established that Saturn is retrograde (#8). The Nodal Axis is *not* emphasized and the parental House rulers are not involved in developmental tension. Still, we know there is a strong issue because of Saturn's "bucket" position in the 4th House. It controls everything!

Mercury is quindecile Saturn (#9): **the mind keyed obsessively and compulsively about the upset in the early home.** Since Mercury rules the 11th and 2nd Houses, there is the suggestion that **the mind's obsession with the father difficulty also includes deep thoughts about being loveable and that it affects the self-worth.** Jupiter is quindecile the Ascendant: **a compulsion to present the Self uniquely that is overdone,** *and/or* **upset and upheaval in relationships.**

Saturn is quindecile the Midheaven: **the career is being used in a compulsive way as overcompensation of other tensions.**

The Sun's quintiles with Uranus and Neptune (#10) emphasize **strong creativity at the core of the life energy.**

Uranus is at the Aries Point, just over the signline (#11): this echoes the Aquarian Moon in that it thrusts to prominence the Uranian dimensions that are **unique, innovative, and individualistic.**

There is a lack of Earth in the horoscope (#12), suggesting impracticality and a lack of day-to-day stability *or* a habit of being overanalytical in order to gain stability in that manner.

The portrait has been painted. Miss Monroe walks into your office for a consultation (not a *reading*, please). You say,

> *Good afternoon, Miss Monroe. Thanks for your interest and faith in making this appointment; please have a seat. We're going to have a good discussion today. Your horoscope suggests a person with strong diversification and intellectual energies that work through a personality that needs to be humanitarian, social, or unique somehow. And you project this to others dramatically, perhaps with a charisma and a sense that you are something other than what you seem. Let's explore this . . .*

[Naturally, there will be dialogue together, not a long one-sided presentation by the astrologer. But for our presentation here, in this text format, "discussion" is indeed focused 100% on the astrologer.]

> *The horoscope* **suggests** *[a key word to use, always] that there is great potential to being thrust strongly into life experience and therefore, open to victimization by it. And this would appear to be related to a difficulty in your early development, possibly regarding your father. The horoscope suggests that he was out of the picture somehow and, through his absence, or in relation to it, you have had your share of tensions, especially when it comes to relationships, to giving love, and some real concerns about your identity, who you are, etc. One could say that your mind is even a bit obsessed with this issue in your life.*
>
> *Through it all, you manage, with great creativity, to build a name for yourself through your career. I am sure that people see you as being unique, special, perhaps prominent on your level. There may be a tendency to overdoing things regarding your presentation of self, perhaps an overexpansion of your uniqueness in order to gain*

significance and/or perhaps you are overdoing things regarding relationships. There are suggestions of upheaval and upset that seem to permeate your relationships. And through all of this, we see issues concerning your sense of stability, perhaps a long streak of impracticality within you.

Please, let's begin; tell me about your early development, specifically regarding your father.

The consultation is off and running and you, the astrologer, are working hard to get Marilyn's experiences of the early home objectified so that she can free some of the issues that lead to exploitation by others, etc. The roots of this analysis come *strictly and without embellishment* from the steps that you have been given and the lesson you have learned.

Summary

1. The quindecile is an aspect measuring 165 degrees (we suggest a 2-degree orb). It is easy to find: It looks like an opposition, but it is 15 degrees shy of an exact opposition. It is formed within the 24th harmonic (360 degrees divided by 24 gives 15 degrees, i.e., successive 15 degree aspects: 15, 30, 45, 60, 75, 90, 105, 120, 135, 150, and 165 degrees).

2. The key words that apply best for the quindecile are disruption, separation, upheaval, compulsion, and obsession.

3. The Aries Point refers to 0 degrees of Cardinal Signs.

4. When the Aries Point is activated, there is the potential of public projection for the person in terms of the planet or point (and in advanced studies, with the midpoint) configured with it.

5. Whenever you see accentuation of the Aries Point that has not shown itself prominently in life, it is an indication that there have been developmental difficulties, typically in the early home life, that have stifled development of the particular dimension suggested.

6. The quintile aspect, measuring 72 degrees, suggests creativity described by the planets involved and their houses of tenancy and rulership (we suggest a two-degree orb). The symbol for the quintile is Q.

7. The suggested steps to be used as an outline for analysis are:

    a. Hemisphere emphasis
    b. Sun-Moon blend
    c. Special aspect structures
    d. Idealism aspects
    e. Peregrination
    f. Significator dynamics
    g. Saturn retrograde
       1. Nodal axis
       2. Parental axis
    h. Quindecile
    i. Quintile
    j. Aries Point
    k. Emphasis or absence of an element or mode

Test Yourself

(See test answers, p. 246.)

1. The quindecile measures _____ degrees.

2. How does the quindecile manifest in a horoscope?

3. Venus, placed in the 10th House, is quindecile Saturn retrograde in the 4th House. Capricorn is on the 5th House cusp. What does this suggest?

4. Discuss the possible manifestations of Uranus in the 7th House quindecile the Ascendant.

5. What is suggested when a planet is in quindecile with the Midheaven?

6. Discuss the mnemonic for the quintile aspect.

7. The quintile measures _____ degrees.

8. What does the quintile suggests in a horoscope?

9. Venus, placed in the 10th House, quindecile Saturn retrograde in the 4th House; explain.

10. What does "Aries Point" signify?

11. What is the significance of planets or points configured with the Aries Point?

12. What does Venus at the Aries Point suggest?

13. What is the symbol for the quintile?

14. What guidelines are suggested to organize analysis of the horoscope?

15. What is the suggested orb for the quindecile?

16. How do we abbreviate the Aries Point?

17. What is the suggested orb for the quintile?

18. What is suggested by Aries Point = ♂ ♄?

19. ☿ ♀ ♂ suggests_____involving_____.

20. What are the guidelines for analysis of the quindecile?

Chapter 12

• • •

Speaking the Horoscope

THE EARLY STAGES OF LEARNING TO WORK with any new endeavor, to apply any new skill, are typically accompanied by a period of nervousness and insecurity. High-risk vocations such as airline pilots, surgeons, astronauts, or law enforcement officers have rigorous training programs that prepare them for "the real action" through simulation of actual circumstances. Entertainers have dress rehearsals that allow ensemble members an opportunity to rehearse a performance until a higher level of comfort and familiarity is achieved. No matter what the endeavor is, practicing, rehearsing, and training over and over again breed confidence.

The process of learning astrology is extremely challenging in the beginning stages. There are planetary symbols to learn. There are translations of those symbols into behavioral faculties of planets. You must learn how to combine planets. There are Signs to learn, planets in Signs, aspects, elements, modes; getting a grip on all of it can seem like climbing a mountain that has no top. It is easy to feel insecure in this process of learning what seems to be an endless array of factors.

Since the process of learning astrology, like living life, is a never-ending experience, we have found that, in the beginning stages, it is extremely helpful to **"speak the horoscope," to bring what you know out of your brain into your expression.** Speaking aloud puts the spoken words into your "working system." The brain in turn recognizes that what is spoken aloud is "active data," more so than the data that is simply read or heard. You may read something over and over again without being able to recall what was read. However, when you say the same words aloud, again and again, the words become a part of you. They are in you. They are yours, and the more you say the words aloud, the more confident you become in saying those words. A singer learns confidence and artistry with a song by singing it aloud many times.

Speaking the horoscope increases confidence, especially in the beginning stages of learning. To speak the horoscope, **simply speak out loud about what you see in the horoscope.** For example, using Bill Clinton's horoscope, begin with the planetary positions in their Signs. Say, *"The Sun is at 26 Leo."* Say it! Say it! Say it five or ten times aloud. Say, *"The Moon is at 20 Taurus."* Say it! Say it again and again and again, loudly and confidently. Say, *"Cancer is on the Midheaven,"* or *"The Midheaven is Cancer,"* or *"We've got a Cancer MC here."* Say it ten times. Feel it in your system. Look at that eastern hemisphere emphasis. Ask yourself what it means and then speak the answer aloud again and again. Go through the entire horoscope this way, repeating its components aloud, and **adding what you know the measurements suggest!**

After you have grown accustomed to speaking the horoscope, seek to increase the speed with which you are able to respond to questions. Quickness of response shows confidence. It shows that you know the subject at hand, that it is second nature. All of this helps to prepare your mind to learn with authority and apply what you learn with efficiency.

For example: name the first six Signs of the zodiac and their opposites. Say them strongly. Say all this strongly and, as you do, increase the speed. Quickly now: what is the Sign opposite Pisces? Quickly, say it aloud!

If you still feel less than confident with this process (even though you *do know* the answer), here is a method that will help: see the wheel in your mind, with the natural distribution of Signs in place (Aries on the

Ascendant). See it in your mind's eye. Close your eyes. Visualize it! See the wheel. You know that Pisces is the Sign before Aries. Aries is right on your left eyebrow. Right over your left eyebrow is Pisces! Do you see Pisces there in the 10:00 position? Now, you see Virgo opposing it, right? Yes!

The wheel visualization technique is immensely helpful. Try it whenever you have quiet time.

Please, speak the horoscope often. This exercise is a major part of your learning now. You will be rewarded quickly with growth in pride and confidence!

Test Yourself

(See test answers, p. 248.)

1. Quickly and out aloud, name the Signs of each specific element in mode-order (Cardinal, Fixed, Mutable).

2. Say the Signs of the zodiac in backward order.

3. Looking at the aspect grid of Bill Clinton's horoscope, say the Ptolemaic aspects.

4. Say aloud what each House means. Say them in quick repetition, and then again.

5. Say aloud the Houses that belong to the Angular Grand Cross.

6. Say aloud the Houses that belong to the Succedent Grand Cross.

7. Say aloud the Houses that belong to the Cadent Grand Cross.

8. Say aloud our all-important paragraph about what is suggested when Saturn is retrograde. Say it several times with different voice inflections (for different emotional situations, different clients, different scenarios of development).

9. Quickly: what does the quindecile suggest and how do you interpret it?

10. Quickly: say aloud what the best way is to locate sextiles in a horoscope.

11. Quickly: say aloud what the best way is to locate trines in a horoscope.

12. Quickly: say aloud what the best way is to locate squares in a horoscope.

13. Say the names of the Signs in zodiacal order, *with* the planets that rule them.

14. What is the Sign that refers to Mutable Earth? Quickly, say it aloud.

15. Say the question and answer aloud: "The Succedent Grand Cross of Houses refers to_____."

16. Say aloud how we see *idealism* in the horoscope.

17. Say aloud what each hemisphere emphasis suggests.

18. Say aloud, quickly, the Signs that Mercury and Venus rule.

19. Say the answer aloud: the Angular Grand Cross of Houses refers to _____.

20. In order, say aloud what the Ptolemaic aspects are.

Chapter 13

• • •

Secondary Progressions

THUS FAR, OUR STUDY OF ASTROLOGY HAS IN-cluded various techniques of organizing analysis of the natal horoscope in order to illuminate identity *potential* in life development. In this introductory study of "Secondary Progressions," we are taking the first step toward *expanding* the natal potentials, toward projecting identity development, based upon those natal potentials, *ahead into time*.

Projection vs. Prediction

Predicting is not just an astrological skill. We *all* predict, all the time. Just think how often you predict the weather, the outcome of a sporting event or an election, what your mood will be tomorrow, how your sales presentation will go this afternoon, how your spouse will react to the news you're bringing home. This is a built-in human sense, a function of the mind within its sense of time; it is a faculty we exercise by leading our past experience with certain concerns under certain conditions into future potentials when similar concerns arrange themselves similarly again.

When you visit a doctor for the first time, you provide a full medical history in order to set the base of past experience upon which to anticipate future development. Financial analysts predict future financial trends from the study of past trends involving many dimensions of life and development. Sports gambling is an industry based on prediction through the "odds" (the mathematical probabilities) of winning or losing in the swirl of variables playing on a given situation. If you are accustomed to driving to a certain distant location, you are able to anticipate driving time and conditions ahead of time based on previous trips, much more accurately than from a map.

In today's astrology, we apply a great deal of intelligence and sophistication to the concept of looking ahead in time; we do that by **projecting ahead**, not by making wild, fatalistic predictions based upon what we know about planets.

A "prediction" can too easily overlook the reality of the life that is being addressed, limiting that life to what we expect planets "to do." **Prediction has to give way to *projection*.** When we project forward in time, *we do so based on the life being lived and* the way *the life has been lived*. In this way, our projections are practical and rational. **To a high degree, the only thing that happens is what *can* happen.**

Two people may be born with extremely similar—even identical—horoscopes, but in entirely different life circumstances in which development will occur. For example, one child may be born into wealth and sophistication in Beverly Hills, California while the other, with the same horoscope, is born in Thailand into a depressed farm family. Although the two will assimilate the same astrological factors, they will not manifest the same outcome. Projecting for these two will be *prediction with sensibility*, without blatant fatalism, and with strong recognition of the freedom of choice that is part of human will.

The Formulation of Prediction Systems

The birth horoscope describes the potential for individuation, potentials that are rewarded, developed, and challenged throughout life development in relation to one's environment. Astrology's systems to monitor this development in time have developed slowly over millennia.

The earliest astrologers who could read, write, and measure (third millennium B.C.E.) were intrigued with the closeness in the number of units (degrees) assigned to clarify the circle and the number of day units that defined the year: the 360-degree zodiac and the 365-day year.[1]

Much later, this enduring fascination was embellished through many references to the sky, the heavenly bodies, and especially their relationship with time that appeared in the Bible (from 550 B.C.E. onward): "Let there be lights in the dome of the sky to separate the day from the night; and let them be for signs and for seasons and for days and years and let them be lights in the dome of the sky to give light upon the earth" (*Genesis* 1:14–15). "For everything there is a season, and a time for every matter under heaven: a time to be born, and a time to die;" and "a Day shall be for a year . . . ." (*Ecclesiastes* 3:1–8; approximately 330–200 B.C.E. forward).

Ptolemy (second century C.E.) formally organized celestial mechanics most impressively in relation to the fact that one degree passes over the Midheaven in four minutes of earth time.

These and many other relativity factors motivated inquiry and inspired study toward trying to develop a system that would give the astrologer a way to gauge the passage of potentials into the future. Space (degree) and time (minutes, months, years) were somehow related, and many attempts at systematization were tried.

While observation of the heavens was indeed most sophisticated, there were no rules for planetary motion yet devised, until Johannes Kepler's discovery of these laws in 1607 provided the base for the first Ephemeris. Indeed, there were still arguments about the Earth being round or flat and, for the longest time, arguments about whether the planetary system revolved around the Earth or around the Sun, which wasn't resolved for almost 1600 years after Ptolemy.

Without an Ephemeris, the ancient astrologers, in order to make their predictions, had to rely upon what they could see above them: the rising and setting of the Sun, its angular shift with the seasons of the year, planetary conjunctions, eclipses, the Ptolemaic aspects of relationship (inferring the opposition through eclipse study), comets, and other stars, etc.

Ptolemy created a prediction-specific, very difficult system called "Primary Directions" that was based on the symbolic concept that **every four**

---

1   The concept of 360 units emerged from Sumerian times in Mesopotamia (and probably from Egyptian sources before that): to determine the area of a circle, six equilateral triangles were drawn to abut each other around a single point; a hexagon is formed roughly outlining the circumference of a circle. Each corner of an equilateral triangle is 60 units (degrees), and six of those angles radiate from the central point to form the hexagon (the general circle) totaled 360 units (6 x 60).

minutes after birth is equal to a successive year of life. Primary Directions were terribly demanding and enduring (for some 1500 years) because of their mathematical sophistication! Who could possibly criticize this extraordinary work? In the Renaissance, great Italian mathematicians worked for decades on Ptolemy's work, not to change the system, but to simplify it.

The system of Primary Directions is practically unheard of in today's astrology because the system is so cumbersome with its orientation to the equator instead of the ecliptic, and because it simply can not grasp symbolically the breadth and length of development and change in our life span.[2]

Shortly after Kepler made the Ephemeris possible in the early seventeenth century—allowing astrologers to know the positions of planets into the future—a new method of equating degrees with years (time) was advanced (probably by the Italian Antonio Maginus). **It was the method equating one year of life to each successive day after birth.** This idea of using one day after birth for one year of life was called **Secondary Progressions.**

In studying the relationship between the Earth and Sun, Maginus realized that the Earth's orbit around the Sun gave the Sun an apparent motion that completed exposure to the entire Zodiac *in one year*. The Earth's rotation upon its own axis once each day gave complete exposure to the whole *in one day*. These two intriguingly related motions lead finally to the equations of *one year equals one degree; one degree equals one day; therefore one year equals one day.*

Calculation

Secondary Progressions are a system of prediction that says each day after birth, *in the Ephemeris*, symbolizes a successive year of life. In other words, if a person is born April 15 and has an inquiry about age eleven, the astrologer looks into the Ephemeris and, beginning with the positions on April 15 at birth, adds 11 days, reaching April 27.

In today's world, the computer calculates Secondary Progressions in seconds. But what is the computer doing when it makes that calculation? Let's use President Bill Clinton as an example. Bill Clinton was born

---

2   Every 4 minutes after birth would give a new horoscope for that next year of life; in 6 hours of time (4 x 15 = 60 m [1 hr] for 15 y; 6 hr = 90 y), 90 years of life would be covered. How much does the horoscope change in just 6 hours? Can that possibly reflect the nuance and dynamism of modern life development?

August 19, 1946 at 8:51 A.M. CST, in Hope, Arkansas. He was elected President of the United States in November, 1992, *at the age of 46.* To calculate secondary progressions for Clinton during his election year (his forty-sixth year of life), the computer goes forward 46 days in the Ephemeris to October 4, 1946, *and calculates a horoscope based on the same birth information as if Clinton's birth date were October 4, 1946.* The new calculated positions are then placed by the computer on an outer wheel around the natal horoscope for comparison with the natal positions on the inner wheel (Fig. 29, p. 184). *The progressed positions must be related to the natal positions, to the potentials shown at birth to be significant for analysis.*[3]

Just as you have learned in natal analysis, the "hard aspects" correspond to things happening. In Secondary Progressions, it is the same. **A hard aspect from a progressed planet to a natal position indicates tension that must be resolved in a common-sense manner** (respecting what is possible brings us close to projecting what is probable), in reference to reality experience. "Soft aspects" do not reflect behavior that normally leads to development. In any kind of progression, you are looking to find out which planets and points in progression make *hard* aspects (conjunction, square, opposition) to natal positions and points.

For example, in the case of Clinton, the SP Sun (note the SP abbreviation) is conjoining natal Venus. The computer alignment is not exact relating the SP Sun to natal Venus, but the degree number tells you how close the relationship is. Note the table in the lower right of the chart form that shows the full positions of the SP planets, i.e., the SP Sun is at 10 Libra 46; only 21' of arc separates SP Sun from precise conjunction with natal Venus. That arc of 21' is about 4 months in our symbolism for the Sun. Four months after Clinton's birthday of August 19 brings us to December 19, 1992, just 2 weeks before he was inaugurated president of the United States! SP Sun conjunct natal Venus.

Clinton's natal Sun is in the 11th and rules the 11th, the House of love given by others, acclaim, etc. Venus is very strong in its own Sign and in the first House (natally). It is the leader of his great social cluster at the Ascendant, ruling the Ascendant. All of this is being illuminated by the Sun in development. It is a time when we would expect great popularity

---

3   In response to software prompts, the astrologer keys in "Secondary Progressed" horoscope, "Secondary Progressed Angles (Midheaven, Ascendant).

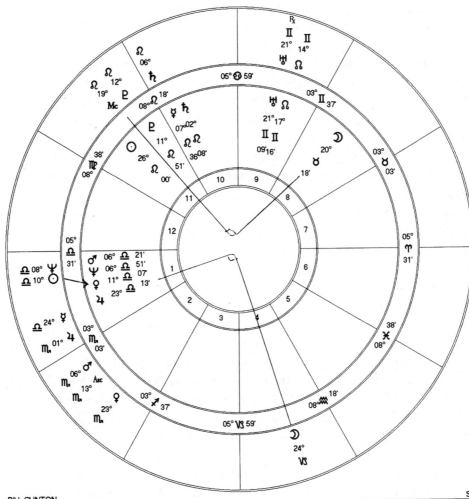

Figure 29
Bill Clinton
Inner Chart: 8/19/46, 8:51 A.M. CST
Outer Chart—SP: 8/19/92, 8:51 A.M. CST
Hope AR, 93W35 33N40

BILL CLINTON

Pl	Geo Lon	Rx	Decl.
☽	20° ♉ 17′ 51″		+15° 32′
☉	26° ♌ 00′ 07″		+12° 51′
☿	07° ♌ 36′ 25″		+17° 18′
♀	11° ♎ 07′ 08″		−05° 07′
♂	06° ♎ 21′ 13″		−02° 08′
♃	23° ♎ 13′ 16″		−08° 00′
♄	02° ♌ 08′ 07″		+19° 56′
♅	21° ♊ 08′ 41″		+23° 13′
♆	06° ♎ 51′ 04″		−01° 23′
♇	11° ♌ 51′ 23″		+23° 22′

SP

Pl	Geo Lon	Rx	Decl.
☽	24° ♑ 05′ 39″		−24° 32′
☉	10° ♎ 46′ 28″		−04° 16′
☿	24° ♎ 59′ 17″		−10° 03′
♀	23° ♏ 30′ 51″		−23° 39′
♂	06° ♏ 44′ 49″		−13° 51′
♃	01° ♏ 54′ 18″		−11° 12′
♄	06° ♌ 55′ 17″		+18° 52′
♅	21° ♊ 46′ 48″	Rx	+23° 16′
♆	08° ♎ 27′ 09″		−02° 02′
♇	12° ♌ 59′ 02″		+23° 10′

Special Note

In our introductory example here, we are looking at the Secondary Progressed calculations *made for the birthdate* within a progressed year. For Bill Clinton this is the birth date of August 19 projected forward to August 19 in his 46th year, 1992 (and that 46th year after birth in the Ephemeris is October 4, something the computer needs to know, but hereafter you do not). So the positions on the outer wheel of the SP 1992 chart on page 184 are for August 19 of that year. (Make sure you use the SP abbreviation for Secondary Progressions to keep references clear.)

Now, think for a minute: the planets will keep on moving after that projected birth moment! The SP Moon will move one full degree for every month within that SP year (the Moon's average motion per day/year is 12 degrees; $12°/12m = 1$ degree per month)! The SP Sun will move one degree in one year (60'), i.e., $5°$ of arc per month.

With the computer, these changes within the SP year are automatically taken care of: we could have put in October 29 or December 21 or even February 7, 1993 (still within Bill Clinton's 46th year, birthdate-to-birthdate), and the movements would be tabulated precisely, but it is extremely important for us to know exactly what the computer is doing.

and good times in his life. (Please note that if Clinton's natal Sun were in the 12th House, with the progressed Sun conjoining Venus, our projection would be altered.)

Note as well that the SP MC at 19 Leo is square Clinton's natal Moon at 20 Taurus! This links his career development (progression) to his natal reigning need to make things as they should be; Clinton's campaign for the presidency and his inaugural speech in January 1993 was about restructuring American life to a standard that it should have.

The SP Venus is applying to a square with the Sun, meaning that it will be in development (because the aspect orb is applying toward exactness) *over the course of the next two years*, as would be indicated in the

Ephemeris. Understand this! The SP Venus is at 23♏ on October 4. The natal Sun is at 26♌. There is approximately a three-degree separation from exactness at 26♏. On October 5 (representing the next year of Clinton's life), Venus will have moved closer. On October 6 (representing the next year), Venus will have progressed even closer. This process continues until Venus makes the exact square, in which case approximately three years of his life (from 1992 to 1995) will pass from the year that he became President, *the entire period graced by the influence of Venus,* affecting the natal need for acclaim.

These progressions do not suggest that this individual becomes President of the United States! What they suggest is a time of illuminated popularity, which, in the life of a politician, can parallel the winning of an election or a time of popularity and fulfillment within Office already won. Applying the same measurements to the life of an adult whose marital status is single could suggest an important time of relationship illumination, such as marriage. The central energy, illuminating popularity and/or relationships, would be the same for anyone experiencing it. However, the manifestation depends on the life being lived.

Hillary Clinton's horoscope is shown here (Fig. 30, p. 187) for her 45th birthday, October 26, 1992, just two weeks before the 1992 election.[4] It shows the SP Moon just past conjunction with the Ascendant (see below), SP Mercury, ruler of the Midheaven, exactly square the natal Midheaven (tremendous career accentuation), the SP Ascendant opposed natal Uranus (high individuation and projection developing during the two to three-year period *before* the election, during the campaign); and the SP Nodal axis exactly on the horizon axis (a tremendous emphasis of coming into public recognition, through her husband, the 7th House).

Nelson Mandela[5] was given his freedom from prison on November 2, 1990. In his horoscope here (Fig. 31, p. 188), we have asked for the SP measurements for November 2, 1990 exactly. This means that the computer has calculated the SP horoscope to Mandela's birthdate of July 18 in 1990 and then gone beyond with the symbolic motions of the planets and points to arrive at the SP positions for the date of November 2, 1990.

---

4 For many years, Hillary Clinton's birth time was thought to be 8:00 P.M. CST, but recent research and discovery by astrologer Frances McEvoy (Boston) has revealed an error in that birth time, and made the correction to 8:00 A.M. CST (see *The Astrologer's Newsletter*, Feb./Mar. 1998, Vol. XVII, No. 6, Boston).

5 Nelson Mandela's birth time was rectified and published by Noel Tyl, and then, two years later, was actually confirmed by Mandela, within two minutes.

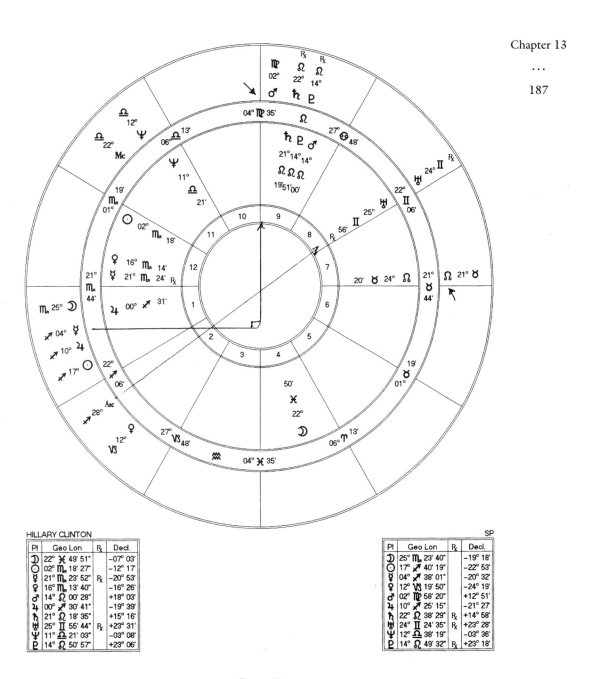

Figure 30
Hillary Clinton
Inner Chart; 10/26/47, 8:00 A.M. CST
Outer Chart: 10/26/92, 8:00 A.M. CST
Chicago IL, 87W39 41N51

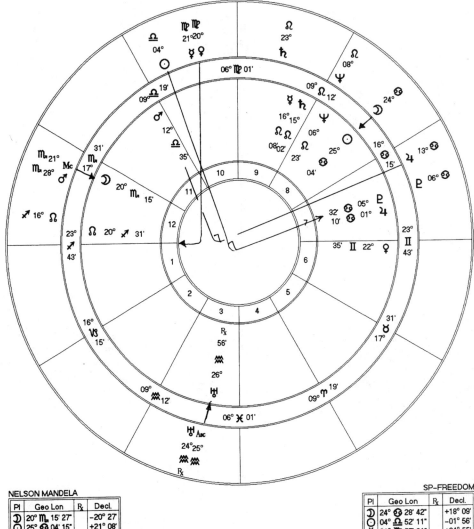

Figure 31
Nelson Mandela
Inner Chart: 7/18/18, 2:54 P.M. EET
Outer Chart: SP Freedom: 11/2/90, 2:54 P.M. EET
Umtata SAFR, 28E47 31S35

We see several telling measurements: SP ASC is tightly conjunct Uranus (what more could one ask for as symbolism of freedom?). The SP Moon has come out of its position "locked away" in the 12th House to conjoin the Sun, which suggests a new beginning because of the New Moon connotation. SP MC is just past conjunction *with the natal Moon*, bringing ego-consciousness in focus with the symbol of his reigning need to gain control of his life. See that SP Mercury and Venus have gotten together in idealistic conjunction and are approaching square to the Ascendant, promising much reform in Mandela's projection and message for the times ahead (Mercury rules the Midheaven and the Public 7th, Venus rules the 11th, acclaim).

The SP Sun is almost exactly square with the powerful Pluto in the 7th House, suggesting the enormous public power ascendancy that began immediately upon Mandela's freedom and led to his becoming President of South Africa in May 1994.

The Secondary Progressed Moon

The measurement of the SP Moon position is the most powerful contribution of Secondary Progressions to prediction technique. The signal the SP Moon sends is *especially important when it goes over the Angles of the natal chart*. This passage over the Angles of the birth chart usually marks a significant change of a person's connection with internal or external environment, or both; a new approach or shift for self-realization.

Passing over the Ascendant, the SP Moon suggests major alterations in life expression. Passing over the 4th House cusp, there is a suggestion of special new beginnings; matters come to an end, and a new period begins, often with a change of residence. Passing over the Descendant, matters having to do with relationships come to the fore. In public personalities, it is a time of a fresh emergence into the public. Crossing the 10th cusp, the Secondary Progressed Moon suggests emphatic focus on the job or career.

For example, look again at President Mandela's horoscope; this time it is set for his Inauguration date on May 10, 1994 (Fig. 32, p. 190). The SP Moon is very tightly conjunct the Midheaven. What could better mark this extraordinary time in his life?!

Note as well in Mr. Mandela's horoscope that the SP Venus is square to his Ascendant. (Indeed, the SP MC is trine to his natal Sun, a background corroboration of this fulfilling time.)

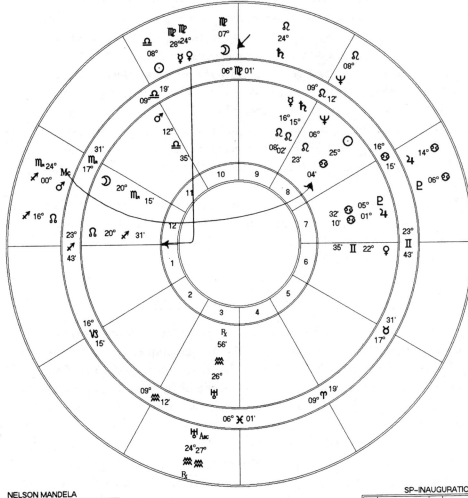

Figure 33
Nelson Mandela
Inner Chart: 7/18/18, 2:54 P.M. EET
Outer Chart: SP Inauguration: 5/10/94, 2:54 P.M. EET
Umtata SAFR, 28E47 31S35

NELSON MANDELA

Pl	Geo Lon	Rx	Decl.
☽	20° ♏ 15' 27"		−20° 27'
☉	25° ♋ 04' 15"		+21° 08'
☿	16° ♌ 08' 00"		+17° 12'
♀	22° ♊ 34' 46"		+22° 00'
♂	12° ♎ 34' 41"		−05° 06'
♃	01° ♋ 10' 03"		+23° 12'
♄	15° ♌ 01' 57"		+17° 13'
♅	26° ♒ 55' 39"	Rx	−13° 16'
♆	06° ♌ 22' 36"		+18° 34'
♇	05° ♋ 32' 29"		+19° 08'

SP-INAUGURATION

Pl	Geo Lon	Rx	Decl.
☽	07° ♍ 52' 05"		+03° 59'
☉	08° ♎ 19' 46"		−03° 18'
☿	28° ♍ 09' 59"		+02° 26'
♀	24° ♊ 55' 59"		+03° 21'
♂	00° ♐ 43' 22"		−21° 20'
♃	14° ♋ 10' 33"		+22° 33'
♄	24° ♌ 17' 48"		+14° 25'
♅	24° ♒ 12' 50"	Rx	−14° 11'
♆	08° ♋ 51' 40"		+17° 57'
♇	06° ♋ 38' 43"		+19° 03'

The Secondary Progressed year can be subdivided into months: the Moon's average daily (yearly) motion is actually 12–13 degrees,[6] which we round off to 12 degrees to be congruent with the twelve months of the year. In analysis of the specific *months* during a progressed year, **simply progress the Moon one degree per month further** from the SP Moon position noted in the outer ring of the given horoscope! The progressed horoscope always represents the progressed year, *beginning with the birth month,* or the progressed year of the event being charted..

Note as well that you can *regress* the SP Moon at sight, similarly: one degree per month *backward* in time, into *earlier* hard aspect configurations.

Returning to Bill Clinton's Secondary Progressed chart (p. 184), notice the SP Moon's location at 24♑. When did the SP Moon cross the preceding Angle? This is how we compute it: 24 degrees (the SP Moon's position), minus 5 degrees (the degree on the 4th House cusp) = 21 degrees, (which equals 19 months). 19 divided by 12 gives 1 year and 7 months *before* November, 1992. That would be the approximate time when the SP Moon would have crossed the all-important 4th House cusp. We can deduce that there was a new beginning, a powerful focus of development, surely related to his realization that he could successfully run for the office of the Presidency, the organization of his campaign. Note that his Moon rules his Midheaven!

Returning to Hillary Clinton (p. 187), the SP Moon had just crossed her Ascendant 4 months earlier (make sure you understand that mental calculation). Now, note that the SP Moon—at the same time—was *square* to her natal Saturn in the 9th ; *and* 7 months yet earlier, the SP Moon was square her natal Pluto! This was the time when her husband's extra-marital affair (Jennifer Flowers) was exposed by the news media, quite a jolt to Hillary's personal perspective indeed, to her personal honor, her projected image.

---

6 In unusual cases, where the Moon's birth date motion approaches 15 degrees, an error may creep in within this calculation shortcut.

A Time for Action

The Secondary Progressed Moon's conjunction, square, or opposition to Saturn are extremely important periods in life-development, times in which the personality will be planning strong career activity or strong changes in general, or, indeed absorbing difficulty/challenge (much as are SP Moon contacts with Angles). These periods of progressed contact occur approximately every seven years (one orbit of the Moon about the Earth approximately every 28–29 days yields, within the SP symbolism, 28–29 years, and the quadrature—28/4—of approximately 7 years. From any beginning point, i.e., from a base contact time between the SP Moon and Saturn (or any other planet or point), successive fourth harmonic (conjunction square, opposition, conjunction, square, etc.) progressed aspects will be made every seven years or so.

For example, for Hillary Clinton (p. 187), SP Moon was square natal Saturn (and conjunct her Ascendant) in June 1992. We can project a cycle from that beginning point by adding successive time periods of 7 years to the beginning mark: June 1992 plus 7 years gives June 1999, i.e., SP Moon is projected within its cycle with natal Saturn (and the Ascendant in this case) to be *opposed* natal Saturn (and square the Ascendant) in June 1999, a critical time in her life, *six months after deliberation by the United States Congress on the impeachment of her husband, the President, for sexual misconduct and lying under oath.* The Secondary Progressed Moon-Saturn quadrature aspects are *calls to action.*

In studying this presentation, have you noticed in Mrs. Clinton's SP horoscope that SP Mars is approaching the Midheaven in the 1992 horoscope (p. 187). It finally arrived at the Midheaven at the time of her greatest life-trial. In fact, SP Mars was *exactly* upon her Midheaven late in October 1998, the exact time when the move to impeach her husband was established, when her personal honor was severely jeopardized in view of the entire world!

Familiarity and experience with Secondary Progressions allow calculation of the Moon's progressed relationship with Saturn without consulting a computer or an Ephemeris. Take the Moon's average daily (yearly) motion as 12 degrees and count ahead in degrees in the horoscope to the first square, conjunction, or opposition with Saturn in the birth horoscope. Then, divide by twelve; *the quotient is the age at which the cycle begins.* This relationship between the SP Moon and Saturn will then repeat every seven years (square, opposition, conjunction, square, etc.). This concept and technique is very helpful as you will see in your work, justifying the repetition here in this presentation.

For example, in Bill Clinton's natal horoscope (p. 29), the distance to Moon conjunct Saturn in his natal horoscope is 72 degrees (a quintile; creative administration). Division by twelve gives age six, the time when his SP Moon-Saturn cycle began. Counting seven years forward successively from the age of six (13, 20, 27, 34, etc.) defines Clinton's SP Moon-Saturn cycle, approximately—enough to alert you to further, more careful calculation and study.

In general, conjunctions, squares, and oppositions from the SP Moon to natal planets are going to mark a time when the behavioral faculty of that planet (or the House it is in or rules) will become emphasized. For example, SP Moon conjunct Venus can indicate a time of heightened romance, the birth of a child, a gala party of importance, a great reception to a new plan, etc.

The Progressed Lunation Cycle

The developing progressed aspect relationship between the SP Moon and SP Sun (not SP Moon to *natal* Sun) is called the *Progressed Lunation Cycle*. It is a cycle of phases and it refers to the "synodic period" of the Moon from new moon to new moon (lasting approximately 29 days).

The cyclic phases of the Moon have become the role model archetype of all cycles of relationship in astrology. The Moon waxes from its new moon to full moon phases and wanes from the full moon to new moon. This basic concept of a phase beginning, reaching a peak and winding down to begin another new phase, increasing and decreasing in light, is what the lunation cycle symbolizes. We take this central archetype and apply it to the relationship between the Secondary Progressed Moon and the Secondary Progressed Sun. This allows us to see the cycle in which we "gain light" and "decrease in light" over the course of a time span that is approximately 28–29 years long.

The monthly lunation cycle begins at the new moon, when the Moon and Sun are in conjunction. The Moon is completely darkened at this point. It cannot be seen. It has no light. This is followed approximately two days later by the crescent of the Moon. At first quarter, the Moon is half full, elevated at the zenith (the Midheaven) as the Sun sets. The zodiacal distance between the Moon and Sun continues to increase in light and is reflected in the Moon's appearance of roundness. When the Moon reaches opposition to the Sun, and is face to face with the Sun, the full moon phase is fulfilled. The Moon is now fully illuminated by the Sun, equal to the Sun in relationship to their distance from the zenith.

The light reflected upon the Moon now begins to decrease as it heads toward the last quarter phase, a time when the Moon is seen at the zenith as the Sun rises. In the days following, the pull toward the Sun compels the Moon to rise later and later, until it becomes lost in the light of the Sun to gain new light.

In the lunation cycle, we are taking this wonderful, poetic relationship between the Moon and Sun and relating it to a 28–29 year cycle of life that allows astrologers to determine, symbolically, whether the person is growing toward fulfillment (full illumination of potentials) or whether they are decreasing in light, heading toward an important new beginning in life.

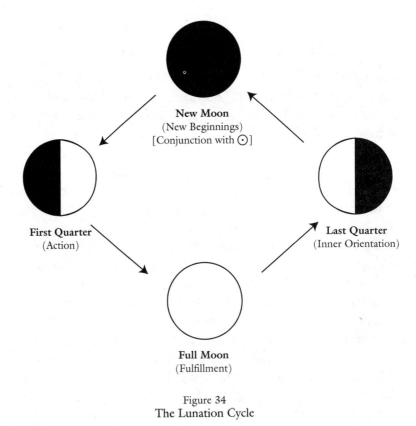

New Moon
(New Beginnings)
[Conjunction with ☉]

First Quarter
(Action)

Last Quarter
(Inner Orientation)

Full Moon
(Fulfillment)

Figure 34
The Lunation Cycle

The cycle begins when the SP Moon and SP Sun are conjunct. This is the New Moon phase of the life cycle. It is a time of important new beginnings, the planting of seeds that will be developed over the duration of the 28–29 year cycle. While the "new beginning" frequently correlates with external events that happen to an individual, it can often symbolize a time when there is an important inner reorientation that is more subtle, less obvious.

With a new path having begun, the life is progressing along the lines of the new seeds that were planted during the new moon phase. The First Quarter phase takes place seven years after the new moon cycle begins. The SP Moon is now 90 degrees from the SP Sun, creating the dynamic tension that you know so much about now. This is a time of action. Things begin to happen *in relationship to what was initiated during the new moon*. It is a time of decision making, of making important commitments.

The Full Moon phase of the cycle occurs 14 years after the new moon phase. Symbolically speaking, if the new moon represents the planting of seeds, the first quarter shows those seeds at the beginning of important development as a visible plant above the ground. Now, in the full moon, those seeds have resulted in a fully developed tree for all to see. Who one is usually becomes fully illuminated. If the path has been earnest, correct, and has been accompanied with hard work, this cycle will usually correlate with a time of reward. There may be the realization that a certain course of action can go no further, thus suggesting a new beginning. Or, it may be the beginning of some kind of an end.

The Last Quarter phase (seven years after full moon) represents the time in the cycle when, symbolically speaking, the leaves begin to fall from the tree. There is a crisis in the formulation and sharing of meaning with people, places, or things. One's inner nature begins to change, and this reflects itself outwardly in a change of values and perspectives. The Self is making preparations for the new cycle ahead by clearing out the things that are no longer useful.

The lunation cycle helps us to see where a person is within a particular cycle of individual growth. Remember, we are either growing toward full illumination or receding from illumination, working toward a new beginning.

Calculating the Lunation Cycle

The easiest way to calculate the lunation cycle is to set your software to calculate square aspects (this includes conjunction, square, and opposition) involving the Secondary Progressed Moon to the Secondary Progressed Sun.

If you do not have access to a computer or software, you can use an Ephemeris to approximate the cycle. For example, look at the Ephemeris section showing Moon and Sun positions for the birth date of August 1, 1954 (p. 197). On this date, the Sun is in Leo and the Moon is in Virgo, **within the new moon phase of the cycle.** (Picture that: see the Leo Sun and place the Virgo Moon separating, in counterclockwise motion, from what had been the new Moon in Leo).

To find the approximate date of the first quarter (working with the symbology of 1 day = 1 year), look to see when the Moon is square (in Scorpio) to the Sun. This date is August 6, when the person is five years old. (Note the square relationship is between two fixed signs, Signs of the same mode, as it should be.)

Now, we want to approximate the year of the full moon. We are looking, from August 6 forward, to the date when the Sun and Moon are in opposition. This will be on August 14. This person's SP Full Moon occurred at the age of approximately 13.

Continuing to find the last quarter, *we see it clearly as August 20*, when the person is 19 years old. A pattern has been set. There is going to be a change in the phase of the cycle approximately every seven days in the Ephemeris.

We now want to find the new moon. Count seven days forward from August 20 and, on August 28, when this person is approximately 27 years old, there was a SP New Moon (note now that the Moon and Sun are both in mutable Signs.). The first quarter is found on September 5 and the Full Moon on September 12, when this person was approximately 42 years old.

The Lunation Cycle in Action

Since I can corroborate the details of my life better than I can detail anyone else's, I will use the lunation cycle in reference to my life as an example. I am the person whose birth date was used here with the ephemeris listing.

My birth date is August 1, 1954. I started primary school in 1959 (first quarter). My teacher immediately discovered that I had musical talent, which was nurtured and supported throughout my school years.

My SP Full Moon was in 1967. That is when I started playing my primary instrument (bass) and developed the ambition to play music professionally. **It is also when I was first introduced to astrology.**

My last progressed quarter in the Lunation Cycle occurred in 1973, a time when major changes took place inside me. I had started playing professionally and began to see life differently. This new way of seeing things reoriented my approach to music and, by 1976, I was associated with one of the leading names in popular music. I also met Noel Tyl for the first time in 1976.

In 1980, just one year prior to my SP New Moon, I was part of a team that won a Grammy Award for our music! That group broke up almost as soon as the award ceremony was over. By now, I had played with or recorded for a plethora of artists. I'd seen more countries than I could remember. Enough was enough. Astrology gained ascendancy in my life. This was the year in which I became a professional astrologer, a New Moon for sure! This SP New Moon was in 1981. I purchased my first computer and astrology software, which changed my astrology radically. I became determined to make a name for myself in astrology. I also got married, my children were born, and developed my ambition to write and produce music.

Ephemeris

GMT + 0:00 Tropical Geo Long	The Moon ☽	The Sun ☉	GMT + 0:00 Tropical Geo Long	The Moon ☽	The Sun ☉
Aug 1 1994	03°♍17'	08°♌12'	Aug 17 1954	27°♓13'	23°♌33'
Aug 2 1954	15°♍57'	09°♌10'	Aug 18 1954	11°♈40'	24°♌31'
Aug 3 1954	28°♍20'	10°♌07'	Aug 19 1954	26°♈08'	25°♌28'
Aug 4 1954	10°♎31'	11°♌05'	Aug 20 1954	10°♉30'	26°♌26'
Aug 5 1954	22°♎31'	12°♌02'	Aug 21 1954	24°♉44'	27°♌24'
Aug 6 1954	04°♏26'	13°♌00'	Aug 22 1954	08°♊48'	28°♌22'
Aug 7 1954	16°♏18'	13°♌57'	Aug 23 1954	22°♊40'	29°♌19'
Aug 8 1954	28°♏13'	14°♌55'	Aug 24 1954	06°♋20'	00°♍17'
Aug 9 1954	10°♐17'	15°♌52'	Aug 25 1954	19°♋48'	01°♍15'
Aug 10 1954	22°♐32'	16°♌50'	Aug 26 1954	03°♌06'	02°♍13'
Aug 11 1954	05°♑05'	17°♌47'	Aug 27 1954	16°♌11'	03°♍11'
Aug 12 1954	17°♑56'	18°♌45'	Aug 28 1954	29°♌04'	04°♍09'
Aug 13 1954	01°♒10'	19°♌42'	Aug 29 1954	11°♍45'	05°♍07'
Aug 14 1954	14°♒45'	20°♌40'	Aug 30 1954	24°♍14'	06°♍05'
Aug 15 1954	28°♒39'	21°♌38'	Aug 31 1954	06°♎31'	07°♍03'
Aug 16 1954	12°♓50'	22°♌35'			

During my first quarter period in the second cycle, several important developments took place in relationship to the seeds that were planted during my New Moon phase: I was called upon to do an astrological radio show. It lasted for three years and was very successful. My articles about astrology began to gain acceptance by the major magazines. Noticing my growth, Noel Tyl invited me to take part in a very sophisticated book project.[7] In music, I was invited to join a team of composers who wrote the music for a weekly television show.

My SP Full Moon began in 1996. I began to do my first lectures in astrology (including invitations to the prestigious United Astrology Congress and Astro2000 conferences). My work was being published frequently. Peer respect and notice among top astrologers came my way. Now, I am cowriting my first book and am an important part of the teaching of astrology in South Africa, a position that has increased my prominence immensely. We could certainly say that who I am is fully illuminated! The seeds that were planted during my New Moon have blossomed. The illumination of my first Full Moon, when I encountered astrology for the first time, has come full circle to a new level!

Other examples of life peaks during individual New or Full Moon cycles: defeated Chancellor of Germany, Helmut Kohl, is just beginning his SP Full Moon (there must be a new perspective for him, framed for his future). George Bush became President of the United States in 1988, one year after his SP Full Moon began. Ronald Reagan's SP Full Moon began in 1977; he became President in 1980. Richard Nixon became President in 1968, one year after his SP New Moon phase began. It is important to note here that, in December 1998, with his life scandal having erupted and impeachment hearing begun, *Bill Clinton was experiencing his SP Full Moon phase,* everything was coming to light.

The Limitations of Secondary Progressions

In comparing Bill Clinton's Secondary Progressed positions to his natal positions, notice that the SP positions of Jupiter, Saturn, Uranus, Neptune, and Pluto have hardly moved at all from their natal positions!

The outer planets move so slowly each day (in our Ephemeris record) that this slowness is translated into very little movement each year in our

---

7 Noel Tyl, *Astrology Looks at History* (St. Paul: Llewellyn Publications, 1995).

day-for-a-year symbolism. In Secondary Progressions, we lose the use of the planets Jupiter-through-Pluto because they do not move enough to create new aspects with other planets in the natal configuration. Just as the SP Moon is so very valuable analytically—because of its swift diurnal motion—so the planets Jupiter-through-Pluto have very little value. The best that can be hoped for is *the completion of an aspect* that is already formed in the natal horoscope, as is the case in Bill Clinton's horoscope, with natal Saturn and natal Mercury in conjunction in the natal horoscope, with a 5-degree orb: SP Saturn closes in on Mercury (his Midheaven ruler) very, very slowly, becoming exact at the height of his scandal late in 1998. This is a fascinating example for sure, but it is also a rare one. The outer planets in Secondary Progressions will rarely be significant factors in astrological appreciation of development.

The creators of the Secondary Progression system in the early seventeenth century did not have this outer-planet slowness problem, since the planets Uranus, Neptune, and Pluto had not yet been discovered; for the great astrologers at that time, the horoscope was overbalanced in favor of the swift-moving inner planets Moon, Mercury, Venus, and Mars. Jupiter and Saturn were the outer reaches, the end of the line, so to speak, the reward in heaven and the end of time.

With the discovery of the outer planets and the increasing complexity of life, much was needed from a symbolic time-projection chart; the Secondary Progression premise, the intriguing involvement of degree, day, year, and cycle, had to be updated and refined. Many theoreticians tackled the problems, but there was always some lack, some variable that could not be harnessed. It was not until the middle of the nineteenth century that the Ptolemaic orientation to the equator was abandoned and the Maginus modernization of Secondary Progressions was improved upon. This updating was accomplished (probably) by W. J. Simmonite, a leading astrology light of Victorian England.

Simmonite devised a system of symbolic predictive measurement that we today call **Solar Arcs**. The system is not difficult but it is masterful, applying the symbolic motion of the Sun in the now-familiar, day-for-a-year formula *to every planet and point in the natal horoscope*, bringing everything forward uniformly in terms of the developing life-energy of the Sun. This creates an enormous number of new aspect-relationships with the natal picture. This is the open door for you into further studies of astrology.

With experience with Secondary Progressions and the all-important use of Transits (Chapter 14), you will have learned an orientation to astrology that is formidable. The polish will come from your further studies in the field, in specific techniques that you will soon call your own, as you now do the many, many measurement and synthesis techniques presented in this volume.

Chapter 14

. . .

Integrated Transits

THE NATAL HOROSCOPE IS MUCH LIKE A loaded gun: the bullets are in the gun and the finger is on the trigger. Secondary Progressions, which we studied in the last chapter, suggest symbolically the aim we take with the gun, and "transits," which we are studying in this chapter, are the actual trigger.

The term "Transits" (tr.) refers to the actual movement of planets in real time.

The planets are always moving; they are always "in transit." Our birth horoscope is a kind of map-photo that captures a specific moment in time *in terms of where the planets are at that moment*. The horoscope chart shows that frozen moment, the transiting planets frozen at particular positions, and it becomes the individual birth portrait.

The predictive system of transits relates measurements of planets-on-the-move at their different rates of motion—where they are in moments of time, future and past—*to aspect contact with the planetary positions preserved in the birth horoscope*.

To a great extent, transits represent energy and activity in the actual environment in actual time; e.g., transiting Mars is like a very flashy, powerful car that is going along (in transit) at a certain speed on a certain path. If transiting Mars comes to where our natal Sun is located (a transiting conjunction), we will have a meeting between Mars and Sun, perhaps a collision (especially if transiting Mars comes to a square "meeting").

Transits—the planetary positions recorded in the Ephemeris on- and off-line—represent the environmental pressures operating upon the individual and how he/she may respond to them.

A planet in transit brings its own intrinsic nature into new relationships within the natal horoscope. In analysis, we primarily look at the transits of the outer planets to the other natal planets and points in the horoscope because—remember—the outer planets, the intrinsically slower moving planets, condition development more emphatically, with more impact, than the swifter-moving inner planets. For this very same reason, transits of the Sun, Moon, Mercury, and Venus are almost always ignored, except in very fine measurements involving a day or an hour. Mars, as a kind of bridge planet between inner and outer planets, usually acts as a catalyst that energizes other developed patterns. **The important, life-changing transits always, always involve the relationship between tr. Pluto, Uranus, Neptune, and/or Saturn to the natal Angles, to the Sun and/or the Moon.**

Astrologically, to appreciate the meanings of specific transits, we use our understanding of planetary/Sign archetypes and House symbolisms. But when we apply this knowledge of transits to the anticipation of events and reactions, we must appreciate humanistically the reality being lived by the "client" who is experiencing the transits. *Not every person responds to specific transits similarly;* and there are many occasions when real life does not allow (admit, support) the occurrence of a signified event; the symbolic transit energy does not manifest in life experience.

On the one hand, we have a grasp of meanings that become potentials. On the other hand, we have a filter for those meanings, an adjustment of how those potentials might manifest, all in terms of what is possible in the life being lived by the client. This is a very important "Reality Principle."

The way we normally protect the sensibility of this process is by respecting the past and using its record to support projection into the future. We record a case history of our client in order to assess reactions to certain transits in the past, in an earlier cycle of transit movement. This helps us anticipate response in a repeat of that measurement in the future, in a future cycle of transit movement. Remember my SP Full Moon when I first was introduced to astrology at the age of 13? I became a professional astrologer at 26 at my SP *New* Moon, and then actually became internationally known and active as an astrologer with my SP *Full* Moon when I was 42. While this is not transit activity, it is a perfect example of a life development pattern in terms of the timing structure of the SP Lunation Cycle; each part of the cycle corresponded to my development in astrology.

Keeping this perspective helps us to avoid the sense of "planets doing something to us" in a fatalistic fashion. By projecting ahead based upon what is *likely* to happen, reasonably, in a person's life, we are being *realistic* instead. **People make things happen; the planets simply reflect this.**

Let's get acquainted with the sense of the most important transits.

Saturn in Transit

In transit, Saturn represents *structure*, either beneficial or restrictive. We can see Saturn as a professor who gives you a test to see how well you have learned your lessons or a supervisor who looks over your shoulder, plans your work, times your work, and teaches you how to do your job better. The idea of necessary controls is vital to our lives; it tells us that we grow through discipline, across boundaries, against pressure. What we learn through a Saturn transit should reward us somehow by restructuring values or strategy. This results in greater efficiency. If this top side does not register, there can be the sense of debility, frustration, delay, even failure. Saturn represents any structure connected with personal security or the threat to it by strict authority or austere confinement. **The Saturn symbolism in transit always carries the dimension of instruction; frustration and delays occur in order for learning (better management of life) to take place. Rewards are given for hard work. The professor rewards you with an "A."**

The TIME STRUCTURE of Saturn Transits

Saturn's orbit around the Sun takes approximately 28 years. Its transit through the zodiac in passage over the Angles and, as well, in aspect to its own natal position in the horoscope, serves as an architectural guide to life development, usually regarding ambition.[1]

When Saturn transits the **Midheaven**, ambition is usually at its highest point of potential development. One is in a position to experience the potential for highest development. This high point of development usually carries through the next seven years (approximately) until transiting Saturn reaches the Ascendant.

When Saturn transits the **Ascendant**, life reaches a peak; a focus of achievement or development that sets the standard for the period to follow (approximately seven years) when Saturn transits the Nadir.

As Saturn moves through Houses 1, 2, 3, if a significant peak standard has not been achieved during the transit of the Ascendant, there is often a period of wandering that follows, a still period in life when one may recede into the background. It can be a period of obscurity that changes powerfully when Saturn transits the nadir.

When Saturn transits the **Nadir**, it typically represents the beginning of a new rise. It is a definitive time of new beginnings, a new start. Life begins to bloom again, possibly through relocation, a change within one's work, etc. So by the time Saturn transits the Descendant, there is a new presentation to others, especially in comparison with the time of Saturn's transit of the Ascendant (opposite the Descendant).

As Saturn continues to transit through the Houses 7–8–9, one is busy working with others en route to again reaching the peak potential of the Midheaven transit.

Saturn's transit over the Angles correlates with very important structural changes in life.

Tr. Saturn's Aspects to its Natal Position

The fourth-harmonic transit of Saturn (the hard aspects) *to its natal position* occurs every seven years in the horoscope. It is so important that it has entered the profile of social development throughout much of the world. Viewing Saturn as ambition, we see the following indicators:

---

1   Grant Lewi, in his book *Astrology for the Millions* (St. Paul: Llewellyn Publications, 1992), gives a masterful presentation of Saturn's transit from Angle to Angle. This book is an indispensable guide to understanding transits, especially the importance of the Saturn transit.

At age 6–7, transiting Saturn squares its natal position; children get their first burst of independence, freedom—out of the home into the school situation.

At age 14–15, transiting Saturn opposes its natal position and we see the adolescent crisis as the teenage years begin, tr. Saturn is staring itself (the natal position) in the face; ambition beckons, but society controls freedom; the adolescent must wait seven more years!

At age 21, there is the social recognition of adulthood, a serious burst to freedom. Mistakes are made, to be corrected probably later, seven years later at 28!

At age 28–30 (and again at 56–60), Saturn returns to its natal position. This extremely important transit is called **the Saturn Return.** The Saturn Return occurs twice (30, 60) during the normal lifetime (three times if you live to be ninety) and at each occurrence it marks deep, conspicuous, important change. There is almost always a complete revision of one's awareness of surrounding conditions, bringing up fundamental realizations that can lead to a complete revision of ideas and plans; by the time the Return has completed itself, one can be living a new life with a deeper purpose, aiming at a more thoroughly comprehended goal. The buildup is usually about 1.5 years: life *should* change direction and/or level.

All of this change potential frequently indicates a dramatic shift in human relations: marriage, divorce, change of jobs, loss of job, death or separation from parents, move to a new locality, or something in the world outside you which alters the course, direction, and pace of life. The Saturn Return can be the most profoundly important period of conspicuous developmental change in one's life!

At age 35–36, Saturn makes the opening square to its natal position: there is a shift of gears regarding ambition.

At age 42–45, Saturn is in opposition to its natal position, just as it was during the onset of the teen years. This is the period of "second adolescence," a time when one sows oats. (At this time, the Secondary Progressed Moon is in opposition to its natal position, giving an emotional intensity while Saturn intensifies ambition. Note that the hard aspect transit of Saturn to its natal position is paralleled by the Secondary Progressed Moon's hard aspect relationship to itself. There is important emotional maturation every seven years that goes along with the important structural changes shown in the Saturn transit.)

At age 49–53, ambition has another shift of gears. There is a reformulation of life's goals.

At age 60 or so, there is the second Saturn Return: a time of retirement considerations.

With Saturn aspecting its own position, we see strong periods within the flow of time. In aspect to the Angles, we have a skeletal structure of time focus. To other planets, we have a measurement structure of specific challenge, events, and reactions that forms identity strongly.

Abbreviated Meaning-Images for the Aspects of Transiting Saturn

Tr.♄☌☉: Usually a time when one is rewarded for diligent work that has been on the correct path, or it is a time when there is failure, delay, or frustration, suggesting a necessity for a fundamental reorganization of affairs. Under this transit, one gets what one deserves, has worked for, on course or not.

Tr. ♄□☉: Readjustment of what happened during the conjunction/opposition.

Tr. ♄☍☉: This can be one of the most frustrating times in life! It suggests introspection and a careful reordering of one's status quo, laying secure foundations carefully and strategically. Things can be as far as they can be from what is desired. It is often a time of hard, hard work and great responsibility.

Tr. ♄☌□☍☽: High sensitivity; emotional challenges; frustration of one's reigning need. Pressure for growth and development. Ambition can pull on the self-image.

Tr. ♄☌□☍☿: Depression; need for objectivity; serious responsibility.

Tr. ♄☌□☍♀: Relationships are challenged, resulting in either a positive restructuring, separation to work things out, a general period of difficulty, or divorce. May also accompany financial difficulties, especially if Venus relates to the 2–8 axis through tenancy or rulership.

Tr. ♄☌□☍♂: A waning of energy; conservatism quelling aggression; frustration.

Tr. ♄☌□☍♃: Brings a sense of practicality to the reward needs.

Saturn transits to Uranus, Neptune, and Pluto should be analyzed in terms of where they are placed in the individual horoscope: the Houses they are in and Houses of rulership are the considerations for Saturn's

sense of restructuring of one's status quo. In general, the transit to
Uranus symbolizes a restructuring of individuality; in aspect to Neptune,
a restructuring of ideals; in aspect to Pluto, a restructuring of one's perspective through hard, hard work or super achievement.

Uranus in Transit

The orbit of Uranus uses 84 years to circle the Sun. It stays in each Sign,
via transit, for approximately 7 years. **In transit, Uranus represents
quick, sudden, unpredictable intensified change, usually in the name
of individuation.** *It intensifies what it touches,* **always giving a situation more urgency at the time than it actually has. In transit, Uranus
is still Bzzzzzzzzz!**

Angular Transits of Uranus

When **Uranus transits the Ascendant**, the emphasis of individuation is
at its peak. One has the need to redefine oneself. If the years prior to the
Uranus transit have been experienced as boring, dismal, or even oppres-
sive, this transit will usually represent the time in life when "the shackles"
come off the oppression. As the Ascendant is in opposition to the
Descendant, if one is married when this transit occurs, the marriage may
be challenged in the face of this new burst of individuation. With very
high reliability, Uranus transiting the Ascendant represents *relocation*.

When **Uranus transits the Nadir**, as at the Ascendant, a time of relocation is very often represented. There will also be important new beginnings and endings with the job/profession (tr. Uranus opposing the MC,
as it crosses the Nadir).

When **Uranus transits the Descendant**, the manifestation is similar to
the Ascendant transit but with more of an emphasis on one's partner,
marriage, relationship. There may still be the sense of a redefinition of
oneself but this occurs now because of someone else, not from within, as
is the case with the Ascendant transit.

When **Uranus transits the Midheaven**, the typical manifestation is
one of sudden developments on the job, career, etc. In the life of a child,
there may be a sudden development in the parental situation because of a
parent's work development that results in relocation.

Uranus Transits to its Own Position

At age 21, **Uranus squares itself** at the same time transiting Saturn squares *its* own natal position, both emphasizing the determined burst of freedom that is typical when one is legally recognized as an adult in most cultures of the world. When **Uranus transits in opposition to its natal position** at about age 42, it represents a strong push to individuation; is the grass greener elsewhere?

When transiting Uranus opposes itself, remember that, at the same time that transiting Saturn and the SP Moon oppose their respective natal positions! This period in life correlates with an intense rejuvenation of individuality, young thoughts, ideas, and energies, disruptions, and sudden breakups. It is the time to do what you have always wanted to do!

At roughly age 63, individual attention to the Self's individuation in the world gives way to paying attention to the Self within personal realms.

Note: Uranus' orbit of the Sun once every 84 years means (when divided by twelve) that it transits one House approximately every seven years. This tells us that there is an important shift of experience for the process of individuation every seven years. It is fascinating, with the accumulation of astrological references to seven year portions of time, how that has entered our Western society and is reflected in traditions, in sayings, and in the very structure of life development.

Transits of Uranus to Planets

Tr. ♅ ☌ ☐ ☍ ☉: The life energy is given a jolt of intensity that frequently represents a breaking of ties, confrontation with new people, places, and things, impulse, self-centered energies, abruptness, sudden shifts in status, rebellious reactions to unfavorable conditions in life, especially in the Houses that the Sun is in and rules.

Tr. ♅ ☌ ☐ ☍ ☽: Emotional intensification with a strong urge to "express yourself." Discontent with things leads to impulsive changes. Individuation rules the roost.

Tr. ♅ ☌ ☐ ☍ ☿: Creativity, nervousness, sudden ideas, travel, mental stimulation.

Tr. ♅ ☌ ☐ ☍ ♀: Relationship intensity, either through the excitement of a new beginning or the experience of a sudden ending.

Tr. ♅ ☌ ☐ ☍ ♂: Impulse, accidents, temperament, strong drive.

Tr. ♅☌□☍♃: A time of potential good luck, profit, and gain if one deserves it.

Tr. ♅☌□☍♄: Ambition is given an intense push; the urge to break free from an old or restrictive circumstance.

Tr. ♅☌□☍♆: A strong alert to spiritual sensitivity or collusion.

Tr. ♅☌□☍♇: The big challenge, the big break.

Neptune in Transit

The orbit of Neptune takes 165 years. In hard aspect transits, Neptune can manifest in an inspired, spiritual or creative way or in tremendous confusion, insecurity, and uncertainty.

Neptune Transits to Planets

Neptune's transit to ANY Angle, the Sun or Moon most frequently manifests as a time of great challenge and difficulty or a strange vacuum, so much so that the ego can experiencs a "wipe-out time."

For example, Bill Cosby, the internationally famous entertainer, suffered two extraordinary turns of events in January 1997 (Fig. 33, p. 210). His son Enis was murdered, and Cosby himself was served papers to appear in court for purposes of child support. These events occurred *on the same day!* Imagine the turmoil in life for this man at that time. Although Cosby was acquitted of the paternity charge, the incident tarnished his "squeaky clean," family-man image. Transiting Neptune was precisely upon Cosby's Midheaven when this happened. This is a slow transit, of course, and the gloom it represented in Cosby's life was protracted through the legal trials of his son's murderer and his work to salvage his public reputation.

Tr. ♆☌□☍☿: Mental confusion and uncertainty or creativity.

Tr. ♆☌□☍♀: Deception, illusion, or relationship idealism, perhaps insecurity; a confused relationship.

Tr. ♆☌□☍♂: A cloud over one's energy focus or an inspired, inspirational push manifesting as a period of heightened charisma in life.

Tr. ♆☌□☍♃: The potential for opportunity can be sharply increased or mysteriously lost.

Tr. ♆☌□☍♄: Ambition can crumble, go to sleep, under this aspect. If one has been involved in illegalities, this transit can manifest the results. Generally speaking, there is confusion and uncertainty about one's status quo, *whatever it may be.*

Figure 33
Bill Cosby
Inner Chart: 7/12/37, 1:39 A.M. EDT
Outer Chart—Tr: 1/15/97
Philadelphia PA
75W09 39N57

Pluto in Transit

Pluto's erratic orbit around the Sun is approximately 265 years. Under most circumstances, it will cross only one Angle of the horoscope in a lifetime; it will make the quadrature square to itself at the same approximate time that transiting Saturn and Uranus make squares to their respective natal positions!

When Pluto transits an Angle (or, as well, the Sun or Moon), conditions in life press for a major change of perspective, usually through some overpowering life event. Pluto transits typically suggest a surfacing of something that has to be eradicated from the life in order for it to function better. It is common for this eradication to involve a significant death in the life. In Pluto transits of the Angles, Sun, or Moon, something will surely come to an end in order for a new beginning (perspective) to take place.

With Pluto's link to empowerment and prominence, the transits can indicate times when one is propelled forward prominently *in beneficial ways* as well, thereby lending a new perspective to the *status quo*. In aspect to Mercury, the mind takes on a new perspective; in aspect to Venus, relationships or finances are highlighted; in aspect to Mars, there is an increase in the potential for accidents through force. In aspect to Jupiter, there is a tremendous potential for gain.

When transiting Pluto is ☌ ☐ ☍ ♄ (or vice versa), there is the suggestion of tremendous difficulty and hard, hard work. It can represent a severely difficult period of loss, filled with trial and error. There is also the potential for one to make superhuman gains during this transit, but it is most typically experienced as difficulty, especially if Saturn is prominent in the horoscope. Saturn's symbolism tries to maintain structure and it is Pluto's job to alter things for a new perspective.

Jupiter in Transit

Jupiter's orbit takes 12 years. In transit, Jupiter expands, rewards, presents opportunities, and generally represents a time when things "step-up." It is important to understand that the wonderful things that can correlate with a Jupiter transit *come to those who have prepared for them. Being prepared **invites** rewards, opportunities, and luck.*

Jupiter transits can also expand something in the natal horoscope that is debilitated by strong aspect and position; a period when that something that is inherently difficult is expanded into even more difficulty.

Jupiter Transits

Tr. ♃ ☌ □ ☍ ☉: During Jupiter's 12-year orbit, Jupiter will aspect the Sun by quadrature every three years. Jupiter-Sun transits can correspond to major periods of opportunity, especially in *conjunction* with the Sun. Reward comes. There is a heightened sense of well being. The transit of Jupiter to the Sun defines the reward cycle.

Knowing where Jupiter is in the present, one can count back one year per Sign to reach the Sun Sign of the person. This establishes the time of the Jupiter-Sun transit for the person and sets the 12-year cycle of conjunction, into the past and into the future. For example, my natal Sun is in Leo. Jupiter is in Pisces right now in 1998, a separation (going backwards in the zodiac to Leo) of 7 Signs, or 7 years. That would be the approximated time (1991) that I experienced my last Jupiter-Sun transit, establishing 1991, 1994, 1997, 2000, 1988, 1985, etc., as the years when my Jupiter-Sun contacts (conjunction, square, opposition) occurred. Think about it. Understand it! (Check your mental deductions against the 100-year transit Tables contained in Noel Tyl's *Synthesis & Counseling in Astrology: the Professional Manual.*)

Tr. ♃ ☌ □ ☍ ☽: One's emotional well-being is enhanced. The reigning need is fulfilled.

Tr. ♃ ☌ □ ☍ ☿: A period of heightened, beneficial learning, moving, travel; a positive state of mind.

Tr. ♃ ☌ □ ☍ ♀: A heightened, expansive period of social, romantic, or aesthetic concerns.

Tr. ♃ ☌ □ ☍ ♂: High energy.

Tr. ♃ ☌ □ ☍ ♃: A 12-year cycle (similar to that of Tr Jup-Sun) and a period in which important plans and ideas are revised. The period may include big new steps that have long-range implications. The squares and oppositions indicate minor shifts in what was initiated in the conjunction.

Tr. ♃ ☌ □ ☍ ♄: Ambition is given a lift.

Tr. ♃ ☌ □ ☍ ♅: Expands the ego and brings opportunity for beneficial self-expression.

Jupiter and Saturn cycles reward needs and ambition, and seem to work together in transit. Jupiter transits its own place at age 24, just after the Saturn closing square to its natal position and before the Saturn Return. Jupiter returns to its own place for the third time at age 36, just after Saturn makes the square opening to its natal position in its second orbit. Jupiter opposes its natal position at the age of 42 when Saturn opposes its natal position. What this tells us is that ambition and reward have *prescribed checkpoints* at very important times of life. It seems that Jupiter provides the reward opportunity after Saturn makes the shift in ambition. Fascinating, isn't it!

From Jupiter through Pluto, we have seen that the transits of these planets all seem to come together at important times in life. The key ages in development are established at ages 7, 14, 21, 28 through 30, 35, 42, etc. The point made here is that **at every major quadrature point of Saturn's superstructure, all the planets say something.**

Mars in Transit

Being relatively as close to the Sun as the Earth is, Mars moves swiftly and does not have a dramatic, lasting impact on life normally. It usually acts as a trigger to other measurements.

The Mars orbit measures 22 months, returning to its natal position approximately every two years of life. The opposition occurs during every other odd-numbered year of age. Conjunctions occur at ages 2, 4, 6, 8, 10, etc. Oppositions occur at ages 1, 3, 5, 7, 9, 11, 13, etc. When Mars returns to its own position, there is the suggestion of refreshed energy in terms of Mars position in the natal horoscope. There can be new starts, renewed energy.

When Mars *opposes* its own position, there is a suggestion that the energies of others are pulling or attacking us. The tension and restlessness that are a normal part of the Mars transit are still there, it's just that the opposition highlights an awareness of this faculty in/from others.

The squares of Mars to its own position suggest adjustments of applied energy in terms of the conjunction and opposition.

In general, Mars transits suggest a stirring up, an assertion of energy in the terms of the planet being transited:

Tr. ♂♂□♂☉: The arousal of one's core life energy in terms of the Sun's House position in the horoscope. The square suggests much ego assertion and drive, while the opposition is an awareness of the energy of others through arguments, fights, etc. There can be fevers, emotional upsets; hot-headedness.

Tr. ♂♂□♂☽: In the conjunction and squares, the emotions are stirred up, manifesting through a show of ego in the terms suggested by the Moon's reigning need. The opposition suggests demands on the Self from others that manifest in temperamental displays of emotion.

Tr. ♂♂ □ ♂ ☿: A heightening of the nervous system; snap judgments, rash decisions, travel mishaps.

Tr. ♂♂ □ ♂ ♀: Passion; glamour; spending too much money.

Tr. ♂♂ □ ♂ ♃: The energizing of opportunity in terms of Jupiter's natal placement. Extravagance, waste, going overboard.

Tr. ♂ □ ♂ ♄: Frustration!

Tr. ♂♂ □ ♂ ♅: Temperament, haste, accidents, anxiety.

Tr. ♂♂ □ ♂ ♆: The stirring up of intuition, imagination; a short period where one's charisma and attractiveness may be heightened.

Tr. ♂♂ □ ♂ ♇: Energy and temperament are stirred up to full potential.

The Mars–Saturn Connection

Saturn, the symbol of ambition, describes the building of ambition, architecturally speaking. This architecture of advance requires new starts of ego energy. When Saturn makes its first square (age 7), Mars will have made three orbits, and be back at its natal position (age 6). When Saturn opposes itself (age 14), Mars will again be in opposition to its natal position (age 15). At 21, Saturn squares its own position at the same time Mars opposes its own position. This interplay between Mars and Saturn occurs throughout life, symbolically showing the relationship between the advancement of ambition and new starts of ego energy.

Integrated Transit Summary

Age 7: Saturn squares its natal position, SP Moon squares its natal position, Mars opposes its natal position, preceded by Jupiter opposition. We are off to school, we grow a bit emotionally.

Age 14: Saturn opposes its natal position, SP Moon opposes its natal position, preceded by Jupiter's return to its natal position. There are the Mars conjunction/opposition to its natal position at the respective ages of 12–14 and 13–15. Uranus has shifted into another House. This represents the adolescent crisis, another step in emotional growth and toward more freedom.

Age 21: Saturn and the SP Moon square their natal positions; Uranus squares its natal position; Mars opposes its natal position: there is a burst of freedom and an enormous social importance attached to this age.

Age 24: Jupiter makes its second return, corresponding to opportunities based upon what happened at age 21 and paving the way for the Saturn Return at age 28.

Age 28–30: Saturn, SP Moon, and Mars Return to their natal positions; Jupiter opposes its natal position; Uranus trines its natal position: a time of conspicuous change, full emotional maturation, opportunity. The new individuality is given support.

Age 35: Saturn and SP Moon square their natal positions; Mars opposes its natal position: a shift of gears regarding ambition and another step in emotional growth pave the way for the Jupiter Return at age 36, a time of opportunity potential.

Age 42: Saturn and SP Moon oppose their natal positions; Mars returns, Jupiter opposes, Uranus opposes, Neptune squares, and Pluto squares! This is a second adolescence, a time when there is a very serious burst of freedom—thus the midlife crisis.

Age 49: Saturn and SP Moon square their natal positions one year after Jupiter returns; Mars returns.

Age 56: Saturn and the SP Moon return; Jupiter returns (age 60); Mars returns, Uranus and Neptune trine: conspicuous change of level.

Age 63: Saturn and SP Moon square.

The Erratic Nature of Transits

It is important to note that transit periods do not always work like clockwork. The slightly erratic nature of the periods is due to the distances between the planets and the Sun. For example, Pluto is extremely erratic. As we have learned, its orbit is 248 years. Pluto was in Aquarius for 21 years, Pisces for 25 years, Aries for 29 years, Taurus for 31, Gemini for 30, Cancer for 25, Leo for 18, Virgo for 15, Libra for 12, and Scorpio for 11 years. This erratic motion is due to Pluto's range of distance from the Sun and its elliptical orbit. It has actually transited inside the orbit of Neptune! Since its move closer to the Sun, it moves more quickly.

Another factor in erratic orbit times, aside from retrogradation, is called long and short Ascension. The Signs Cancer, Leo, Virgo, Libra, Scorpio, and Sagittarius are called Signs of long Ascension because they take longer to ascend above the horizon than the other six Signs, called the Signs of short Ascension (Capricorn through Gemini).

As a result of this phenomenon, **certain transits will last longer through certain signs than through others.** Saturn, for example, spends an average of two-and-a-half years per Sign, but the transit time spent in Signs of longer Ascension is longer (several months) than in Signs of short Ascension.

Retrogradation and Orbs

Because of the phenomenon of retrogradation, a planet in transit will typically aspect a planet or point *three times!* In most cases, the first and/or last contacts will have the most emphasized manifestation in life.

It is important to understand the idea that the exactness of an aspect refers to the completion or peak of a process *already in development.* For example, if transiting Saturn is exactly square a person's Venus, we expect a positive restructuring or severe testing of relationship, possibly ending in breakup, divorce, etc. At what point did the relationship actually begin to break up? It did not, all of a sudden, come to an end on the day that transiting Saturn squared Venus! The transit simply indicated the peak of a process that had been in development already!

Understand that an orb of application and separation for a transiting planet aspecting a natal planet represents a "span of consciousness" (a marvelous Tyl description). Things do not usually happen in life on the precise day an astrological aspect is exact; there is a gradualism, a build-up, and afterward, an easing up of significances. With transits, we are talking more about specific time periods than we are exact dates.

In general, when an outer planet is making an aspect, its influence will be felt in the life within two or three degrees of its exactness.[2] The influence will begin to recede when the planet is two degrees separating from partile.

Analysis

Whew! You have learned a lot about transits, and very soon you will have the feel of these transits, knowing the characteristics of planets-on-the-move and the nature of fourth-harmonic aspect influences on the natal symbols of needs and behavioral faculties.

Here are three guidelines to help you get comfortable with the analysis of a transits:

- Noticing that a specific transit is significant within a horoscope (hard aspects from outer planets to natal positions and Angles are the most significant), you first examine the symbolism (archetype) of the transiting planet, with reference to the House location of

---

2 We use the term "partile" when referring to an exact aspect.

the planet being transited and the House ruled by the planet being transited.[3]

- To gain a sense of the energy development in process, examine the natal position of the transiting planet.

- Check to see if other transits are in effect at the same time (don't forget the Secondary Progressed Moon).

For example, Figure 34 (p. 218) shows the horoscope of actress Demi Moore. Between June and August 1998, Moore's life underwent two very serious changes through the death of her mother and the breakup of her marriage due to her husband's relationship with another woman.

The transits are set for mid-July and you see transiting Uranus exactly square Mercury. Mercury is placed in the 8th House natally (affairs of death; her husband's resources) and rules the 4th (a parent) and 7th Houses (relationships), all of which were intensified.

Transiting Saturn squares its natal position, a shift of gears, an adjustment in terms of what the natal synthesis of *her* Saturn—the love received from her partner (Saturn ruling the 11th).

Figure 35 (p. 220) shows the horoscope of Chelsea Clinton again, with transits set for September 1, 1998, the time period when her father made it publicly known that he had been dishonest in his discussions of the Monica Lewinsky scandal.

Transiting Pluto is squaring her Sun (note: the aspect is not exact, it is *applying*, and promises quite a difficult time ahead with regard to the change in her life perspective due to the scandal). The Sun is in the 4th House (a parent) and rules the 10th House (the other parental house). This is a clear symbolism that spells the change of perspective she certainly experienced through a very trying period in her life.

In addition, transiting Uranus (ruler of the 4th) is in exact opposition to her Moon, suggesting emotional intensification and excitation, corroborated by transiting Mars conjunction to her Moon. Seeing these indications of parental upheaval almost forces you to analyze the horoscopes of her parents to see what was happening during the same time period.

---

3 You will also find that the symbolism of the planet being transited becomes the focal manifestation, regardless of the House it is in or the House it rules. For example, a transit of, say, Pluto to natal Venus is usually going to manifest a change of perspective in terms of Venus, regardless of House tenancy or rulership. In this example, the inclusion of the House being tenanted and the one that planet rules will bring in additional factors that are being affected by the transit.

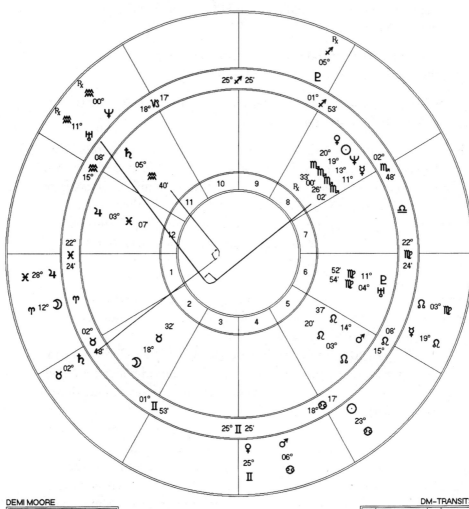

DEMI MOORE

Pl	Geo Lon	Rx	Decl.
☽	18° ♉ 32' 20"		+12° 42'
☉	19° ♏ 00' 17"		−17° 28'
☿	11° ♏ 02' 00"		−14° 15'
♀	20° ♏ 32' 30"	Rx	−22° 01'
♂	14° ♌ 36' 45"		+18° 12'
♃	03° ♓ 07' 28"		−11° 32'
♄	05° ♒ 40' 24"		−19° 35'
♅	04° ♍ 54' 16"		+10° 24'
♆	13° ♏ 26' 13"		−14° 14'
♇	11° ♍ 52' 28"		+19° 18'

DM–TRANSITS

Pl	Geo Lon	Rx	Decl.
☽	12° ♈ 40' 54"		+01° 54'
☉	23° ♑ 08' 00"		+21° 27'
☿	19° ♌ 46' 39"		+14° 29'
♀	25° ♊ 26' 27"		+22° 28'
♂	06° ♋ 22' 28"		+23° 58'
♃	28° ♓ 03' 06"		−02° 00'
♄	02° ♉ 48' 35"		+10° 08'
♅	11° ♒ 29' 11"	Rx	−17° 59'
♆	00° ♒ 59' 18"	Rx	−19° 36'
♇	05° ♐ 33' 19"	Rx	−09° 11'

Figure 34
Demi Moore
Inner Chart: 11/11/62, 2:16 P.M. MST
Outer Chart—DM Tr: 1/15/98
Roswell NM, 104W31 33N24

Now, let's look again at Hillary Clinton's horoscope (Fig. 36, p. 221) for the same time, the height of Bill Clinton's scandal, September 1, 1998:

Transiting Saturn is in opposition to her Sun (this can be one of the most frustrating times in life) and transiting Neptune is applying over the signline to a square with the Sun (ego wipeout time). Transiting Pluto at 5 Sagittarius is squaring the Midheaven (a major change of perspective in profession, in public recognition). Transiting Mars at 7 Leo, moving about 30' of arc a day, is at its natal position *conjunct Pluto* (here in the 9th House, calling legalities and attack into the picture).

Now, follow the notes about the horoscope: tr. Saturn is retrograde early in September 1998, which means it is transiting backward into a second opposition with Hillary Clinton's Sun (her Sun rules the 9th as well); and then there will be a Station, and Saturn, in direct motion, will make a third opposition (the final one) and start to separate from the Sun. This takes place in March 1999.

At the same time, tr. Neptune moves to 2 Aquarius *square the Sun* in February 1999; tr. Uranus moves to 14 Aquarius exactly opposed the natal Mars-Pluto conjunction, exact in March 1999; and tr. Mars will have transited on to 2 Scorpio, exactly conjoined the Sun in February 1999.

It is clear (and indeed alarming) to see all of this energy symbolically so focused in February and March 1999. A very tough time is ahead for Mrs. Clinton. What will emerge to order her life?

Chelsea and Hillary are absorbing the same transits as everyone else in the world at that time—the transits being where the planets are around the Earth—but **the manifestation within an individual life is suggested by the relationship of those transiting positions to the natal configurations** that *are* Chelsea, that *are* Hillary.

Bill Clinton absorbed them too. Look at his horoscope (Fig. 37, p. 223). In the time period we are studying, September 1, 1998, tr. Saturn was at 3 Taurus, opposed Hillary's Sun and **tightly square Bill's natal Saturn in the 10th!** Transiting Neptune was at 29♑, making an over-the-signline square with Hillary's Sun and was **opposing his natal Saturn!** (This means that Bill's natal Saturn natally is exactly square Hillary's natal Sun, a very, very difficult relationship within a partnership, from one horoscope to another!)[4]

---

4 You will learn with experience that when Saturn and Neptune in transit are aspecting the same planet or point, there is a suggestion of anguish that permeates the time period. Here, in Bill Clinton's horoscope, we see that anguish being in terms of career matters, of ambition, of the public honor.

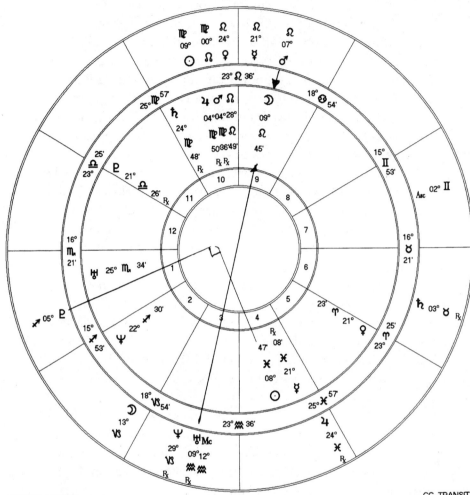

Figure 35
Chelsea Clinton
Inner Chart: 2/27/80, 11:24 P.M. CST
Outer Chart—CC Tr: 9/1/98
Little Rock AR, 92W17 34N45

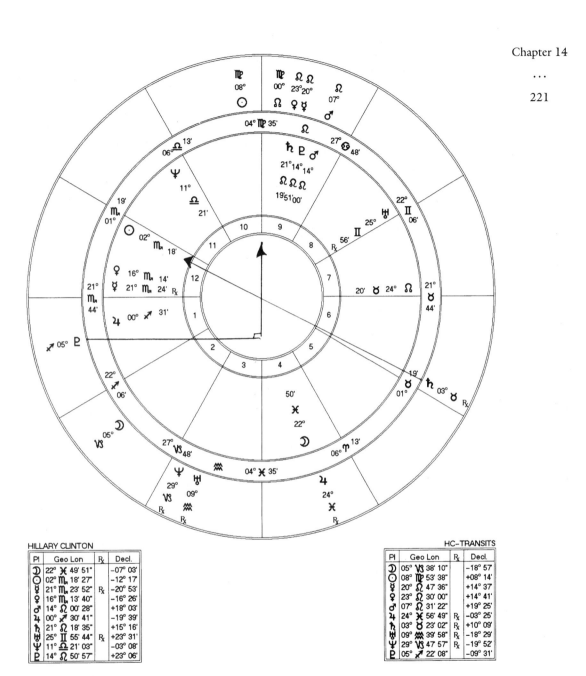

Figure 36
Hillary Clinton
Inner Chart: 10/26/47, 8:00 A.M. CST
Outer Chart—HC Tr: 9/1/98
Chicago IL, 87W39 41N51

HILLARY CLINTON

Pl	Geo Lon	Rx	Decl.
☽	22° ♓ 49' 51"		–07° 03'
☉	02° ♏ 18' 27"		–12° 17'
☿	21° ♏ 23' 52"	Rx	–20° 53'
♀	16° ♏ 13' 40"		–16° 26'
♂	14° ♌ 00' 28"		+18° 03'
♃	00° ♐ 30' 41"		–19° 39'
♄	21° ♌ 18' 35"		+15° 16'
♅	25° ♊ 55' 44"	Rx	+23° 31'
♆	11° ♎ 21' 03"		–03° 08'
♇	14° ♌ 50' 57"		+23° 06'

HC–TRANSITS

Pl	Geo Lon	Rx	Decl.
☽	05° ♑ 38' 10"		–18° 57'
☉	08° ♍ 53' 38"		+08° 14'
☿	20° ♌ 47' 36"		+14° 37'
♀	23° ♌ 30' 00"		+14° 41'
♂	07° ♍ 31' 22"		+19° 25'
♃	24° ♓ 56' 49"	Rx	–03° 25'
♄	03° ♉ 23' 02"	Rx	+10° 09'
♅	09° ♒ 39' 58"	Rx	–18° 29'
♆	29° ♑ 47' 57"	Rx	–19° 52'
♇	05° ♐ 22' 08"		–09° 31'

When we add yet another dimension, the picture becomes even more fascinating! Monica Lewinsky's horoscope is shown here (Fig. 38, p. 224) with her transits set for February 1, 1998, just after the scandal about her relationship with President Clinton became public.

Transiting Saturn is exactly(!) **conjunct the Descendant** (a new showing of Self to the public, indeed); transiting Uranus is exactly conjunct her Jupiter in the 4th (shaking up the home life, for sure) and nearly exactly square her Moon, suggesting sudden intensification in relationship and/or within the public. Note that the Moon here rules Monica's Midheaven: the Uranian transit zaps this situation into enormous prominence in terms of her work (and job strategies were central to the affair as it has been disclosed) and public honor.

And let's hope you spotted the key of it all here: tr. Neptune at 00 Aquarius is exactly opposite Lewinsky's Sun! Her ego has been wiped out in this relationship scandal with the President of the United States.

It is important to note that, if Lewinsky were a classical composer or an artist, the Neptune transit would have had a different potential manifestation. If Hillary Clinton were in a different society, living at a different level, say as a farmer in New Zealand, she may have still experienced ego wipeout but it would have been related to what could happen *living life at that level*. Remember, the only thing that will happen is what can happen. Always, always look at the person's life first instead of seeking to control that life through descriptive astrology.

Remember, you do not need to do a double-wheel printout to see transits. They occur continuously and capturing them on one date or another by computer is very time consuming. Simply find a century ephemeris and refer to that for the years to come, or better yet, use the tables in the Appendix of *Synthesis & Counseling in Astrology: The Professional Manual*, by Noel Tyl. You can see transits past and future **at a glance!**

For further study of transits, we recommend strongly the book *Planets in Transit* by Robert Hand (Gloucester, MA: ParaResearch, 1976).

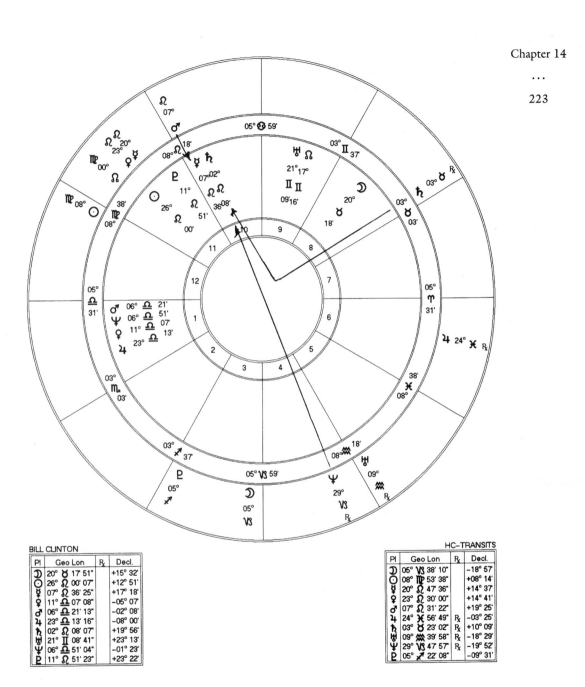

Figure 37
Bill Clinton
Inner Chart: 8/19/46, 8:51 A.M. CST
Outer Chart: BC—Tr: 9/1/98
Hope AR, 93W35 33N40

BILL CLINTON

Pl	Geo Lon	Rx	Decl.
☽	20° ♉ 17' 51"		+15° 32'
☉	26° ♌ 00' 07"		+12° 51'
☿	07° ♌ 36' 25"		+17° 18'
♀	11° ♎ 07' 08"		−05° 07'
♂	06° ♎ 21' 13"		−02° 08'
♃	23° ♎ 13' 16"		−08° 00'
♄	02° ♌ 08' 07"		+19° 56'
♅	21° ♊ 08' 41"		+23° 13'
♆	06° ♎ 51' 04"		−01° 23'
♇	11° ♌ 51' 23"		+23° 22'

HC-TRANSITS

Pl	Geo Lon	Rx	Decl.
☽	05° ♑ 38' 10"		−18° 57'
☉	08° ♍ 53' 38"		+08° 14'
☿	20° ♌ 47' 36"		+14° 37'
♀	23° ♌ 30' 00"		+14° 41'
♂	07° ♌ 31' 22"		+19° 25'
♃	24° ♓ 56' 49"	Rx	−03° 25'
♄	03° ♉ 23' 02"	Rx	+10° 09'
♅	09° ♒ 39' 58"	Rx	−18° 29'
♆	29° ♑ 47' 57"	Rx	−19° 52'
♇	05° ♐ 22' 08"		−09° 31'

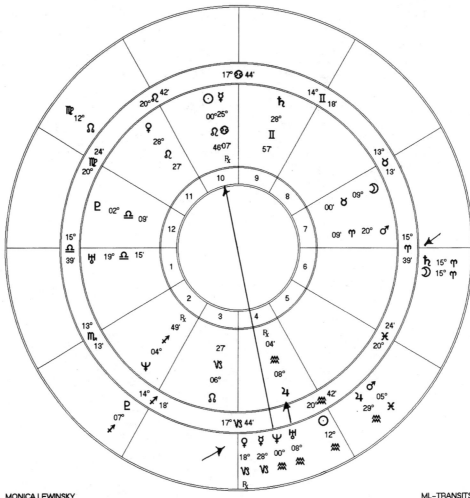

Figure 38
Monica Lewinsky
Inner Chart: 7/23/73, 12:21 P.M. PDT
Outer Chart: ML—Tr: 2/1/98
San Francisco CA, 122W25 37N46

MONICA LEWINSKY

Pl	Geo Lon	Rx	Decl.
☽	09° ♉ 00' 12"		+18° 44'
☉	00° ♌ 46' 22"		+19° 59'
☿	25° ♋ 06' 33"	Rx	+16° 20'
♀	28° ♌ 26' 43"		+13° 29'
♂	20° ♈ 08' 31"		+04° 53'
♃	08° ♒ 04' 24"	Rx	−18° 57'
♄	28° ♊ 57' 29"		+22° 22'
♅	19° ♎ 15' 09"		−06° 59'
♆	04° ♐ 48' 55"	Rx	−19° 29'
♇	02° ♎ 08' 40"		+14° 03'

ML–TRANSITS

Pl	Geo Lon	Rx	Decl.
☽	15° ♈ 05' 09"		+03° 13'
☉	12° ♒ 46' 35"		−16° 58'
☿	28° ♑ 46' 07"		−21° 54'
♀	18° ♑ 48' 05"	Rx	−14° 55'
♂	05° ♓ 52' 38"		−10° 15'
♃	29° ♒ 23' 03"		−12° 30'
♄	15° ♈ 30' 26"		+03° 55'
♅	08° ♒ 56' 20"		−18° 36'
♆	00° ♒ 08' 23"		−19° 46'
♇	07° ♐ 39' 41"		−09° 43'

Summary

1. "Transit" refers to movement position of a planet in real time, in the NOW. The technique of transits measures how the movement of planets in actual time affects development in life through aspects with the planetary positions in the natal configuration.

2. Transits (which are recorded in the Ephemeris and are an included feature in most astrological software packages) represent the environmental pressures operating upon the individual and how he/she may respond to them.

3. A planet in transit brings its own innate nature into new relationships within the natal horoscope. In analysis, we primarily look at the transits of outer planets to the other planets and Angles in the natal horoscope.

4. The important, life-changing transits always, always involve the relationship between Saturn, Uranus, Neptune, and/or Pluto to the natal Angles, Sun, or Moon.

5. Transits are used to project times ahead based on the life that is being lived, the reality that is unfolding in development. Transits are not fatalistic indicators for the future.

6. The Saturn symbolism in transit always carries with it the dimension of instruction: frustration and delays occur in order for learning (better management of life) to take place.

7. The transit of Saturn in conjunction, square, or opposition to its natal position defines the core of social development in most world cultures.

8. In transit, Uranus represents quick, sudden, unpredictable intensified change, usually in the name of individuation.

9. In hard-aspect transits, Neptune can manifest in an inspired, spiritual, or creative way for development, or in tremendous confusion, insecurity, and uncertainty.

10. Neptune's transit to any Angle, to the Sun or Moon most frequently manifests as a time of enormous challenge and difficulty, so much so that the ego often experiences "wipeout."

11. When Pluto transits an Angle (or the Sun or Moon), conditions in life press for a major change of perspective through some overpowering life event; frequently the death of someone significant in the life is involved.

12. In transit, Jupiter expands, rewards, presents opportunities, and generally represents a time when things "step-up."

13. Mars transits have an energizing, ego-oriented manifestation. Mars stirs up whatever it touches.

14. Transit periods do not always work like clockwork. The slightly erratic nature of the periods is due to the distances between the planet and the Sun.

15. The Signs Cancer, Leo, Virgo, Libra, Scorpio, and Sagittarius are called Signs of long Ascension because they take longer to ascend above the horizon than the other six Signs, called the Signs of short Ascension (Capricorn through Gemini). As a result of this phenomenon, certain transits will last longer through certain signs than through others.

16. Because of the phenomenon of retrogradation, a planet in transit will typically aspect a natal planetary position or point three times. In most cases, the first and/or last contact will have the most emphasized impact.

17. In transits, we usually use a three-degree orb in application to and a two-degree orb in separation from partile (exactness of an aspect).

Test Yourself

(See test answers, p. 248.)

1. What is a transit?

2. How is the position of a transiting planet found?

3. What is the purpose of transit analysis?

4. The transit of _____ to _____ defines the reward cycle.

5. "Ego wipeout" refers to _____.

6. Which planet's transit relationship to its natal position is so important that it has entered the core of our social development?

7. You see in a horoscope that transiting Uranus will conjoin natal Venus in the 5th House. What does this suggest?

8. In example #7, Libra is on the cusp of the 7th House. What dimension does that add to the synthesis?

9. What is suggested by Pluto's transit in conjunction, square, or opposition to Saturn?

10. What is the meaning of the term "integrated transits?" Demonstrate your answer.

11. You see in a horoscope that transiting Pluto is going to conjoin the Sun. Leo is on the 4th House cusp and the person has a critically ill parent. What does this Pluto transit suggest?

12. Using the above example, assume that Leo is on the 10th House cusp of an ambitious person who is 35 years old. What does that suggest?

13. What is our suggested orb allowance with transits?

14. What does the term "span of consciousness" refer to?

15. What is a Saturn Return? When does it occur?

16. Why do transits through some Signs last longer or shorter than through others?

17. Why is Pluto's orbit so erratic?

18. The secondary progressed Moon's hard aspect relationship to itself parallels which planet's transit?

19. What does a Uranus transit of the Ascendant suggest?

20. A simultaneous transit of Saturn and Neptune to Venus suggests _____.

While this book has come to an end, your course of study has not!

Congratulations! You have learned so much astrology so quickly, now let it all sink in, get smoothed out, and, most important, pick up corroboration from real life. Work with your friends, research what you've learned, and gain confidence for what you know.

Then, the course continues: you follow Progressions into the totally absorbing, rewarding study of Solar Arcs; you follow transits into patterns that become dramatically strategic rather than simply descriptive; astrology becomes part of your way of appreciating life and helping others do the same. *You live life learning more.*

...

Appendix

Answers to Test for Chapter 1 (p. 18), by Noel Tyl

1. ♇ ♆ ♅ ♄ ♃ ♂ ♀ ☿ ☽ ☉ .

2. ☉ ☽ ☿ ♀ ♂ ♃ ♄ ♅ ♆ ♇ .

3. Sun/life energy; Moon/reigning need; Mercury/how we need to think, also communication, mobility, movement, the mind, the nerves, lungs arms, and more; Venus/how we need to relate, social drives, beauty, aesthetics, the throat, lower back, kidneys, bladder, and more; Mars/ applied energy, getting things done, adrenaline, agitation, force, anger, the head region, fevers, and more; Jupiter/ enthusiasm, hope for reward, expansion, things legal, ethical, churchy, educational, international, the liver, upper leg, sciatic nerve that runs down the outside of the thigh; Saturn/necessary controls, time itself, father and authority reference, conservatism, tightness, coldness, strategy, ambition, difficulty to test value, the skin, knees, the bones, and more.

Uranus/Bzzzzzzzzz intensity! The sense of electricity, invention, individuation, going against convention, the avant-garde, the nervous system and ankles; Neptune/something other than it seems, dissolution, murkiness, fogginess, inspiration or bewilderment, confusion, camouflage, imagination, aesthetics, the blood and feet; Pluto/empowerment, the sense of perspective, an adverb of scope, how much, how big, how important, how long, affairs of death for new beginning, the genitalia and alimentary canal.

4. Intensity, sharp mind, nervous thrust of thought, biting fingernails?

5. Loveliness, grace, strong interest in nice things, aesthetics, possible vanity, social awareness.

6. Tremendous passion about and within relationship, making things happen in terms of relationship and romance; so much attention to things Venusian that a waste of emotions can be expected.

7. Planets represent needs expressing themselves in the relationship with other planets, other needs; my need for caution (Saturn), for example, will probably be upset by the need for aggression (Mars) if the two are related together in the horoscope. Might that result in indecisiveness?

8. Mercury is closest to the Sun. Mercury can get burned up here and inspire fanatacism! When the mind and all that energy get together, it's something special usually!

9. Saturn, of course; besides being quite a distance from the Sun—the end of the line, so to speak, for the ancients—it just looks like it should be somewhere else, away from these inner planets!

10. ♃.

11. The human being in the center of all, energized within the scheme of things.

12. The mind, through caution, discipline, or authoritative restriction, learns to manage, learns to cope with life, and eventually over time gains wisdom; or there is such difficulty experienced that melancholy, depression, or withdrawal is revealed in the mental state.

13. The opportunity of Jupiter could change your life, but such a gain does not usually last a long time; a new level may be achieved, but things settle down. But with Neptune, a tremendously deep change is probable, often into the psyche, and it is felt over a protracted period of time (since Neptune's orbit is so very slow).

14. Jupiter, the biggest planet, its mythological archetype speaking of grandness and power, in contact with Mercury, the mind; would certainly suggest far-reaching thought (or communication) processes.

15. Sun and/or Moon in relationship with Pluto; but astrologers learn that sometimes there is too much here, and in development this perspective is often pushed down, censored, not encouraged, and as a result there is frustration and underachievement.

16. With Mars: intense, bright, loquacious, nervous, fast; with Saturn, careful, quiet, sparing, anchored, strategic.

17. ♄ Saturn.

18. Venus: social needs, awareness.

19. Absolutely not! There is an energized Bzzzzzzzz! Tremendous impulse instead of deliberation, which would be introduced only by Saturn.

20. Jupiter: there is a hint of the numbers 2 and 4 in the planetary symbol, and 24 is the number of years Jupiter takes to orbit the Sun 2 times.

Answers to Test for Chapter 2 (p. 38), by Noel Tyl

1. ♈ ♉ ♊ ♋ ♌ ♍ ♎ ♏ ♐ ♑ ♒ ♓
   ♓ ♒ ♑ ♐ ♏ ♎ ♍ ♋ ♌ ♊ ♉ ♈

   I can do each line in nine seconds.

2. ♈-♂ ♉-♀ ♊-☿ ♋-☽ ♌-☉ ♍-☿
   ♎-♀ ♏-♇ ♐-♃ ♑-♄ ♒-♅ ♓-♆

   This took me 17 seconds. It was interesting to feel what my mind was "saying" as I added each ruling planet successively to each Sign, and it helped the speed of recall to order the work Aries-Mars through Virgo-Mercury on one line and Libra-Venus through Pisces-Neptune on the second line. This is because of the supportive grouping of the Signs organized as opposites, the way they are arranged always across from each other around the horoscope wheel!

3. The archetypes of the Signs came from observed "behavior" of the planets within them: certain planets seemed to behave powerfully (and other ways) in certain signs; planets were given "rulerships" of certain signs because of certain affinities among the planet, the zone in the heavens, and correspondences with events on earth.

4. Signs: ♋︎♒︎♏︎♓︎, ♌︎♍︎♐︎♒︎, ♎︎♈︎♉︎♋︎, ♑︎♓︎♊︎♐︎. Aquarius sticks out because is not a Water sign like the others in the group; Sagittarius sticks out because it is not a Fixed sign like the others in that group; Taurus, not Cardinal; Capricorn, not Mutable.

5. Sagittarius.

6. ♈︎♋︎♎︎♑︎. We always initiate conceptual thinking with the sign of Aries, the beginning of everything.

7. Cancer.

8. ♑︎♉︎♍︎. It's good form to list elemental groups in the order Cardinal, Fixed, Mutable, the same order they appear in the progress of the zodiac, e.g., Aries, Taurus, Gemini.

9. "MY MOON IS DEFINITELY, ABSOLUTELY, FOR SURE, IN ARIES!"

10. ♊︎♍︎♐︎♓︎. Here again, the mutable Signs are listed in the order they appear in the zodiac.

11. Thinking about, especially conscious of, communicating about home security, emotional security, feeling that things are safe.

12. ♋︎♏︎♓︎. Note how we start with the Cardinal, go to the Fixed, and end with the Mutable.

13. Stolidity, resistance to change, needing to keep things as they are or to improve them to where they should be, with a probable dimension of idealism or aesthetics as part of the package.

14. ♉︎♌︎♏︎♒︎. All these "fixed" signs look solid and anchored, don't they! And they are in the proper order of zodiac flow.

15. Prissiness; the need to be discriminatingly correct, fastidious about it all; proper social behavior, convention.

16. Mars in Aries suggests a hot poker, a ramrod, battering ram, a charging train, the sense of attack. Mars in Capricorn suggests determined, patient, lethal strategy, the hard drive to get things done one way or another, thoroughly. Note that the images take on the rulership dimension of the Sign: Aries is ruled by Mars, so Mars in Aries is a double dose of Mars! Mars in Capricorn takes on an implicit synthesis with Saturn, since Saturn rules Capricorn. Another way to look at it: Mars is working in Capricorn's corporation here, Saturn is the CEO; Mars takes on a different demeanor to please the boss, but the objective remains the same, to make things happen!

17. ♎︎≈♊︎. Note here, the zodiacal order begins with the Cardinal sign in Air, goes to the Fixed, and then, to get to the Mutable Air Sign, it crosses over Aries. While our sense of circle has a beginning point in Aries, it really has no end; a sense of cycle takes over, over and over, and over again through the Signs, as years follow years.

18. My Moon is extremely delighted, and thrilled with the opportunity, I might add and I do believe I've said that correctly—to be in Gemini, because, from all my reading and so much life experience, I have found that knowing how to spell *coelacanth*, a fossil but still-living fish deep in the Pacific, is much more fulfilling than completing my income tax form, but then again, if I were to think about this a bit further, I . . . !

19. The need profile has difficulty with emotional orientation and often reaches out to a large construct that will provide that orientation. Often there is a lack of success with up-close and personal emotional exchange. The large religious, social, or even cosmic relationship may seize life to make it significant.

20. Get out of my way!

Answers to Test for Chapter 3 (p. 59), by Noel Tyl

1. I've done this too many zillion times already; I really don't want to do it again, Basil; but I do know that the first six Houses relate to development of the self, and the following six to experiences of self in interaction with others and the world at large; I created the idea of focus-initiation in the Angles, organizing for value in the Succedent Houses (2, 5, 8, 1), and distributing it all one way or another through the Cadent Houses (3, 6, 9, 12). You teach this section just beautifully!

2. Cusps.

3. To tell the celestial mailman where to deliver the planets in relation to the birth location and the birth time! The cusp signs and degrees keep things organized.

4. A zone of experience in personal development, with many different but related levels of interpretation, from the psychodynamic to the nakedly material.

5. The horizon, the contact we have with others, symbolized from breathing in the first breath to exhaling it, from self-awareness to awareness of others, from Yin to Yang, from dawn to twilight, from uplift to retreat.

6. Absolutely not. In the 3rd House, the birth time is between midnight and 2 A.M., usually, but then again, I know some people who really don't know what time it is! Ever!

7. The Midheaven, the highest point in the horoscope.

8. Succedent Houses, their dynamic is organization, following focus and initiation in the Angles and getting ready to give things over to distribution dynamics in the Cadent Houses (III, VI, IX, and XII).

9. The Meridian line.

10. There sure is: the sign is the archetype reflecting the ruling planet, part of the quality matrix of need formation and behavior; the House is a mundane zone of experience down into which the Sign-planet combinations are brought. It is in the Houses where synthesis relates to reality experience.

11. The apparent path of the Sun; astronomically it has a tilt from the Earth's equator of about 23 degrees, reflecting the Earth's tilt, which allows us to have seasons.

12. I told myself that, I sure did. I think you introduced the dilemma gradually and clearly. Thank you!

13. The Sun sets at that point, it comes down; the Self gives way to the lights of others and to the refreshment of night.

14. Cadent Houses distribute the substance of personality; communicating, working with others cooperatively, publishing and traveling, seeking inspiration, etc. [I just sort of keyed into the four Cadent Houses in my answer; not bad, eh!]

15. Immum Coeli. The "I.C."

16. Mercury (the need to think a certain way) in Virgo (refinement) in the 5th House (creative matters): *Mercury in Virgo in the 5th* (or ruling the 5th, as I know you will be teaching us soon).

17. Saturn (older, wise through weathering all those difficulties and instructive controls) in the 7th (marriage experience, partnership): *Saturn in the 7th,* and perhaps I could have said Saturn with Venus in Libra in the 7th, just to overdo the picture of possibilities.

18. On paper they do; yes, "in the horoscope."

19. Sun in Pisces (core energy; archetype for intangibles) in the 3rd (mindset experience): *Sun in Pisces in the 3rd* with the *Moon in Libra in the 10th* (the personality form, reigning need, connected with the popularity archetype and focused in career-concern experience). Grrrreat question!

20. The Angles, without any doubt.

Answers to Test for Chapter 4 (p. 66), by Noel Tyl

1. Greenwich, England.

2. Earth Time must be converted to Star Time (Sidereal Time); the latter begins when the Sun enters Aries and spends 24 hours, while Earth Time spends one year.

3. The Sun appears to travel one degree of arc every four minutes of clock time.

4. Daylight Saving Time makes the clock "spring" forward an hour; horoscopes are calculated only on the Standard Time of any time zone, so the computer must adjust the DST backward one hour to get the standard time.

5. Los Angeles is located at 120W00 longitude (120 degrees west of Greenwich), which is 8 time zones (120/15), i.e., 8 hours difference from Greenwich. L.A. is west therefore it is *earlier than Greenwich*, –8 hours (subtract, minus).

6. East of Greenwich equates to an addition of one hours per time zone (every 15 degrees longitude), PLUS.

7. The Sun's apparent movement is what has established the longitude line system every 15 degrees around the Earth.

8. The time of birth captures the exact position of the Sun, Moon, and planets in their various paths.

9. The birth date, the birth time, the birthplace, and the time zone, with special attention to the possibility of Daylight Saving Time during the Spring and Summer (or in time of wars in the past, "War Time," which was actually years-long enforced Daylight Saving Time; your computer knows all this!!)

10. 43 degrees East longitude equates to: 43 ÷ 15 = 3, almost to the beginning of the 3rd time zone east (later than) than Greenwich. Probably 3 hours later on the nose!

Answers to Test for Chapter 5 (p. 89), by Noel Tyl

1. There sure is: the trine projection from Taurus is to Virgo (two Earth Signs), specifically 29 Virgo in this case. Four Libra is just five degrees further on, certainly within orb for the Sun. There is a trine here, over the sign line.

2. The hard aspects are aspects of highest developmental tension. I would rank them like this: Square, conjunction, opposition.

3. Conjunction (0), sextile (60), square (90), trine (120), opposition (180).

4. Orb.

5. Project a specific degree area forward or backward two Signs, i.e., 60 degrees.

6. 120.

7. Sharp, developmentally tense ego-energy; potentially disruptive, rebellious, inventive, innovative, unique (all the things that make cooperative relationship difficult).

8. Positions at similar degree areas in Signs of the same mode (Cardinal, Fixed, or Mutable).

9. Yes, but this study plan has not yet introduced them.

10. Opposition, i.e., the "Full Moon" idea, seeing the light, being aware of extremes.

11. Conservatism, perhaps wisdom, a careful approach to need fulfillment, perhaps a very supportive paternal figure.

12. Sextile and Trine (60 and 120 degrees, respectively).

13. We work most with the hard aspects, because this set of developmental tensions is stronger, manifests more clearly, and promotes change more dramatically than the keep-things-as-they-are senses of the soft aspects. People want to talk about change, and they remember best those things that have prompted change in life.

14. Mercury in relation with Saturn: hard aspects suggest some depression; soft aspects, conservatism.

15. The Sun in hard aspect with Pluto. Pluto is empowerment, indeed, but in the square to the Sun it suggests difficulty for the empowerment to bloom within orderly societal development. There is usually a parental

damper put on things or a painful control exerted; routinized behaviors follow in reaction that often add up to underachievement.

16. Uranus strong with the Sun.

17. Noting the need and behavior symbolism of the planet, framing an image in terms of its Sign placement and relating it dynamically to another planet as conditioner; the intrinsically slower-moving planet conditions the intrinsically faster-moving planet, which is the reactor.

18. A dose of idealism, fanned by religion, law, or aesthetics, usually. Any conjunction relationship among the Sun, Mercury, and/or Venus will do the same, classically. We will see, I know, that idealism is an enormously important defense mechanism within development!

19. Venus conjunct Mars: Mars conditions social/love needs with high energy and forthrightness; Venus sextile Mars: Mars conditions Venus supportively, richly; Venus square Mars: Mars conditions Venus sharply, strongly, usually with romantic upheaval or difficulty in expression and/or relating; Venus trine Mars: a stronger manifestation of the sextile; Venus opposed Mars: a full awareness of the potential of things sexual, romantic, socially aggressive.

20. By our working definition, the intrinsically slower-moving planet conditions the intrinsically faster-moving planet, but both of these planets are slow moving and very "heavy." Still, we can say that Saturn meets its match in Pluto, that Pluto pushes enormous change, even rebirth, into being over a long period of time; usually something must be broken down before it is reconstructed or is reborn with this aspect. A good analogy: the muscle is broken down in the process of building it up bigger and stronger. "No pain, no gain!"

Answers to Test for Chapter 6 (p. 103), by Noel Tyl

1. A Grand Trine is formed by three or more planets relating by trine aspect among all three signs of the same element.

2. The Grand Trine relates behavioral faculties of a similar kind (motivational, social, emotional, practical) into a circuit of interreliance. The circuit becomes an important self-protection, a behavioral construct defending the Self in development. This defensiveness works against relationships and tends to be self-isolating.

3. Fire: closed circuit of motivational self-sufficiency; Air: social or intellectual self-sufficiency; Water: emotional self-sufficiency; Earth: practical self-sufficiency.

4. A square or opposition aspect from yet another planet to any corner of the Grand Trine tends to register as a disruptor, a window opener, a freedom or safety valve for the behavioral construct. This is very important because the Grand Trine stores up a lot of energy; the routinized behavioral patterns keep energies in a highly defensive mode; opening the window, breaking up the routinization through understanding and trust of maturation within development can free up and release lots of fresh energy. Development can be rejuvenated without so much fear.

5. Career (ambition) is essential for the person to prove him/herself; one is not ordinarily defensive or diffident when one is successful! AND: the problem behind the defensive structure—necessitating it—in the first place was probably linked to the paternal relationship (the 10th House).

6. A minimum of three, i.e., one of the corners or two or three could be a conjunction with another planet, increasing the number of planets involved within the construct. The more planets involved in the structure, the more massive it is, the more telling it is within personality development. If one of the potential corners for the Grand Trine is the MC or the ASC, we have a tendency to the Grand Trine defensive behavioral construct: the feelings are all there, but the rigidity of the pattern is much less, usually.

7. An opposition axis squared by another planet (or conjunction of planets).

8. A reservoir of energy: the awareness of energies within the opposition axis is charged, jolted, illuminated, graced . . . whatever . . . by the symbolism of the planet square the axis.

9. Tremendous, eruptive opportunism? A great power drive for success. Working with the "really big picture"!

10. Strategic control to the sense of the opposition axis.

11. Cross purposes, bringing strongly into awareness the affairs of one of the Grand Crosses of Houses.

12. The Grand Cross suggests dilemma more than the T-Square; the T-Square suggests energy management more than the Grand Cross.

13. Cross purposes or related concerns of major magnitude.

14. Parents, identity development, and relationships; tension among them all.

15. Self-worth/money, giving and receiving love.

16. The mindset and education somehow foundering or incomplete, insecure, undermining cooperation with others, forming relationships on the proper level of equality.

17. In Cardinal signs the energy is geared to taking action, making things happen; in Fixed Signs, the energy tends to protect the status quo, defends the fort, so to speak.

18. Saturn retrograde: the defense is often an overcompensatory, privately held superiority complex, which can be symbolized by the Air Grand Trine.

19. YES . . . and you are most tricky! If the Sun goes 2 or 3 more degrees over the Sign line into Taurus—well within orb of a trine aspect for the Sun—with Taurus being an Earth Sign, the early degree area there would trine the Moon and Mars also in Earth Signs in very early degrees. The powerful presence of the Aries glyph threatens to overshadow Taurus, the next Sign!

20. A closed circuit of emotional self-sufficiency working overtime to protect enormous ego energies; we could expect tremendous public exposure (Aries Sun) and powerful relationship activity (Moon in Libra), always threatened with disruption (square from Uranus) because of something problematic in development; privately, the defensiveness might make this person a conspicuous loner (the isolating tendency of the Grand Trine; quite separate here, since the major aggressive, Cardinal, attack thrust to the public is so prominent).

Answers to Test for Chapter 7 (p. 115), by Noel Tyl

1. Three: Angular, Succedent ("following" the Angle), and Cadent ("falling" into, distributing into the next Angle). These three Grand Crosses of Houses echo the Angular-Fixed-Mutable orientation from the Ascendant to the 2nd and to the 3rd House in the natural distribution of the Signs (Aries, Taurus, Gemini).

2. Angular, Succedent, Cadent (see #1 above).

3. Angular: identity formation, parental interaction, relationships; Succedent: self-worth profile, giving and receiving love; others' values and resources (with which we create exchanges in the process of interacting with

others); Cadent: point of view, mindset, and communication profile, cooperation, higher education and new environments, some suppression of some kind.

4. That which gives a sign, indicates something. From the Latin *significare*, to indicate.

5. Neptune; anywhere in the horoscope, Neptune will make reference to wherever Pisces makes its mark.

6. Developmental tension of significance in the early home, giving rise to patterned behaviors carried into adulthood.

7. The significator of the 2nd House is under developmental tension.

8. It is somehow *necessary* for there to be developmental tension with one's parents in order for identity to form, to stimulate individuation. The question becomes to what degree and how that tension has been internalized, assimilated.

9. It is somehow axiomatic that the ease/comfort with giving and receiving love from others (including establishing intimacy) is dependent upon development of a secure self-worth profile.

10. The mindset affects cooperation dynamics interpersonally and societally.

11. With Cancer on the 7th cusp, **we know that Capricorn is on the Ascendant!** Very tricky, Mr. Teacher! Capricorn is ruled by Saturn, i.e., Saturn is the significator of the Ascendant. Here in the example, Saturn is in the 2nd House of self-worth conjoined with the Moon, and the Moon, we know, ruling Cancer, is the significator of the 7th. Put all that together and we have some difficult identity development (Ascendant) because of a debilitated self-worth profile, which, in turn, makes relationships difficult (the 7th).

12. Two times in a row!! **With Leo on the Ascendant, we know that Aquarius is on the 7th!** Uranus is the significator of the 7th and here, in this example, Uranus is conjunct the Sun, ruler/significator of the Ascendant in the 6th House. With the significators of the Ascendant-Descendant axis joined together in zappy tension, we can suspect a wild relationship history (breakups, unusual people, stops and starts) maybe occurring too often in the work place. Emotional ties could very well upset cooperation in the work environment; everything is stirred up here as this person tries just about anything to prove personal specialness.

13. How sweet it is!

14. The Ascendant.

15. The 2nd House.

16. The 3rd House.

17. Difficult dynamics of cooperation with others, a disrupting mindset, opinionation diverted from the norm; unpredictability.

Answers to Test for Chapter 8 (p. 129), by Noel Tyl

1. It's a sight line phenomenon: the view from a rotating Earth out to and through an orbiting planet, with position measurement determined by reference to the stationary zodiac behind the planet. When the observation point on the Earth gets ahead of the planet at certain places in its orbit, the planet seems to slow down and go backward in zodiacal measurement. It is like being on a train, seated on the right side, looking out the window. Your friend is walking alongside the train in the same direction, waving good-bye to you. The station stays still, of course. BUT, as you pick up speed in the train, a straight sight-line through your friend to a reference point on the train station wall, for example, changes and *gives reference to your friend in locations he has already been, i.e., going backward!*

2. The "Station" made by a planet is the time period when it appears to stand still longitudinally, just before "going Direct out of retrograde movement" or "going Retrograde out of direct movement." With computers doing the measurements today, the Station period is very brief; in older practice, the Station period was given an entire day of duration, and much more importance.

3. Counterpoint suggests another level of behavioral significance within the symbolism of a planet in retrograde motion. Often, there is the sense of "hidden agenda" in development.

4. No. Only planets are retrograde—and perhaps a few astrologers I have met!

5. The outer planets—Uranus, Neptune, and Pluto—have very long retrograde periods. Their significance in terms of counterpoint seems negligible. However, in overall patterning in the horoscope—as we will study in the next lesson—outer planet retrogradation is important. And, indeed, with these slower moving planets, generational significances can be hypothesized.

6. A counterpoint in our thinking process, a second agenda, doublespeak? If Mercury is ruler of the Ascendant, there will be a clear tie to concerns in identity development.

7. A counterpoint in our relational behaviors, our motives, our fears. If Venus is ruler of the Ascendant, there will be a clear tie to concerns in identity development.

8. A counterpoint in our deployment of energy; the energy usually goes in before it goes out, going in for censorship, editing, checking, substitution, etc. If Mars is ruler of the Ascendant, there will be a clear tie to concerns in identity development.

9. Jupiter retrograde suggests a contentment being alone . . . but we are not sure here.

10. Saturn retrograde is enormously significant indeed; and your teacher has been most kind with accrediting its discovery and development to me. SO, you better know this without my help!!

11. The Lunar Nodal Axis defines the two opposite points on the ecliptic where the Moon crosses in its epicycle path around the Earth. One is North, the other is South; they are always opposite each other. The North is shown in the horoscope and the South is implied. The axis is best appreciated, not as two points or a straight line, but as a great circle.

12. Always opposite.

13. The Moon symbol of the feminine and the Sun symbol of the masculine come together in the symbolism of fecundation. The inspiration within this process support a mother-related concept. Any planet or point tightly configured by hard aspect with the Lunar Nodal Axis will suggest— almost invariably—an enormous significant maternal concept in development. There is a full range of possibilities indeed, but one begins with the analytical focus of the planet or point configured with the axis, its symbolism and the House matters signified by the planet.

14. The Saturn retrograde phenomenon will involve crucially the dynamics of relationship, all life long. There is the feel of unfinished business here and it threatens to undermine relationships constantly.

15. Venus retrograde suggests a counterpoint in relational needs and behaviors, a second agenda; as the ruler of the Ascendant, it is suggested strongly that the relational needs are part of difficulty in identity development. The Venus position in the 5th House introduces a difficulty

(or lack of fulfillment) in the process of giving love. It is fascinating how these references all work together to form a consonant profile of developmental concerns.

If I might add—and try to follow this push forward in learning—with Venus ruling the Ascendant as a given, let us say the Sign is Taurus; knowing the 5th House is usually trine to the Ascendant, this Venus would probably be in the next Earth Sign, Virgo; Venus in Virgo within this hypothetical analytical construct suggests a tightness, a discrimination, a perfectionism, a defensive idealization about emotional expression which becomes part of this vignette of difficulty as well! As ruler of Libra, this would put Venus in the 5th in Aquarius, an avant-garde intensification of relational needs; the retrogradation would inhibit this or perhaps no one can be special enough (the retrogradation), etc.!

16. By default within the Saturn retrograde phenomenon, the maternal reference comes to the rescue.

17. An overpowering importance with the maternal image—or feminine figures influentially permeating developmental times; or a mother never known, longed for, shaping the life in absentia.

18. An involvement of the mother of zapping individuality into being—or perhaps a highly individual relationship with the mother; or a highly unusual mother.

19. The "spill-over" effect is the interrelating of areas in development: a major concern in one area reaches out holistically to affect concerns in other areas; it is a kind of psychodynamic domino effect!

20. Two degrees; with experience—from my experience—one learns to reach out a bit more if reality suggests such maternal involvement. Always: the tighter the orb the more reliable the deduction from the aspect.

Answers to Test for Chapter 9 (p. 143), by Noel Tyl

1. It is that way in life! The first impression is involuntary; our senses pick it up and formulate it in so many ways. We immediately evaluate myriad perceptions whenever we meet someone, experience something, or even hear an idea! What's more, first impressions have an enormous reliability, proved even in rigorous psychological tests; first impressions are valid and enduring.

2. Conspicuous hemisphere emphasis. It is almost always there. If it isn't, we can just go on to the Sun-Moon blend, the dominating aspect, etc.

3. A grouping of planets in one hemisphere (even one quadrant sometimes) that is conspicuous.

4. The profiles emerge from the sense of the Angular House in the center of the hemisphere (the 1st for the East, Self; 4th for the North, early home, one parent; 7th for the West, others; 10th for the South, the profession, another parent).

5. The inclination to be swept away, even victimized by events outside oneself. There seems to be a lack of anchor. NOTE: very often, hemisphere emphasis denies formation of an opposition aspect; it isn't there for anchored awareness (polarity), and the winds can blow development onto a different course!

6. "Unfinished business in the early home." These exact words carry a powerful punch in horoscope discussion with someone with a decided northern hemisphere emphasis.

7. Developmental tension with the significators of the 4th and 10th parental axis.

8. "Defensiveness." This concept, this *word*, says it all for someone with a decided eastern hemisphere emphasis.

9. "Giving oneself away to others." This concept, these *words* say it all for someone with a decided eastern hemisphere emphasis

10. This is a tough question, dear teacher, at this level of our study. We must look for the reasons behind the developmental profile; what difficulties have been met, behaviors adopted because of the difficulties, and the person's own opinion of the developmental process.

11. A hemisphere emphasis faced by a singular planet in the other hemisphere; this is a singleton, and it is usually very powerful in the analysis.

12. We get the hemisphere emphasis in mind and recognize the power of the handle, the singleton, utilizing rulership routings (significator dynamics) etc. Synthesis tends to come together quickly, the more and more factors we relate and the more and more we *anticipate* such interrelationship of horoscopic factors.

13. A planet alone in a hemisphere (if another planet shares the hemisphere, it is probably retrograde, a kind of "bow" to the other planet, which is not retrograde, i.e., alone in its placement). There can be a singleton, a lone planet, that is retrograde.

14. Opposite the eastern hemisphere, in the West.

15. This is a tough question, but that's how we grow with our knowledge! Here we have the tendency to give the self away, to be helpful, supportive to others; the energy to do this will be Mars in Sagittarius, which is strong opinionation, using knowledge as the foil, the representation of the Self. *Communication (Mars signifies the 3rd House here) tells people who this person is.* Now does this suggest developmental concerns underneath it all? Yes, and we would have to look further to see what all this is driven by.

16. This is a counterpoint referring to the *other* hemisphere as prime focus.

17. Enormous defensiveness linked to the Saturn retrograde phenomenon, with the anxieties played out with difficulty in relationships.

18. Being swept up by life circumstances, with the impetus somehow linked to one of the parents, a unique, special parent (Uranus). This is a description of the horoscope of John F. Kennedy, whose extraordinary father propelled the erstwhile college English professor into politics and history.

19. The East, i.e., coming out of the defensive posture.

20. The answers are legion. I'll abstain!

Answers to Test for Chapter 10 (p. 151), by Noel Tyl

1. Perhaps it is more poetical than astronomical: the Sun shines on all planets in the System, of course, but its light that is revealed upon the Moon, the only body that revolves around the Earth, carries a special message for us in the scheme of things.

2. The life energy.

3. The Reigning Need of the personality.

4. Energy caught up with emotional/home security charges the personality's bid, drive, pursuit to be *numero uno*; undoubtedly a major boiling pot (Fire/Water) of overcompensation for developmental difficulties.

5. Refinement, adjustment, rescue.

6. Hard aspects add developmental tension to the Sun-Moon blend; the rocks in the soil against which our roots press in order to reach the Sun.

7. An enormous ego-energy potential somehow having difficulty finding expression, finding form (the New Moon birth is well know for a

weakness in developmental progress in the earliest years especially), from the diffusion of the Neptune (conditioner) opposition. At best, much aesthetic and idealization could be introduced here, toning down and adjusting ego fire; at worst, a frustration blinded with diffused thinking, bewilderment, etc.

8. Adjustment would be through the introduction of ethical concerns; perhaps the Sagittarian and Neptune components introduce religiousness.

9. Sun in Cancer and the Moon in Taurus.

10. The water part will make the fire more acceptable; *the Moon leads the blend* and usually ameliorates the Sun's energy by fashioning it into the best form for real life.

Answers to Test for Chapter 11 (p. 173), by Noel Tyl

1. 165 degrees (the 24th harmonic; 360/24 gives 15 degrees, the increment in the family of quindecile—*quin-deh-chee'-lay*—aspects).

2. Extreme focus, disruption, separation, compulsion, even obsession.

3. Tremendous developmental focus to resolve a legacy of inferiority feelings taken on through the Saturn-retrograde phenomenon, focused strongly on the ability to give love easily, trustingly. There is every suggestion here of a fear of intimacy. Corroboration and extension possibilities: with Venus in the 10th (parental House) and Capricorn on the 5th, Libra is probably on the self-worth 2nd, i.e., Venus, within the quindecile with Saturn, rules the 2nd! Venus would then rule the 9th as well (if there were no interception in this horoscope), because Taurus would be on the cusp of the 9th: This would add the dimension of education, learning, etc. to the development problem: either the education was interrupted, diminishing the person's resources further into the debilitation of the Saturn retrograde phenomenon, and/or education becomes the enormous overplayed focus to prove one's self worthy, etc. in over-compensation.

4. Hyper-individuated behavior focus tends to upset relationships.

5. The job/profession becomes the *sine qua non* of identity.

6. The classical man inscribed within the circle (for the studies of divine human proportions) with circumference contact by 2 hands, 2 feet, *and* the head, adding intelligence to the four-square orientation of action depicted by contact with just the arms and legs (without the head); five points of contact instead of four (360/4 = 90; 360/5 = 72).

7. 72 degrees (see #6 above).

8. Special creativity.

9. The Saturn Retrograde phenomenon deeply affects one's possessive traffic with emotions; there is probably an obsessive fear of intimacy.

10. Public projection of some character trait, developmental concern, or behavior. It is brought forward into prominence. If it is not displayed, it has somehow been diverted in a short-circuit of development.

11. See #10 above.

12. Social relations, the attitude of romance (sometimes views about money), vanity, etc. shown clearly and in forward fashion; there can be a vain strut to personal demeanor. Always in terms of the sign holding Venus, of course.

13. Q.

14. I've got the whole list—and then some!—eternally memorized; I regard it as my private property; and it's a secret . . . but trust me, I *do* know! And every astrology student *should* know too! [Seriously, see p. 172, #7.]

15. 2 degrees (for just about all minor aspects).

16 AP.

17. 2 degrees.

18. Extreme projection of administrative strength and power. The word "lethal" comes to mind—Robert Kennedy's Mars was not near the AP, but *it was peregrine in Scorpio* in the 7th House, ruling his Ascendant! One can feel that enormous power, unbridled, inviting enemies (being in the 7th House); and along with his Moon in Capricorn, we begin to feel a similar concept to Mars in Capricorn at the Aries Point!

19. Lots of focused anxiety involving the nerves, the mind, the opinions, and whatever Houses are involved.

20. Feel the tension in the Houses outlined by the aspect, internalized for expression through the signs holding the planets. Fit the quindecile analysis into the first impression being developed throughout your list of guidelines for analysis.

Answers to Test for Chapter 12 (p. 183), by Noel Tyl

1. I want to assure you that I have spoken over 15,000 horoscopes in 30 years. It still amazes me how any new information that my brain absorbs doesn't become truly "mine" unless I speak it several times. It's much like hearing a new joke: the first time you retell it, you stumble and leave out details, etc. The second time you tell it, you improve. By the fourth time, the joke is yours, and you are adding your own touch to it!

2. At first, you might feel silly speaking out loud for a 10- or 15-minute session! Well, that goes away quickly once you get into it! Make sure you're private, comfortable, and serious. You simply will not believe how helpful this is!

NOTE: Answers to oral test for Chapter 13 not necessary.

Answers to Test for Chapter 14 (p. 227), by Noel Tyl

1. A transit is a planet in motion at any given moment of time.

2. In an Ephemeris or in a comprehensive table included in a very special 1,000-page text I know extremely well!

3. To tune natal potentials in with developments in the living environment.

4. Tr. Jupiter to the natal Sun and/or natal Jupiter positions. Once the cycle begins, there is a nifty 12-year reliability to it.

5. Transits of Neptune to the Angles of the horoscope (conjunction or square) or to the Sun. Conjunctions appear stronger than squares in this case.

6. Saturn.

7. There just has to be an affair of some kind—but, if the transit occurs in early youth, and some heavy portents are also occurring through the suggestion of other planets, at the same time, we can expect child abuse.

8. It makes the affair more serious, more probably marriage orientated.

9. Great difficulty. Something must be corrected or given way, before a new perspective can be established.

10. How the planets in quadrature transit team up at critical times of life development, working mainly upon the infrastructure established by Saturn mechanics.

11. This suggests a very important time of challenge to that parent. It could also suggest an in-law in trouble, since, with Leo on the 4th, Scorpio is probably on the 7th, i.e., Pluto refers to the spouse. Then, working from the 7th House, we see the 4th in our example as the MC of the 7th, the spouse's parent!! THAT should excite you for further study! (Starting at 7, count the Houses counterclockwise as if the 7th were the Ascendant of your spouse!)

12. Tremendous personal ascendancy. Scorpio would probably be on the Ascendant here. Ascendant and MC would be synthesized in terms of Sun, Leo, and Pluto!

13. 3 and 2: 3 applying—and 2 separating. It's a good rule of thumb to capture the gradualism of most event occurrence in our life.

14. Orb . . . the awareness and gradualism of development in life.

15. At 28–30, transiting Saturn returns to its natal position; life should change direction and/or level conspicuously. If it doesn't, I'm sorry! What got in the way?

16. Short or Long Ascension.

17. Long elliptical orbit has recently brought it into closer proximity to the Sun, therefore it has speeded up.

18. Saturn.

19. Intensification of individuation, possibly upsetting relationships (opposite the Descendant), and almost definitely relocation for better opportunity.

20. A real rough time and confusion about relationship, anguish in terms of Venus rulership.

Suggested Further Reading

Hand, Robert, *Planets in Transit*. Para Research, Gloucester, MA , 1976.

Lewi, Grant, *Astrology for the Millions*. Llewellyn Publications, St. Paul, MN, 1992.

Lewi, Grant, *Heaven Knows What*. Llewellyn Publications, St. Paul, MN, 1994.

Tyl, Noel, *Synthesis & Counseling in Astrology: The Professional Manual*. Llewellyn Publications, St. Paul, MN, 1994.

Index